When Clothes Become Fashion

When Clothes Become Fashion
Design and Innovation Systems

Ingrid Loschek

Oxford • New York

English edition
First published in 2009 by
Berg
Editorial offices:
1st Floor, Angel Court, 81 St Clements Street, Oxford OX4 1AW, UK
175 Fifth Avenue, New York, NY 10010, USA

This book has been sponsored by
**Institut für Angewandte Forschung der
Hochschule für Gestaltung, Technik und Wirtschaft, and Pforzheim.**

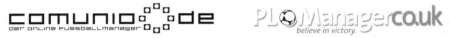

Originally published in German as Wann is Mode?: Strukturen, Strategien und
Innovationen by Dietrich Reimer Verlag, Berlin, 2007

Translated into English by Dr Lucinda Rennison, Berlin

Library of Congress Cataloging-in-Publication Data

Loschek, Ingrid.
[Wann is Mode? English]
When clothes become fashion : design and innovation
systems / Ingrid Loschek ; [translated into English
by Lucinda Rennison]. — English ed.
p. cm.
Includes bibliographical references and index.
ISBN 978-1-84788-366-7 (pbk.)
ISBN 978-1-84788-367-4 (cloth)
1. Fashion.   2. Clothing trade.   3. Fashion design.
4. Aesthetics.   5. Costume—Psychological aspects.   I. Title.
TT507.L7413   2009
746.9'2—dc22
2009020277

British Library Cataloguing-in-Publication Data

A catalogue record for this book is available from the British Library.
ISBN 978 184788 367 4 (Cloth)
ISBN 978 184788 366 7 (Paper)

Typeset by Apex CoVantage, LLC, Madison, WI, USA
Printed in Great Britain by the MPG Books Group, Bodmin and King's Lynn

www.bergpublishers.com

Contents

List of Illustrations

Introduction

Recent years have seen the start of various thought processes which are changing the relevance of fashion decisively, considerably advancing its scientific aspirations. Cultural sciences and theories of art, design and media, as well as sociology including gender studies, provide key impulses to innovative starting points of research and help to push progress from costume studies towards a science of fashion. At the same time, however, fashion runs the risk of being presented exclusively as an example of the continuity of change, or for its everyday quality.

The humanities provide a freedom of thought that promotes innovations and is often path-breaking as well, since it is not purpose oriented—rather, it is almost an intellectual service. The analytical and complex ideas of the humanities mean that they are capable of mediating culture and art in the broadest sense. In an art–theoretical context, the architect Rem Koolhaas formulated an appeal concerning 'the necessity and desire for seriousness' (2006), which I would echo with respect to fashion. Precisely because of their reference to analogies from the past, the humanities are oriented towards the future. The humanities are not exotic subjects or luxury studies suitable only for senior citizens but are highly relevant to visions of the future and also to current practice.

As yet, no theory of fashion has been developed to provide its mono-causal explanation, taking into account the complexity of fashion and differentiating between clothing and fashion. An approach evaluating fashion as a system in accordance with Niklas Luhmann's contemporary social theory suggests itself on the way towards such an explanation. According to this theory, fashion displays self-perpetuation through its continual generation of new creations from within, without being part of the economic, art or media system. Clothing and fashion are explained both causally and in conjunction with their social demands.

Strategies of invention that are relevant for the design of clothing are revealed on the basis of creativity and knowledge. 'Creative destruction' and evolution as the development of the new on the foundation of what came before are both processes by means of which inventions become innovations. They represent research and development, which have become a matter of course in all business fields. It is also the task of fashion theory to perceive and recognise these factors and, finally, to evaluate them.

Furthermore, its iconographic interpretation means that fashion theory makes a contribution to the history of fashion, founded on contemporary avant-garde fashion in this context. In fashion we find the high end and the low end; as with the distinction between serious and popular music, we have haute couture and designer fashion on the one hand, and everyday clothing on the other. We must take both into account along with their respective claims to innovation.

Equally, scientific research will always operate from the premises of the age and in the context of its social demands. New methods and analyses will develop when the tools of research lose their edge and questions lose their social relevance. While the emphasis was on semiotics in the 1960s, on human behaviourism in the 1970s, and on communication science and gender studies during the 1990s, innovation research at the start of the twenty-first century calls for new starting points of scientific study. Here in particular, theory should be given access to practice. Explanatory diagrams are provided within the strategies of invention and the structures of innovation, which are regarded almost as a 'grammar' of the new. They are legible as a tool for design and production, but also for journalism and the media, and indeed for anyone with a keen interest in fashion. The familiar insight that 'there is nothing new in fashion; everything has existed already' is opposed by the equally common insight that applies to the truly innovative: 'Who is supposed to wear that?' The permanently new has become a customary assumption in fashion—a reality in the sense of 'real is what is effective'—, but we must question and assess this notion. Looking from products to the basic structures helps to clarify what is truly innovative. Models of thought from other disciplines will be included in the theory of fashion in order to test its logic.

Finally, I will examine the social constructs of communication, time, space, meaning and gender, via which innovation—and, with it, new fashion—is accepted, modified or rejected. Here, it is a matter of concretising what fashion theory has to offer, providing an answer to 'What is fashion', starting out from the question 'When is it fashion?' On the one hand, clothing is very concrete; a product that apparently surrounds us all the time, one that permanently contains us. On the other hand, however, fashion is extremely abstract, since it is negotiated within society. The aforementioned social constructs are what make clothing into fashion. Fashion requires the places and means to reach its addressees. In a similar way to art, in fashion the attention of the viewer is captured so that he can be approached with further messages—some of which are encoded, symbolic in form. If the message is not verbalised by the designer himself or herself, it is the task of fashion theory to formulate and convey it. As with all products, clothing cannot reach its market without communication. Clothing needs images and texts for its global mediation. It employs semiotics to make it recognisable as a social reference.

Fashion science visualises the structures and strategies of fashion. In the broadest possible sense, fashion journalism is fashion theory. However, much of the existing scientific discourse on fashion has not (yet) arrived in fashion journalism, partly due to a fear—in my opinion unfounded—of demanding too much from the reader, partly because of the journals' worries over the loss of advertising customers. Not least, these factors hamper fashion criticism, especially in German-speaking countries, criticism that is a matter of course in the fine and performing arts as well as in literature.

Fashion has abandoned chronology and—parallel to today's social structure—is now characterised by diversification. This state of affairs makes it logical to examine fashion along with its plurality of styles and to demonstrate the conditions under which fashion may be evaluated as applied art or design.

The aim is to visualise the social system of fashion with its full complexity, from its evolution through subsequent distribution to its perception and final acceptance. The Institute for Applied Research at the University of Applied Sciences in Pforzheim has made it possible for me to carry out diverse studies in this field, as well as—along with Comunio.de—to translate the German version of this volume, *Wann ist Mode? Strukturen, Strategien und Innovationen.* I also thank Fotostudio Them for most of the photographs and their copyrights. Of the many creative works cited in this book, I have included images of a few significant examples; for readers who wish to view some of the other creations described in these chapters, I draw their attention to the wealth of images on the Internet and in digitalised picture archives.

Ingrid Loschek

Part I
Fashion Theory

Does Fashion Need a Theory?

Like any theory of art and design, fashion theory endeavours to interlace scientific methods and creative design processes in a productive way, in order to establish a self-reflective form of cultural practice. Theory in the sense of perception and reflection is also a creative process and a form of design. Its field of application is universal, for it refers to everything that can be observed. Research is concerned with uncertainty, with searching and thought processes and with contingencies (context, coincidence). However, this does not mean that it has no method.

Complex value concepts in art or fashion are never transferred from the object to the viewer via contemplation alone; they are negotiated or mediated in a *communicative* way (cf. p. 139). This communication is not realised in one direction but is based on reciprocal interaction between the designer, object and viewer. Fashion (like art) incorporates categories of creative techniques and innovative processes as well as the potential for social exchange. It is presented as an internal viewpoint—that is, reflection that develops from the genuine practice of the creator (artist, designer)— and also as an external viewpoint, which is its social, aesthetic or cultural role. On the one hand, this means that the subject of a fashion theory is the methods and techniques of creative design, the structural features of clothing products and their visual and verbal representations. On the other hand, it examines the legitimating principles and social contexts of fashion that develop within a culture.

The insights presented systematically in the following are intended to constitute knowledge and enable experience in a manner oriented to activity and process. To this purpose, hierarchic distinctions such as the one between theory and practice will be suspended. In the sense of the statement 'Everyone knows what is beautiful—that is why there is so much that is ugly,' theory may increase the quality of both design and utility. A scientific analysis leads to objectivising, although—like every human judgement—this cannot be entirely neutral: 'Furthermore, artistic-scientific research promises to develop a critical iconic model, which reveals the iconic creation of the meaning itself' (of fashion; author's note).[1] For Otl Aicher, a key designer and the founder of the Academy of Design in Ulm, good design results from its link to the sciences rather than its link to art. The former include aesthetics, perceptual theory, colour theory, design analysis, semiotics and cultural sociology.

The *sensory perception* of structural qualities, like the visual perception of the colour, form and texture of a brightly coloured piece of cloth, is one thing; the *recognition* of what it is—for example a dress—is quite another. It is the quality of meaning, the recognition of a board with four legs as a table, which requires socially or individually acquired knowledge. Aristotle writes in his *Metaphysics*: 'Knowledge, also, and perception, we call the measure of things for the same reason, because we come to know something by them—while as a matter of fact they are measured rather than measure other things.'[2] The physiologist and physicist Hermann von Helmholtz recognised as early as 1850 that '[s]ensations, like the eye's recognition of areas of colour within our field of vision, are signs to the consciousness; the brain must learn to interpret their significance.'[3] The American Charles S. Peirce, who—together with Ferdinand de Saussure—is considered the founder of semiotics at the beginning of the twentieth century, also started out from the assumption that perception occurs through the conversion of sensory impressions: 'We have no ability to think without signs.'[4] In this way, both Helmholtz and Peirce emphasise the act of translation undertaken by the brain in the process of perception. Peirce distinguishes between what is perceived (the percept) and our perceptual judgement. The percept is the sign linking the object and a perceptual judgement. Access to objects always comes about via the reproduction of the percept as a sign. The sign has the form of a sensory impression—in other words, the form of an image, a sound and so forth. The percept is interpreted as something. A sound may be a voice, the ringing of a telephone or the sound of a radio. Standing amidst a grey fog, for example, and concluding that it is smoke (e.g. as a result of the smell or because the sun is shining around about) and furthermore that there is a fire somewhere nearby, one makes a perceptual judgement. Perceptual judgements are an extreme form of abduction, since they generally come about in an unconscious and largely uncontrolled manner, and because we are unable to deny them as a result of our permanently active senses. Another example is a piece of cloth which—on the basis of experience, the form or the white shirt surrounding it—one can recognise as a necktie. The more often repeated perceptual judgements are confirmed, the more often they will be internalised as true and subsequently develop into habits of thought and behaviour, like the wearing of a necktie together with a white shirt.

In *philosophy,* recognition or cognition is the mental processing of what we have perceived. Perception according to *psychology* is the sum of various steps of sensory information—reception, interpretation, selection and organisation—and, indeed, of only the information that is received for the purpose of the perceiver's adaptation to his environment or its alteration (modification). Perception varies due to the individual content of the perceiver's memories, moods and thought processes, which are used to construct a mental model. As a consequence, every living creature has its own perception.

The theories of philosophy, psychology and semiotics can be linked with current insights of *neuroscience,* since the organ of cognition is not the eye but the brain.

The eye is simply a tool in cognitive processes. All '*criteria of interpretation* lie in the brain and are devised by the brain itself'.[5] The brain provides 'constructed realities' that it creates for itself. Neurobiologists like Gerhard Roth and Wolfgang Singer make clear that essentially, the human brain is a system that serves itself; in other words, it is self-referential. The self-referential system of the brain develops its own perceptual criteria and seeks its own criteria for evaluation (in contrast to a computer that is only 'aware' of the rules by which it works; this is also why it works so reliably—it does not evaluate!). The brain has no 'fixed wires' at all; it remains flexible. It is based on a self-generated system that continues to be a subject of research. It is described as 'creative chaos', but also as a binary system of decisions that operates at a rate of 100 million per second. A flexible brain is the obvious prerequisite to humans' lifelong ability to learn and relearn, but also to imagine new things and accept them, and indeed to constantly organise and reorganise itself. *As a consequence of the neuronal concept of reality, it is possible to conceive and/or to recognise the innovative.* Man is not a rigid identity: "The brain learns through its own activity. It is incapable of remaining in one and the same state, and precisely this is the deeper meaning of the self-referential . . . Of course the brain has constant contact with its surroundings. Its semantic self-containment—that of the self-referential—means that the brain can certainly be stimulated from outside but the significance of this perception can only emerge through the brain." Furthermore, not only is the process of seeing a process largely controlled by the brain, but a person's viewpoint is as well.[6]

The brain does not reproduce external realities; it provides internal constructs of reality. These internal constructs of reality are responsible for what each of us perceives as unusual or inconsistent, what each individual remembers or forgets, and what each individual may become accustomed to. They determine when perception is especially easy or difficult, and which stimuli trigger increased attention. These internal constructs of reality—among other things—are responsible for individual taste and individual emotions. Or to put it another way: individual thought and emotional longings or fears design our reality. For that reason, the limits of design lie in the power of imagination and in each individual's readiness to accept it.

In order to avoid creating 'cognitive blind spots'[7] and arrive instead at the similar realities so important for communication, there is a need to develop awareness (cf. pp. 26, 91). This awareness points to things, such as to a necktie, but it also serves to question matters of course like the necktie. 'If we wish to coexist with other people, we must recognise that their certainty . . . is as legitimate and valid as our own,'[8] according to the Chilean neurobiologist Humberto Maturana, whose research focuses on the biology of cognition.

Transferred to a theory of fashion, this means that we need constructs and appellations—a sleeve as opposed to a trouser leg, or a narrow or wide sleeve—in order to not only perceive but also recognise an item of clothing and communicate about it. These constructs and appellations are schemata and concepts with which we can structure perception and recognition, thus becoming capable of action. They are taken into account by the constructor, tailor, fashion creator or designer—who dresses an arm in a sleeve and legs in trousers or stockings and not vice versa—and they function as a basis of communication or, respectively, they evolve through communication.

Vestimentary[9] constructs have been passed down orally since the beginning of historical time, and since the sixteenth century as drawn construction plans—so-called patterns. Since then they have been available in books of patterns and constructions, and as concepts in fashion lexica and encyclopaedias. Concepts help to define and sort explanations, but they themselves are not the explanation. Accordingly, fashion theory cannot subsist without descriptive costume studies and fashion history as its basis; these analyse styles, forms, cuts and materials on the basis of both objects (artefacts) and visual or verbal descriptions, and place them in the relevant historical contexts. In addition, the specifics of clothing arise as a result of their combination with the human body (cf. p. 158)—in formal respects, but also with respect to appellations like leg/leggings, neck/neckline. But what is the quality of meaning when a seam is fashioned like a neckline, or the other way around, as in the models Viktor & Rolf presented in their summer 2006 collection? This kind of innovation results in tremendous uncertainty and usually meets with rejection due to our previously acquired or learnt knowledge. In order to become available as an insight, a pullover with front and back sections each consisting of four sleeves so that the whole consists of ten sleeves—like a model Rei Kawakubo produced for Comme des Garçons in 1982—must be 'newly' perceived and also renamed as a new construct. Ten sleeves on one pullover does not exist in our universal cultural memory.[10] (There is specialist knowledge in fashion, too; however, it is typical of the everyday culture of fashion that people refer not to specialist knowledge but rather trivially to 'insider knowledge'.) In clothing, a reference to man—anthropomorphism in the sense of man having two arms and therefore a pullover requiring two sleeves—continues to be valid knowledge. Notwithstanding this, clothing is not measured against human body forms a priori; it also follows its own rules of design (cf. the crinoline), which are asserted insofar as they are evaluated positively in a society.

On the one hand, fashion is explained from the perspective of sensory perception, on the other hand from the basis of a theoretical recognition of social constructs. Following the system theory of Niklas Luhmann, the definition of clothing and fashion evolves through form and medium (cf. p. 25). The 'what' that we see is followed by turning to 'how' we see it. In other words, after the 'what' has been clarified as a traditional definition, observation of the 'how' begins—as individual, cerebrally synthesised processing. The essence and significance of fashion are thus analysed individually, above and beyond the form of clothing.

Fashion Does Not Explain Itself

What do Marcel Duchamp's *Urinoir,* which he interpreted as the art object *Fountain* in 1917, and a dress full of holes that Julien McDonald created, which he defined as a lace dress in 1997, have in common? Neither work 'functions' without the underlying tension between what is visible and the statement made about it. In 1917, Duchamp submitted the urinal as an artwork for the annual exhibition of the Society of Independent Artists in New York. His claim was that the context—the art exhibition, the mode of presentation (pedestal, angle), the signature of the producer (he signed the industrial product 'R(ichard) Mutt' using a name based on the manufacturer, J. L. Mott), the title *Fountain,* and art-theoretical reflection—made this trivial serial product into art. Duchamp was not allowed to leave the pissoir basin in the exhibition, and only one single photograph of it exists, in the second edition of *The Blind Man* (New York, May 1917); the urinal itself was thrown away.

Marcel Duchamp was the first artist to thematise the function of art along with its purely visual principles of contemplation, and to question it by involving philosophical and technological insights. Literally, he drew attention to the limited information of visual reception by showing how a change in meaning could be brought about through the intellectual reception or, respectively, nonreception of a work. Duchamp came to the conclusion that *the viewer 'makes' art.* Duchamp's conclusion can be transferred to fashion, inasmuch as *the viewer 'makes' clothing into fashion.* This meets the extravagant haute couture model's claim to be fashion, just as an item of clothing becomes the fashion only when it is worn by a specific group within society.

Duchamp's works survived as Readymades. This term, which Duchamp himself chose for an existing manufactured object placed in an artistic context, established an art trend that led—among other things—to Pop Art. On the theoretical level, Marcel Duchamp recognised that the importance of art, or rather of the claim to be art, pointed the way for Modernist art. The previously valid understanding of art was thrown into question and subsequently reformulated. In 1924, the important art theorist André Breton wrote his *Manifesto of Surrealism,* so helping Surrealism towards a better understanding and ultimate recognition. Interpretation is also a vital cultural achievement.

Interpretation and theoretical references convey the value of what has been perceived and have a reciprocal effect on perception, in the sense of 'you only see what you know'. The 'view beyond the familiar aspect of things' visualises a different level of values. As a consequence of this, Wassily Kandinsky took the opposite path. He wrote and published his theory 'Concerning the Spiritual in Art' in 1912, before he painted his first abstract picture. (Today, there is no lingering doubt that Kandinsky backdated his 'first abstract watercolour' from 1913 to 1910.) He deemed this measure necessary, as a nonreflexive experience of art 'remains . . . ineffective, for the visible aspect of the work with its external mundanity is, as a rule, already familiar to the viewer'.[11] But in fashion, where every model is known as a com-modity and judged as such, the need for explanation is usually rejected; as a result, there is no fashion criticism as such. In contrast to art, little or even no substance is expected of fashion due to its assumed mundanity. In fashion, an increase in cultural evaluation is achieved by declaring the intentions of the visible, for example in the case of intellectually connoted models by Alexander McQueen (cf. p. 55) or Hussein Chalayan (cf. p. 63).

As active permeation and interpretation, declarations connect a fashion design to various cultural value levels (tradition, space, everyday), pinpoint the tensions constituting the model and increase interest in this way—for fashion always points to something extra-vestimentary such as the body, eroticism, emotions or music.

At the beginning of the twentieth century, artistic aspirations were defined in *manifestos*. The avant-garde in contemporary art and film declared itself via manifes-tos and dogmas in which aims and ideals were laid down, the need for innovation was expressed, and delimitations and breaks with tradition were demanded in a radical and ultimate way. It is wrong to believe that art and design (clothing) explain themselves today: 'Today, artists occasionally express the opinion that their work speaks for itself, implying that aesthetic practice and theory come about in (the same) work and cannot be separated from one another. Accordingly, they maintain, the theory is contained in their works; the artist has said . . . everything in the work . . . Additional statements would only represent meaningless watering down and simplification. Quite apart from the fact that not everything can be expressed or represented conceptually: this elitist refusal to enter into discourse can also be interpreted as arrogance' (or uncertainty— author's note).[12] Without the desire and willingness to grasp something intellectually, there would be no academic study of literature, art or philosophy.

Silke Peters, art theorist and independent artist, has been calling upon people since the beginning of the twenty-first century to write manifestos again and has founded an Internet forum to that purpose.[13] A manifesto (from the Latin *manus,* hand) clari-fies what is described and makes it 'tangible' in a way that is not possible through pure contemplation; the intellect thus experiences it as ergonomics (the universal law of work) and a connotative extension of visual reception. But manifestos are no lon-ger fashionable. Surely we ought to be able to expect programmatic statements and the mediation of perspectives from artists/designers themselves. Today this seems to be a positive taboo. But designers and artists seldom master the ability to describe their own work well, even in the case of such eloquent personalities as Karl Lager-feld (who talks rarely about his creations and more often about himself) or Vivienne Westwood. Ultimately, of course, it is not their profession. Analytical or formal-aesthetic discourse on art and fashion is left to art or fashion theorists, specialist journalists and historians. If fashion journalism succeeded in describing the signified in fashion—its ideology and rhetoric above and beyond a description of form and material—the fashion press would gain *the capacity for criticism* above and beyond its commercial character. Furthermore, declarations would make avant-garde fashion comprehensible and perhaps acceptable as a result. It is the task of fashion theory to analyse the aesthetic premises, performative impulses, social characteristics and economic conditions of fashion, and to make these universally comprehensible.

Roland Barthes and 'The Fashion System'

The French philosopher and semiologist Roland Barthes investigated the language used in French fashion journals of the 1960s (at a time when there was a comparatively large proportion of text in fashion journals) in his publication *Système de la mode* (1967).[14] This was the first large-scale analysis of a nonlinguistic sign system (fashion) and its linguistic, that is written mediation. In this work, Barthes explains the existence of a vestimentary linguistic code, along with its poetics and rhetoric. By becoming the subject of magazines—and to the present day, (almost) every debate with it is associated with this medium—clothing fashion develops from a 'reality' into a code and is thus translated into the mode of the written sign. This means that Barthes sees fashion as a 'narrative'[15] before the object. It is therefore language through which fashion is constituted, it is language that arouses the desire for consumption and defines the 'collective imaginary'.[16] Barthes pinpoints language—and not images, as is now the case—as the essential strategy in the diffusion of fashion. In this context, the literary theorist Gerhard Goebel provides a memorable example based on jeans advertising from 1981: a woman and two men wearing jeans are leaning on a railing, and in the background we see the silhouette of a big city (New York). In addition, within the image there is the text 'New Man, c'est aussi la liberté'. (According to Roland Barthes, the pictorial advertising here is given meaning only by the added text.) Goebel analyses: 'New Man' (the brand of jeans) means 'new fashion', means 'New York', means 'new man' or rather 'freedom'. 'A specific product points to "fashion", as well as to a part of the world and beyond that to a specific ideal, a more or less ideological and certainly affectively charged value: product—fashion—world—value; this could be the basic formula of the message, not only of fashion advertising but also of fashion news as such, for fashion reports in the relevant magazines are no more than concerted advertising for the products of several manufacturers.'[17] The jeans advertisement just described expresses 'the dialectic distinction and affiliation—being different and being "in"— that constitutes recognition of the actual value of the fashion sign',[18] according to Georg Simmel (sociologist) and, in accordance with Luhmann's system, the binary code—'in' and 'out'—in the system of fashion (cf. p. 25).

–2–

Textiles as Material

Apart from fur, leather, rubber and other so-called non-wovens, the substance of clothing—for which the collective term is *material*—is usually woven, that is it is a textile. Preparation work is necessary in order to produce textiles (from the Latin *texere,* to plait, weave)—preprocessing such as spinning and weaving, knitting or milling. The textile is used as a cover and as delimitation, whether of the human body, products (table, chair) or spaces (tent, tapestry).[1] To benefit these functions, the textile is received as 'nonconcrete', almost as a medium comparable to the paint in painting. Fabric is the medium for the tailor, and the medium of clothing is thus its substance. Textiles display qualities of the 'nonmaterial' due to their extreme adaptability and manifold states as a flat surface, fold or plastic form, as well as their multiple characteristics like rigidity (stiff silk) or mobility (wafting, swinging), density (non-transparent) or delicacy (transparent). Ecologically, the textile may be a pointer to renewability (wool), but also to nonpermanence (natural silk). Great cultural-historical and iconographic significance is attributed to textiles as a result of their material condition and their varied surface designs (colours and patterns). In archaeology, however, textiles have been and often continue to be undervalued.[2]

Since the end of the twentieth century, high-tech textiles as well as ecologically and ethically acceptable textiles have been coming to the fore. Textile research institutes focus globally on climate and body control microfibres, thermal shape memory fabrics, and colour changing and retro-reflective materials, but smart textiles have not reached the major market yet. One of the biggest challenges is to imitate the most intelligent—natural skin—which is one of the tasks of bionic and biomimesis. Though still in experimental stages, innovations such as dissolving fabrics developed by designer Helen Storey in collaboration with scientist Tony Ryan, are sparking pioneering impulses in organic textiles and eco-fashion. Despite continuous efforts within both the exclusive prêt-à-porter and the ready-made clothing industry, the general interest in eco-fashion is still marginal.

–3–

Clothes as Form

If the human body is seen as a spatial form, the skin represents the demarcation line between the inside and the outside. Clothing then becomes an extension of this corporal space boundary and the interface between a person's corporal space and the external space of the environment (cf. p. 146). This extension may be realised with several layers of protective fabric, and by means of physical apparatus creating distance such as the crinoline or brassiere. Clothing is always connected to the body, whereby on the one hand it forms a spatial extension of the body and alters our image of the body's surface and form; on the other hand, it imposes the materiality of the clothing onto the body and alters it in this way, for example by means of lacing and tying.[1] This connection with the human body does not signify wearability in the sense of social tolerability—'Who on earth is supposed to wear that?'—but is an exclusively physical connection. Where it is not given, clothing is art; that is clothing is used as a form by the system of art (cf. p. 167). Clothing,[2] including accessories like bags or shoes, always refers to the human body, that is it emblematises the form of the human body (however, this is not a causal explanation of clothing; cf. pp. 12, 136) and is observed as such. Tailors' dummies and display mannequins function as a surrogate, namely as representatives of the human body form. As an ideal living body, the model (mannequin, from the Dutch for 'little man' and jointed doll) is located at the interface between the inanimate tailor's dummy and the imperfect 'normal body' of the wearer.

Clothing—as a 'second skin'—shares its character as the encasing of space with architecture, the 'third skin'. In contrast to clothing, architecture is the encasing of an 'air space' in which people spend time, move around and store things. In contrast to architecture, people carry the covering clothing around with them. Exceptions are borderline objects such as Lucy Orta's *Habitent* from 1992, a rain cape that can be transformed into a tent. Clothing points to a basic model that is both *plastic* and *sculptural,* in the sense of a material draped or wound around the body (plastic) or of material that is fragmented, cut out (sculptural) and sewn together. The creating (Latin *creare*) of material forms like clothing should be understood as a process from one material state into another, for example from the sheep's fleece via the woven piece of cloth to the draped or sewn item of clothing. An item of clothing is the result of a process constituting material and form. Thereby, the pattern sheet (the paper pattern) is the enduring form that guarantees the possibility of infinite reproduction (cf. p. 127). The two-dimensional pattern indicates both the flat expanse and the third dimension of dress and body. Lines on the paper mark the lines of the cuts; here the material will develop depth or rather gain a plastic form. In itself, the tailoring process is a sculptural technique (from the Latin *sculpere,* to cut). During the process of sewing together the pieces, positive forms (protrusions) on the paper and their transfer onto a soft fabric lead to negative forms (indentations) in the clothing. The sewing together of individual parts as well as the marking of pleats or darts result in the plastic form (from the Greek *plastos,* formed) of the clothing. Individual plastic forming is also achieved by means of lacing, as was customary before the origin of the art of tailoring. A plastic casing—a second skin in a more exact sense—has become possible only with the use of extremely elastic materials beginning in the 1960s. All such creations also allow additional modifications and the lacing up of the body.

A mass of historical evidence attests to the idea of the body as a spatial form. This evidence ranges from the work of Leonardo da Vinci, who mirrored the division of the earth's surface into individual provinces by Ptolemy by chopping up the body into limbs, segments and chambers, to Sigmund Freud, for whom the body appeared as a sum of sexual erogenous zones concentrated primarily on the body orifices (oral, anal, genital zones), and finally to Erving Goffman, who drew attention to the culturally specific evaluation of different body regions, pointing out that among the American middle classes, for example, little effort is made to 'protect the elbows from contact, while particular attention, as a rule, is paid to the body orifices'.[3] In addition, there is James Laver and his reference to the changing erogenous zones in fashion.[4] Clothing not only takes into account all these spatial figurations like limbs, erogenous zones and body orifices; it limits existing forms or adds to them. Clothing designs the body. The original purpose of all extensions of the body (coverings, carrying apparatus) was, on the one hand, to retain body energy or to gain it, bringing evolutionary advantages to man as a species, and on the other hand, the global expansion of his living space.[5] Strategies like body painting, hangings and clothing served the purpose of physical and psychological survival. The clothed or otherwise designed human body is perceived as a unit. Clothing as well as body painting and other body designs make man into a social addressor (cf. p. 156).

Everything cultural (from the Latin *cultura,* meaning the cultivation of body and soul, processing, ennoblement, agriculture, building) can be viewed as a form of clothing or dressing up and as a form of delimitation and exclusion: the tent, the house, walls, ceiling, the carpet, tiles, the painting, the car, the aeroplane, the sculpture (the dressing of the corporeal), music (the dressing of sounds), literature (the dressing of words), agriculture (the dressing of nature). Fashion is the dressing of clothing; it is the interface between creation and social communication, between form and medium (cf. p. 25).

Production in the Historical Context

A *survey of the historical order of clothing and craftsmanship* promotes an understanding of clothing forms, their production and innovation, and fashion as a system (cf. pp. 19, 21).

In Roman antiquity and the Middle Ages, a distinction was made between the *artes liberales* (of higher standing) and the *artes mechanicae,* the 'liberal' and 'working' arts. The *artes liberales* included—divided into two disciplines—grammar, rhetoric and dialectics as well as arithmetic, geometry, astronomy and music. First and foremost, the *artes mechanicae* included *ars lanificium*—work with wool, including all tasks involved in the production of clothing. In addition, the following were attributed to the *artes mechanicae*: seafaring, agriculture, hunting, healing and acting. Architects, painters (since they only copied reality) and sculptors were described as 'labourers', a concept—as *ouvrier*—that already existed in French. It was not until the fifteenth century that the humanist and neo-Platonist Marsile Ficin introduced painting and architecture to the liberal arts and the 'artisan' was further separated from the artist or 'artiste'.

Before the twelfth century, clothing was usually made in convents or within the family, meaning that the tailor's profession did not evolve until the middle of the twelfth century. In France at that time, a distinction was made between the work of the tailor and that of the sewer. Then, later, the appearance of clothing was separated between religious (much to the annoyance of the Church) and state-political contexts of meaning and function. This division is documented by repeated attempts at containment (bans on luxury) or binding regulations in the shape of so-called clothing orders. The development of fashion as an individual form of clothing is documented from this time onwards. The preacher Berthold von Regensburg wrote at the end of the thirteenth century: 'And wenches, ye exceed all manner of decency with dresses and fine skirts, sewn with such frills and folly, ye fain be ashamed.'[6] Both iconography and literary sources make clear that the reasons for differences in fashion were not only political and social, but mainly individual erotic demands; clothing emphasized the relevant intentions. In contrast to the artist personality developing at the beginning of the sixteenth century, however, the producers of clothing, the tailors, enjoyed little to no prestige. Artists like Albrecht Dürer also functioned as fashion advisors and designers. Their influence on the development of style was irrelevant, however, with the exception of Jacques-Louis David at the end of the eighteenth century and the artists of the Reform Movement at the beginning of the twentieth century.[7] As opposed to the sewers, but also to the cobblers and later the corset makers, the tailors were not organised into a guild. For this reason, the profession was often practised by Jews, to whom access to the guilds was denied anyway. This state of affairs continued until the French Revolution in 1789, when the guilds were abolished. The tailor had little influence on the design of fashion; as a rule, the client received any recognition for the clothing that he wore. The criteria of one's being fashionable were based on the contrast between being noticed and not being noticed (binary code) as a resource of individual aesthetic and/or erotic attention. In the course of the eighteenth century, the milliners—who were responsible for updating the embellishments of clothing and for accessories—appeared as 'fashion advisors' more frequently, especially in Paris. They belonged to the guild of the *marchands des modes* (French for fashion merchant) and were thus part of the economic system.

It was not until the mid–nineteenth century that autonomous forms of fashion with a designated signature emerged in Paris—known as *haute création* or haute couture—apart from a very few tailors known by name in the European metropolises of the eighteenth and early nineteenth centuries. The status of the haute couturiers involved a new self-understanding; they were granted autonomous aesthetic responsibility, which allowed them to seek out their clients and to negotiate with customers concerning both the aesthetics of the creation and their own fee. The haute couturiers' pecuniary reward was measured by abilities judged not as exclusively artisan, but rather as creative and intellectual. Reward was given to the idea, quite apart from working hours and material. In this way, the definition of the price of an haute couture dress was raised from the level of objective calculability (with respect to both made-to-measure and the already existing ready-made clothing) to the level of subjective evaluation. The haute couture dress was understood as a concrete original (comparable to a work of art) and led to copying of the cut and surrogates of its expensive materials (cf. p. 127). Correspondingly, the founder of haute couture, Charles Frederick Worth, is quoted as claiming that 'one of my waistlines is worth an oil painting'[8]. Subsequently, design was set above handicraft skills. The French imperial family under Napoleon III supported this attitude, regarding the couture *création* as the marketing of luxury goods which—also in the fields of porcelain or silks—was always adjudged a pillar of the French economy.

But why were handicrafts regarded with less respect than intellectual work, even by the ancient Greeks? Denis Diderot, the son of an artisan and an encyclopaedist and enlightener, struggled in isolation to demonstrate to other key figures of the Enlightenment that the production of concrete objects could also represent an intellectual art (cf. p. 176).

–4–

Fashion as System

If fashion is verified as a social system, there is no longer any need to categor-
ise it as a 'phenomenon'.[1] This analysis is based on *Social Systems* by Niklas
Luhmann (1984), which is currently one of the most frequently applied theories in
German-speaking countries, not only in sociology but also in sciences as diverse as
psychology, management and literary theory. Luhmann's social system—despite
the many difficulties of terminology—offers a suitable basis on which to grasp
fashion intellectually. Fashion as a system is equated with the systems Luhmann
laid down such as politics, economics, sport, religion and art.

Luhmann himself did little to investigate fashion. He mentions fashion, among
other things, when he refers to 'symbolically generalized communication media',
which also include morality and language but are not systems in themselves. Furthermore, Luhmann cites fashion—*la mode*—as an example, at first in connection with
the emergence of modern societies, in contrast to the former *le mode* (cf. p. 133).
He writes: 'The discovery of fashion [*la mode,* author's note] begins to undermine
the enduring validity of forms [*le mode,* author's note] and thus the possibility of
hierarchizing humanity. Aptitude in terms of temporal conditions becomes more important than position.'[2] This statement may be true as such, but not with its restriction
of time to 'since modern society'. Individualisation—as well as changes in the shape
of dress, particularly with respect to embellishment and accessories—is already evidenced in the mediaeval period; among other things, by repeated attempts to restrict
it through (local) clothing regulations and bans on luxury.[3] However, the notion of
individuality emerged within the community, while—according to Luhmann—today
the individual is denied any possibility of identification with the whole of a functionally diversified society.[4] Luhmann starts out from a functional differentiation of modern society on the basis of social communication, which has led to the distinction and
emerging independence of various functional social systems. Such a system, such
as politics or sport, fulfils a function that cannot be fulfilled by any other functional
system. A system must be autonomous, self-referential and operatively closed.[5] This
will also apply to fashion, if it proves to be a system. It means that only the fashion
system produces fashion and not, for example, the economic system. Fashion is not
a clever invention of capital for the purpose of constantly renewing individual attire.
Fashion even endured as a self-referential system, as autonomous design, in times of

war. Even the frequently cited reciprocal relation of skirt lengths to the state of the economy is quite inapt. Capital has merely adopted a system that had already mastered the production of luxury goods in the age of darkest feudalism.

The exclusion of the economic system as a producer of fashion (not as a producer of clothing) is verified in the chapter 'When Is Fashion?' via its demonstration that the basis of fashion is communication. The fashion system consists of the immaterial process of communication, fired by the material clothing. Fashion can emerge only when there is communication about clothing and it is termed as fashion. This leads to the paradox that couture and design creations—a priori, before any type of distribution—are referred to as 'fashion' and yet an already widely distributed mass 'fashion' is also known as such. This paradox is explained by the terminological ambiguity of 'fashion' (cf. p. 133) and by the development process of clothing and fashion (cf. p. 19). Communication about fashion simultaneously unifies, organises and regulates fashion and develops a form of flexible self-description. Every social communication must develop mechanisms that make the constant reproduction of basic occurrences possible.[6] Fashion journalism and journalists (observers of the second order) represent the communicative interface between clothing, fashion and clientele (observers of the third order). Luhmann attributes journalism to the system of media. In journalism, it is a matter of *linguistic, cognitive and media-relevant* explanations and analyses, and of the mediation of images (photo journalism).

The self-referential nature of fashion does not signify an autarkic sealing off. If no connective operation (another fashion) takes place, systems (costumes), but also their parts (e.g. hoop skirts) come to a standstill. Fashion as a system does not lead to the assimilation of the environment, but to a *structural linkage,* for example with other systems such as economics, politics, mass media, music, art or sport. This structural linkage is crucial to a reflection of the zeitgeist in fashion. The context is significant for structural linkage: from the standpoint of economics, fashion is a component of the economically significant environment; from the perspective of fashion design, economics is an important constant of the environment as relevant to fashion. In fashion, this exchange with the environment or other social systems is considerably greater than in the case of clothing characterised by religion or ethnic traits or of a uniform; for this reason, fashion is dynamic, open to innovation and less socially isolating. The environment or other systems have a supportive and also a blocking or neutralising impact on fashion.

Conflicts ensue when the differing attitudes of expectation towards the system are not satisfied. As examples, one could cite—despite a liberalisation of role-linked behaviour[7]—the idea of being dressed like a banker or the view that fashion makes people younger and/or beautiful (whereby the terms 'young' and 'beautiful' are negotiated in a socio-communicative way as well). Fashionable exaggerations are also understood as 'malfunctions' within fashion itself and thus as conflict.

Self-referential System of Operative Closure

Self-referential means that systems refer only to their internal operations yet remain open in a cognitive way. If we examine fashion as an external observer, it proves to be *a self-referential system of operative closure,* which develops dynamics in interchange with the environment and varies its state without altering its systemic structures as such. Systems of this type are characterised by the fact that they are not influenced causally from outside, but adjust their internal organisation (own production, tailor, ready-made clothing and haute couture, prêt-à-porter, designer fashion) in case of changes in the environment. This is known as self-organisation and may be understood as a paradigm of organised complexity.

Fashion is a *self-referential system* focused on self-organisation and the cyclic auto-reproduction of systemic elements. Since they always refer to themselves alone, in endless recurrence, they are necessarily closed on the level of their inner control structure. Thus the core area of fashion exists independent of environmental influences; it exists 'as itself'. Man's system of altering the appearance of his external body (body design) is timeless and global; only the forms change. The global power of fashion and its self-referential system (its autopoiesis) is expressed in precisely this 'ruthlessness' towards independent cultural features and social conventions.

The term *operative closure* indicates that every communication refers to a previous communication within the same system, at the same time offering the opportunity to connect with a further fashion-specific communication. Under special circumstances (e.g. following the emergence of the Punk movement), contacts to the environment (structural linkage) are adopted to increase reproduction. In self-organising systems there is no given hierarchy between organising, designing or controlling components. All parts of the system represent potential designers. Correspondingly, design, production, distribution and consumption are all part of the system and equal in value. The fashion system increases its attractiveness through performance (fashion show, pose, video clips), models, media, advertising and leading figures as well as by means of manipulation, for example by using image processing.

The theory of the *self-referential system of operative closure* explains—in a comparable way to Darwin's theory of evolution—how so many temporally and culturally different body designs and ethnic forms of clothing, costumes, military and civilian uniforms and fashions could be generated from the original development of body design (painting, hairstyling, covering up). On the one hand, environmental stimuli have an effect on systems, altering their structures (system–environment–paradigm), while interchange with other systems has an influential effect as well, such as the fashion system interchanging with the political system or the economic system. (Remember that fashion is not produced by the economic system; it is only tied to the economic system by structural linkage.) The absolutist political system influenced a hierarchic fashion structure, the democratic system a heterogeneous structure.

Comparable to the complexity in music—serious and popular music—clothing exists as haute couture and as a mass product. As a result of popular consumption, mass clothing becomes the 'semblance' of fashion. The fashion system determines for itself which factors (communication, time, space or meaning) are significant as input, or upon which it relies, and on the other hand, it defines the output that it will provide (in the sense of an input-output model).[8] Fashion as a unique creation represents an elite product, while fashion in the sense of clothing represents a mass need. In the sphere of conceptual art, fashion demands inclusion in cultural politics and the exhibition business (cf. p. 200).

In the following, I will attempt to examine fashion as a system heuristically in the spirit of Niklas Luhmann's sociological system theory.[9]

Function

Fashion is a system operating worldwide, throughout states, nations and organisations, and it does not stop at the borders of such entities. Even in times of crisis, such as during the First and Second World Wars, there were border-crossing fashions.

Systems like fashion (and the same applies to economics, science, politics, sport etc.) offer no access; they have no social address. In other words, 'fashion' is entirely without leadership and centre; there is no logical place where it can be reached. Neither organisations like the Fédération Française de la Couture, du Prêt-à-porter des Couturiers et des Créateurs de Mode in Paris nor New York Fashion Week, nor so-called fashion institutes or fashion-industry associations provide a central address for 'fashion' as such, and they do not define what becomes fashion, but try to pinpoint trends (cf. p. 27).

Autopoiesis

The organisation of fashion is a form of autopoiesis, which means that structures organised in this way change their structure only internally; they may be subject to irritation, but it is impossible to intervene into them. Autopoiesis means that all systems must arrive consistently at new forms/contents[10] if they are not to collapse, and this is also true of the social systems of religion, politics and fashion.[11] In other words: autopoietic systems (and not only, but also fashion) are dependent upon the production of innovations in order to continue. In fashion, this capacity for continuance is guaranteed by precisely defined items of clothing, patterns and parameters for draping, specific styles including so-called classics and basics, and of course by the colours, patterns and qualities of the materials. All of these provide a foundation for continuation as well as negation.

Stability

Fashion proves stable due to its systemic form of autopoiesis and its 'human interest' (the addressor; cf. p. 156). Or to put it in another way: its stability is the outcome of autopoiesis and 'human interest'. Fashion arrives at stability as a consequence of its instabilities (cf. contingency), in a way comparable to the neuronal (contingent)-network of the brain or the dis-order of chaos.

Code

The codes of systems are highly abstract and assessed as standardised difference. Fashion follows the binary code of 'in'–'out', which implies fashionable–old-fashioned. By contrast, the system does not distinguish between beautiful and ugly. This attribution arises from outside as a social understanding, a social negotiation, and also involves individual taste (cf. p. 9). The (supposedly) ugly can be extremely aesthetic, like punk or gothic fashion, according to the concept of the 'aesthetics of the ugly'.[12]

Form and Medium

Clothing is regarded as form, fashion as the medium. Since the form of clothing represents the foundation for the medium of fashion, fashion is form *and* medium. Whatever we see, it is form; the medium cannot be seen or rather the medium becomes visible only as the form of clothing. This means that we see only the clothing, not the fashion. If art makes use of the form 'clothing', the outcome is an imaginary reality or a 'doubling of the reality' of painting/photography and clothing. The difference between form and medium leads to the fashion system of 'in' and 'out' (binary code). The form/medium distinction is one made by an observer. Here, only forms (pullover/skirt/trousers etc.) are touched by the act of definition, even when it is a matter of the medium 'fashionable'/'unfashionable'. In other words, the medium can be defined only through the form. Furthermore, energy (a distributor, an operation, an 'outer determination') must be added to the difference, temporarily stabilising the form. The social application comes about via communication. There is no communication from fashion to fashion, for the question of which clothing is fashion is an exclusively social, communicatively negotiated definition. In this way, in turn, the fashion medium proffers a flexible self-definition.

Meaning

The meaning of a system develops from the meaning of observation. The meaning of observation is quasi the medium of the system. *The meaning of the observation of fashion is the new.* The new can be observed as a difference from the old, from other forms of the new, or from the conceivable future. The new is meaningful only when it is followed by another new thing. This results in the possibility of ongoing connectivity: 'Meaning is the continual actualization of potentialities. But because meaning can be meaning only as the difference between what is actual at any moment and a horizon of possibilities, every actualization always also leads to a virtualization of the potentialities that could be connected up with it.'[13] Put simply: *fashion remains fashion, because the fashion does not remain the fashion.* Possibilities for the future are thus kept open: 'The future is no longer blocked by prescribed true purposes; it is infinitely open, containing more possibilities than can be actualized.'[14] Meaning is an instrument of differentiation; first and foremost, its function is to make selections. The new is the function that makes self-referential selections.

The meaning of the observation of clothing (which is not a system in itself, but only the form on which fashion is founded) is *fixation on the human body.* Clothing's fixation on the body is derived from the evolutionary advantage of retaining body energy (animals do not need any dead, extrinsic material as covering). In addition to this, the vestimentary fixation on the body is prescribed by a community's communicative agreement on morality. (Morality is not a system in itself.) As long as clothing and accessories—however outrageous they may be—are connected to the body, they belong to the fashion system. It does not matter whether they have great affinity for the system of art or the system of economics.[15] The body itself is always the body observed: 'The "human body" is not described as an object with an "inside" and "outside", but as the product of observation by the consciousness and society (. . .) Thus, all spatial metaphors disappear that suggest an image of the "world in the world".'[16] Perceptions are the 'levels of contact on which the psychic system maintains or seems to maintain relations to the body'.[17] The consciousness operates through the medium of perceptions, 'since the sensory categorizations referring to it [the body, author's note) can be organised only in society (even in the case of the observing consciousness); this body cannot be exempted from the fragmentation that is defined by functional differentiation.'[18] Functional differentiation—like that currently existing in sport and medicine—is countered by a demand for holistic observation. Clothing (also self-painting and tattooing) and the body are perceived as a single unit. Differences are established by means of comparisons based on observation. Every design of the body is socially negotiated. Clothing, as well as body painting and other designs of the body, makes 'the person' into a social addressor (cf. p. 156). As such, the body is not an address.

Programme

The programme of fashion consists in the design of clothing by means of patterns, seams, pleats, draping, colours and patterns. In addition, the programme includes practices of dissemination such as style guides, creation of brands, fairs and fashion shows (comparable to competitions within the sport system). Style guides are proposals of stylistic design developed by trend scouts—as observers of the environment—and made available to either the design or marketing department of a fashion company or studio. Trend scouts may belong to either the fashion system or the economic system (cf. pp. 24, 96). Distribution and multiplication is realised by magazines and advertising as a part of the media system and by displays (including window displays) as part of the economic system.

Symbiotic Mechanisms

Fashion (even when it is extremely unusual designer fashion) refers to the body through the form of clothing. When no reference is made to the body, this is a question not of fashion but of art making use of the form of clothing (cf. p. 169).

Complexity

The world is complex only to the observer. The complexity of fashion is observed as the plurality of available clothing and styles, as well as the diversity of epistemological explanations and historical developments. Complexity is not a quality in itself. Complexity is selective relativisation of the fundamental openness of human attitudes and actions; it is reduced by the formation of social systems. The fashion system determines the factors it holds significant, whether avant-garde or conventional, sporty or elegant, and so forth.

Contingency

Contingency (from the Latin *contingere,* possibility, chance) refers to a fundamental openness and uncertainty. Our perception of the world and of fashion is contingent, since it is based on distinctions and constructs that could be otherwise or could be made otherwise and are therefore unstable, in the sense of 'everything could always be completely different'. For example, the intentions behind the clothing of film and pop stars or protagonists in music videos or TV soap series (like all intentions) are considered nonarbitrary. In addition, personal taste is a chance aspect (contingency), and the result is an example of fashion's instability.

Furthermore, fashion is subject to the special form of *double contingency.* In other words, as observers of the first order, designers observe the environment including nature, living creatures or system-immanent products like ethnic clothing or street creations and develop these into model creations. There are also designers (fashion is contingent) with great artistic affinity and unusual perceptions, like Rei Kawakubo or Viktor & Rolf, who arrive at something new by starting out from an idea, an emotion, an experiment, or a deviation (cf. p. 60).

In turn, the fashion designers' creations are observed by fashion journalists, buyers and dealers—as observers of the second order—as well as selected and presented to their clientele. This selection is based on experience and on feedback from sales figures, but also on individual taste that seeks to represent a target group. Observers of the second order have a structural linkage to the economic system and the media system. Style advisors including leading personalities and media designers belong to these systems. The customer is a third-order observer[19] who observes the media and the offers available in the shops and orients herself/himself accordingly.

Correspondingly, fashion is 'interplay between contingency and non-arbitrariness'.[20] Both play a part in fashion, as fashions depend very much on how fashion is observed and communicated at the different levels of presentation. In other words, the course of action taken by mass fashion, for example, will be made dependent on the successful communication of luxury prêt-à-porter or designer fashion. (In each case, the other's next step is thought out in advance and influences one's own course of action, as in a game of chess.) Not least due to its contingency, fashion is not necessarily concerned with the beautiful or the true or—in any way or form—with authenticity.

Zero Methodology

The term zero methodology conveys a paradox based on zero as a number signifying nothing, yet making any other number placed to the left of it signify more than it would alone. This means that zero also includes something that it ought to exclude. The paradox lies in the creation of value by means of something with no value; arriving at something positive by means of something negative.

In fashion, for example, luxury brands like Hermès or Louis Vuitton introduce limits on certain articles like the Kelly Bag in order to achieve their aim for desirability and exclusivity—so that a product becomes a fashion. In this way, they (consciously) increase the 'danger' that the article will be copied. In turn, the copy prompts many people—also those outside the 'luxury society'—to want the article. As a result, it becomes the fashion (fashion is not fashion until a group within society has agreed on it). The paradox lies in the promotion of distribution and desirability, including aura, by means of limitation.

To sum up, it can be said that Niklas Luhmann's theory of social systems enables us to grasp both the structure and the strategy of fashion in concrete terms. It helps to rescue fashion from its apparently inexplicable nature, or rather transfers it from the category of a unique phenomenon into something that can be defined and analysed. On the basis of Luhmann's system theory, it is possible to explain the communicative definition of fashion, change and difference as the 'as-is state'—the zeitgeist of fashion.

Part II
Invention and Innovation

Curiosity includes everything pertaining to man's drive to see and disclose scandalously the inside that remains concealed, still to be revealed, behind the overlapping layers of our construction and its ultimate unknown.

Hans Bellmer

–5–

When Is Invention?

Inventions encompass new ideas before their marketing phase. Inventions are expressed as abstracts, blueprints or concepts according to the medium, including the realisation of prototypes. In the fashion business they may be drawings or models and also include the collections shown on the catwalk. Innovations emerge only from inventions' saleable realisation or 'application' in the sense of evaluation—according to the classic theory of innovation (cf. p. 87). The discovery of something new emerged in the prehistorical context of searching for evolutionary advantages in terms of increasing the energetic efficiency, through provision of food, physical protection and territorial expansion. The following evolutionary developments conduced to an increasing competence in social communication, which human behaviourism pinpoints as a biological predisposition of humanity.[1] However, the ethnologist Helge Gerndt points out that in Europe, curiosity has been considered a positive trait only since the modern age (cf. pp. 90, 152). Before that, the fear of the unknown and the unfamiliar, which was not part of tradition or convention—in particular for political and religious reasons—was much stronger than the desire to explore the uncertain and the insecure.

When Is Creativity?

Making something is the extension of the ego into the self-organised world.

Otl Aicher

'Creativity is a natural quality . . . It is the capacity for evolution . . . In reality, human creativity is something natural and simple . . . it is just that man's image of his own creativity is too lofty', according to physicist and Nobel Prize winner Gerd Binnig.[1] Creativity is not a quality demonstrated by humankind alone, as is so often but mistakenly assumed; it exists in the natural world to an equal extent. Nature also produces 'the pointless but beautiful' and 'the useful yet unimposing'; the aim is evolution, although nature lacks the power of imagination, any 'imaginative foresight'. Binnig suggests that creativity also exists in everyday life, for no one process resembles another—at the most, it is self-similar. Minimal differences, variations and combinations can also lead to the new (cf. pp. 101, 113). The evaluation of the creative—its value—is dependent on the observer; or rather, it is negotiated communicatively in the sense of *When is creativity?*

Artistic-creative or innovative design, however, is a question not of the so-called normal creativity shared by every person to the same extent—in the sense, for example of building sandcastles—but of original conceptual and design potentials. It includes a host of cognitive dispositions such as analogue, analytical, metaphorical, associative and quasi 'playful' thinking, as well as curiosity and a wealth of imagination, quite apart from constructive abilities and knowledge. In the current context, being creative means introducing the world to a new, not yet existent design, a genuinely new element or an original solution to a problem. The key factor in innovation is the generative moment. One interesting study on creativity offers an additional aspect: in his book *Born to Rebel*,[2] science-historian Frank Sulloway examines how family dynamics and the order of siblings influence children's personality development and their creative genius. Using the example of scientific revolutions, Sulloway demonstrates that firstborn children tend to take over established views of the world. Those born later are more likely to rebel, to be the ones who trigger revolutionary upheavals in scientific thought.

Man owes his creativity to the dichotomy between his rational left and intuitive right cerebral hemispheres. Here, the decisive factor is how the two hemispheres communicate with each other, namely the process that occurs in the corpus callosum (a dense, fibrous connecting structure cf. p. 8). The rational left cerebral hemisphere generates knowledge, and the right hemisphere generates intuition and imagination; both are necessary for a functioning innovation. Without the communicative neuronal network in the brain, no innovative designs—including vestimentary innovations— would ever come about. They would either have outstanding aesthetics but be unwearable in the sense of not being body connected or hampering the body's movement (that is, a textile sculpture or virtual reality), or they would be structurally flawless but miserable in appearance. Computers do not possess a 'right brain hemisphere', meaning that they are only 'half human'. As a consequence, they are incapable of distinguishing between good and bad design. Computers have no emotions; the weeping cyborg is a fiction. This implies that the creative will always be something subjective and biological. The computer does not calculate things that cannot function in theory, either—in other words, it takes no risks. The willingness to take a *risk*—in both material and emotional respects (e.g. being laughed at)—that constitutes part of creative innovations is characteristic only of nature. The biological brain is carbon based. All carbon compounds are unstable, meaning that components stored in them can be lost—the process known as *forgetting.* The so-called brain of the computer is based on silicon and therefore stores all information indefinitely. Human brains change, lose their productive efficiency and forget—but this also means that they and only they can change perspective and think subjectively, which gives the human being not only his creativity but also an individual personality.

In terms of speed and precision, the computer is light years ahead of the human brain. The speed of today's largely computer-based production and distribution is therefore disproportionately greater than that of human creativity. Realisation has caught up with invention and, in the figurative sense, mass production with the designer model. But our effort is usually expended in an attempt to adapt to the computer's speed and not the other way around, in trying to promote the 'slowness' of human creativity and thus the generation of something that is actually new.

This demand for speed means that we underline the dominance of the left cerebral hemisphere to the disadvantage of the right, abandoning our natural balance.[3] However, great expenditure of time alone should not be confused with creativity.

Furthermore, the computer brain is based on the binary system of zero (0) and one (1). It accepts the validity only of an 'either—or', a definitive yes or no. But human thought is more complex, allowing a 'perhaps'. Here, parallels can be drawn to *fuzzy logic,* that is to the unspecific, nonquantifiable 'fuzziness' that exists—with differing intensity—between polar opposites and permits the possibility of a 'perhaps' with an open outcome. The space between the two extremes, which is beyond the binary logic of the computer, represents the actual, independent sphere of creativity. In other words, creativity can be found not within the binary 'either/or', but in the *open perhaps,* in fuzzy logic, in the place where an artistic-creative interpretation takes effect. On the other hand, without the computer it would not be possible for us to calculate, for example, the stability of a building that has sprung from the imagination.

Creativity and Knowledge

In the mid 1990s, the psychologist Hans Jürgen Eysenck conjectured that creative achievements might be connected to particularly weak filtering of stimuli in the brain. This filter function in the brain helps a person to select the most relevant from a wealth of impressions, to distinguish between the unimportant and the important. If the filter is especially permeable, it may present a prerequisite to unusual associations—which Eysenck regards as a typical characteristic of creativity. On the other hand, our very routines—like the automatic process of climbing stairs—contribute to the unburdening of thought, freeing the brain to process important current information.

In addition, experience—that is, knowledge—helps our judgement and the finding of associations in current information (cf. also p. 91): 'For this reason, a lot of knowledge is a good prerequisite to creativity, for it enables the routine mastery of complex structures and thus increases the amount of conceivable connectivity. It increases, so to speak, the number of possible links in the semantic field . . . Knowledge helps creative people to recognise problems in situations where they may not exist for the less creative.'[4] Knowledge can be seen in the sense of 'redundancy producing efficiency'[5] which is then available to the creative individual. By contrast, intelligence is decisive for creativity only up to a point. According to remarkable findings in intelligence research, creativity is not bound to increase further above an IQ of 120—a good, above-average intelligence level. Looking at the sphere of high intelligence on this basis, it seems that creativity does not necessarily increase in relation to intelligence.

Creativity and Freedom

Another essential precondition to creative production is freedom: freedom of thought, emotion and action. The philosopher and art theorist Boris Groys reinforces the dictate of freedom (apart from the fact that the cultural environment and society will define what is new to them): 'The new may not be planned consciously in the context of a strategy oriented towards success.'[6] This means that innovative or avant-garde fashion design should and may—according to prevalent social demands—be unwearable. In the applied arts, purpose-free activity in the sense of 'the journey is the reward' often resembles escapism, but it creates an indefinable sphere of experience. Innovative design does not mean restriction to simple reaction or adaptation. One may assume that the designer consciously aims to create something new from the outset. Freedom also means a readiness to take risks.

The common view that 'necessity is the mother of invention' should be contradicted, for it applies only to the means to escape the situation of direct necessity.[7] Beyond this, necessity has a paralysing effect, like all pressure and threats: it narrows the imaginable horizon. In fashion, this pressure is exerted by a demand for wearability or usability and saleability. Cultural structures and the desire for recognition restrict creative production to the same degree. As a result, some designers finance their creative free space via second, conventional collections or design contracts with the fashion industry. To some extent, haute couture represents such freedom, for in extremely turbulent ambiences like the fashion world, the generative moment is all the more demanding. Brilliant designers like John Galliano are valued so highly with good reason. The LVMH luxury concern—owner of Dior, among other brands—grants Galliano considerable creative freedom (cf. p. 89).

Often enough, freedom for personal creativity is generated as a result of frustration and disappointment over what already exists. In other words, creative activity is triggered because routine does not function, that is there are obvious faults in it. Mary Quant, Jil Sander and Gabrielle Chanel were dissatisfied with existing fashion, could not identify with it, and thus began to realise their own concepts. These ideas can develop into a personal design language and a consistent style: in the case of Azzedine Alaïa into the erotic, in Jil Sander's work into the purist and in Alexander McQueen's creations into something sexist or even morbid.

Creativity and Emotion

The creation of models and their acceptance are linked to sensations. Sensations are defined as emotions triggered by perception or memory. The dynamics of clothing develop from seams, pleats and hems that result in flat areas and lines. Their design is accompanied by emotions, as inwardly directed reflection (a psycho-physiological process).

Consequently, a line may be perceived as 'sensual' or a form as 'severe'. Sensations are connected with individual preferences or personal character, but also with the collective memory. Does a formal anomaly constitute freedom for the designer/artist—but bear the risk of exclusion from society for the wearer? A suitable example is the collection *Dress Becomes Body Becomes Dress* (also known as *Body Meets Dress,* 1997) by Rei Kawakubo, in which thick padding over one shoulder was documented in the media as 'Quasimodo-like' and thus interpreted as a disability, as an anomaly (cf. p. 42).[8] This overforming was rejected regardless of the fact that in the eighteenth century moulded shapes one metre wide on both hips—the *panier à coudes*—were also quite anomalous but sanctioned socially as fashion. These historically sanctioned fashion aesthetics have continued to exist as such within the cultural memory. The cultural memory[9] is a dominant characteristic in questions of fashion in particular; incompetent comments on historical references, for example, are run of the mill during revivals. But these mental images have no claim to authenticity, being no more than memories of images.

Genius

The term *genius* can be traced back to the Latin word *ingenium*: a natural-born talent. The essence of this talent is seen as original productivity, which employs confident intuition to access new areas of creativity. The person who has genius—that is, a brilliant creative power—is also known as a genius. It was not until the Renaissance that people began to describe an artistic creative potential or the source of inspiration as genius. The key significance for invention is that the so-called genius develops ideas that no one has had previously and, in the words of Immanuel Kant, that 'genius must be considered the very opposite of a spirit of imitation'.[10] In addition, Kant established that genius 'cannot indicate scientifically how it brings about its product, but rather gives the rule as nature. Hence, where an author owes a product to his genius, he does not himself know how he conceived the ideas, nor is it in his power to invent the like at pleasure, or methodically, and communicate the same to others in such precepts as would put them in a position to produce similar products'.[11]

In science as in art, the concept of genius is viewed today with increasing scepticism, or it is emphasised only in an historical or socio-intellectual context. However, psychology and neurophysiology still investigate the phenomena of special intellectual gifts and above-average original creativity.

Inspiration and Idea

> imagination is as important as knowledge
>
> Rob Edkins, 2D:3D Ltd.

In general, inspiration is understood as an intellectual force that brings forth new ideas, which may be triggered by experiences, encounters or dreams. An idea is understood as something that suddenly occurs to someone or is synonymous with a thought. In this context, however, we are not interested in ideas that lead to automated actions like climbing stairs (even though this could also be realised in an entirely new way). Rather, the idea is interesting as the starting point of creativity. Ideas and inspirations, although they sound very much like givens, presuppose thought and knowledge. The production of ideas is based on personal theories, which fit with the science involved. Neuroscientist Semir Zeki[12] sees the production of ideas as a neuronal activity, while representatives of systems theory explain the development of ideas on the basis of communication and observation.

In order to develop creative ideas, it is possible to apply various techniques and strategies such as brainstorming or lateral thinking. Edward de Bono is regarded as a leading teacher of creative thought. He has developed a number of techniques intended to promote the finding of new ideas and to help people to free themselves from ritual patterns of thought; one of these techniques is lateral thinking.[13] Lateral thinking is divergent, nonlinear and unconventional—even to the point of illogical— thought as opposed to vertical, linear, conventional thought, which de Bono also calls parallel thinking. Numerous experiments have indicated that it is extremely difficult to abandon stored schemata and routines. Lateral thinking can help people to step out of the existing rules, systems and taboos.[14] Such 'stepping out', according to sociologist Erving Goffman as well, demands analysis and synthesis, an inductive and deductive approach and divergent and convergent thinking.[15]

To inspire not only means to illuminate but also to stimulate and fill with enthusiasm. The designer must stimulate and rouse enthusiasm—not only his own enthusiasm, but that of others as well. Psychologist and health researcher Mihály Csikszentmihályi refers to a state in which people become completely absorbed in their activities as the 'flow effect'.[16] At the highest level of concentration and tension, the self is forgotten; subjectively, people experience a sense of merging with the environment followed by the opposite: an expansion of the self and personal satisfaction at having reached one's aim. The flow effect triggers and represents the essential basis of euphoria, which can lead to much greater productivity and achievement.

Artistic-creative people have different potentials for creativity and innovation. The following examples can be cited in reference to the important fashion designers of today's avant-garde:

> Metaphorical thinking and creative associations—McQueen
> Deviation, subversion and play—Viktor & Rolf
> Lateral thinking in analogies and images—Chalayan
> Discovery of cognitive order in chaos—Demeulemeester
> Autonomous cognitive decisions—Margiela
> Competence in the strategy of realisation—Beirendonck

To sum up, it can be said that creativity comes about in the interaction between individual thought and an environmental or emotional context. In the fields of art and design, creative actions evolve especially when there is superfluous attention or frustration.

Strategies of Invention in Fashion

Provocation

The British psychologist Edward de Bono explicitly cites intellectual or sensory provocation as a creative technique. In such cases, the characteristics of an object or a state of affairs are altered consciously in order to generate paradoxical, unrealistic or unusual consequences. Starting out from these, an attempt is then made to produce new results. The provocative, the shocking and the radical originate in thought processes before being realised as something tangible and perceivable.

Provocation is no more than an inducement to become involved in whatever is shown. It consists of a conscious stimulus to trigger an excessive reaction, but ultimately the person provoked is responsible for this reaction himself. The aim of provocation in clothing design is a fresh perception of both vestimentary coverings and the body. A fresh perception (cf. p. 91) is provoked by means of a new covering (clothing) of the body, in a similar way to the disguise and wrapping of objects and buildings by the artist couple Christo and Jeanne-Claude, for example. The provocation lies in the crossing of borders and rules, on both real and intellectual levels, as well as in a deviation away from perceptual and emotional norms. Provocation can be understood only against the background of the times and local conditions. Historical examples thus call for historically competent, expert judgement.

Vestimentary provocations function on complex levels of design; through extreme overforming and/or extreme sexualisation of the body, through political-religious associations, or through a provocative presentation of clothing. However, the new is not radical or provocative or obscene a priori. Provocation develops when the 'communicative contract' between the clothing and the consumer is broken, resulting in shocked rejection or euphoric acceptance. Alexander McQueen's genius, for example, is founded on the integration of provocation that develops as a result of the wide gap between his creations and the general image people have of clothing. As a rule, his creations demand an interpretative effort from the recipient before they are accepted.

While the extreme as such—the extremely beautiful or the extremely functional—is not necessarily at all shocking, the *obscene*—as extreme sexualisation—seeks to violate shame or another elementary emotion and to shock by that means. The mere use of the word *obscene* (the very utterance of which is often obscene) already triggers an association with 'the concept of shamelessness in a way that prevents the recognition and definition of the truly obscene when it appears. Our speechlessness in face of the shameless is already part of its social impact'.[17] The presentation of McQueen's Spring/Summer 1996 collection, *Highland Rape,* and his *Vulva Dress* (cf. p. 55), functioned in the same way; the ensuing outrage surpassed all explanation.

Whereas the spectacular, including opulence and glamour, attracts the eye—that is our attention—and creates meta-stimuli, provocation affects people's moral sensibility and moral codes. 'Scandal' and 'propriety' define what could be called 'moral taste'. 'In the vague area between the "indecent" and the "immoral", this taste regulates the sense of shame. But as a medium intended to stabilise our morality, shame is even less reliable than the Ten Commandments', publicist Roger Willemsen wrote in his essay 'On the Obscene'.[18] 'Obscene' creations—Antonio Berardi's *Voodoo,* 1997/1998, Thierry Mugler's *Bum-Décolleté,* 1995, John Galliano's tanga-slip trouser suit made of newspaper print material for the Dior Autumn/Winter 2000/2001 collection, or Vivienne Westwood's *Dressing Up* collection, 1991/1992, including the leather corsage *Statue of Liberty* and a leather codpiece (the French braquette of the fifteenth century) sewn onto the skirt—'according to the common definition, can be recognised by their undisguised intention to create lust, separating this lust from the creation or its techniques'.[19] Vivienne Westwood succeeds in attenuating the provocative by means of humorous caricature or intimations of human weakness. Some examples of this are a fig leaf sewn onto tights, the slightly slipped bustle-cushion, or a well-formed male torso embroidered onto a corsetlike (cuirass) top.

Clothing *without a body* exudes neither emotions nor erotic provocation (cf. p. 202). They emerge only in connection with the body—in its pose, as staging on the catwalk or in verbalisation. Feelings and attractions like eroticism are articulated less by the designer's actual model and more from the outside, by photographers, journalists and advertising (e.g., Gucci's advertisements in 2003), quite apart from the wearer. The designer fashion of 2006 was characterised verbally in the journals as 'nude', for the frequently used colour nude visualised an imaginary nudity.

Immorality is not classified negatively a priori, either in art or in fashion, as long as it is not presented in *public,* that is not on the street but in an art gallery or on the catwalk. So-called problems emerge when the media expand the private sphere and make public what has been offered in a closed context. 'Extreme, utopian, even morally unacceptable positions may find representation within the art system', Boris Groys admits.[20] In response to the following question referring to an RAF emblem on T-shirts: 'What is art's attitude to the cannibalisation of an RAF emblem in a de-historicised Pop cosmos?' Groys answered: 'Both spheres communicate with each other. The Pop culture also adopts functions of modern art; it lends shape to the suppressed, to the forbidden.'[21] Provocation in art resembles revolution in politics.

Since provocation is always dependent on the *attitude of the viewer,* it occurs only outside the environment in which it has developed. Thus, the fashion of punks, rappers or goths meets with agreement or admiration among those groups themselves. Fashionable provocations from the street (as long as they are not tolerated) are disproportionately greater than those from the catwalk, since they emerge in public space and not within the exclusive context of a fashion show. Provocation may also be pure masquerade, like the dressing-up event held by youths in Tokyo's Yoyogi Park every Sunday. One of the aims of a mask is also to provoke, of course. Since the 1980s, kids and adolescents—from chambermaids to female Nazis—have been meeting in the park for role play that offers them a means of escape from everyday life. The innovation content of all these is their being the origin of ingenuity and invention. If innovations do not emerge—as is usually the case—it is a matter of simple copying, as with those kids in Tokyo.

John Galliano's haute couture for House of Dior is less a provocation and far more an aesthetic discourse with and about fashion; *mode pour mode* in the same sense as *l'art pour l'art.* His fashion design becomes an autonomous art form through trans-vesti, ethnic and gender cross-dressing; these means also form the basis of masquerade and are celebrated around Galliano's own person. Galliano himself represents the high point of his *défilé* (instead of or in addition to the bride), when he accepts his ovations dressed up and styled according to the collection's theme.

By contrast to extremes, which may enjoy the justification of the extraordinary—as in 'especially heroic', 'especially efficient' or 'especially beautiful'—exaggerations tend to lead into the corner of provocation. They lack justification within normal sensibilities and are relegated to the category of the pathological, like exaggerated perfection, for example. If the limits of social tolerance are crossed, the outcome is a provocation. However, the limits of social tolerance are subject to constant change, which is the very reason that innovative creations and thus new fashions are accepted. Constant changes in social tolerance and sanctions also determined the rejection or toleration of the dandy in the nineteenth century and the homosexual at the end of the twentieth century. In different ways, the dandy and the homosexual reject conventional masculine connotations; they are 'unauthentic' men. Both are 'aesthetic rebels': one due to the exaggerated accuracy (generally regarded as a quality with feminine connotations) of his fashionable appearance, the other due to his wearing of an earring (which is historically a male tradition as well),[22] for example, which has now become a universal male embellishment due to a shift in the tolerance limit.

Resource of Attention

The process of devoting attention is characterised by an orientation towards and choice (selectivity) of certain objects, with an associated lack of attention paid to other objects. This kind of attention process is characterised by increased alertness and activity, while selectivity functions as a filter to distinguish between important and irrelevant information.

The brain has a limited processing capacity; it cannot process an infinite number of stimuli consciously and simultaneously. It must therefore select the information that is important to the organism and requires attention, and identify which information is less relevant and can therefore be blotted out. If attention is not given to information within five seconds, it is lost. Here, the question arises of what criteria the brain employs to judge the relevance of stimuli. On the one hand, new forms of stimuli are given attention (reaction of orientation, curiosity) in this way. On the other hand, however, attention is directed towards emotionally charged information, which is an indirect marker of importance for the organism. The more emotionally charged a sign is, the more easily we can direct our interest towards it. Movement, colour and contrast increase attention. Because there is limited attention available— and this attention represents an economic, personal or social value—the gaining of attention is an important aim in the process of being perceived.

Form—Overform—Deform—Multiform

Architect and cultural historian Bernard Rudofsky saw the 'purpose of fashionable creativity' in the 'alteration of the human body'.[23] On this basis, he designated fashion creators as *trompe-l'œil artistes,* for they realise a visual illusion with respect to the human figure. The only decisive factor for clothing is the way that it is linked to the body—by whatever means—whereby superlative forms also give rise to superlative attention.

Every product, including the 'product' man, is a unity composed of differences. In fashion design, these differences result from the components—the pattern or materials—which are assembled or draped according to traditional rules or in new, previously unseen combinations and juxtapositions. The differences and combinations are close to infinite. For centuries, the forms of Western or, more precisely, central European culture were the forms viewed as mandatory for fashionable clothing. Their overforms ranged from the hennin (female headdress up to 90 cm high dating from the late mediaeval period) to the Spanish ruff (up to 60 cm in diameter) and the *panier à coudes,* the high-court hoop skirt of the Rococo, which extended up to 80 cm at each side. Today, the human body is usually overformed or rather deformed by shoulder padding, plateau soles and the push-up or Wonderbra.

The boundaries between overforming and deforming are fluid. Vivienne Westwood and Jean-Paul Gaultier exaggerate or heighten female forms to create hypernormal attractions (cf. p. 52). By contrast, Rei Kawakubo shifts padding in dresses until it no longer only overforms, but deforms the body, questioning customary aesthetics. Kawakubo develops her textile deformations from deconstructing the human body, not clothes as in the case of Margiela, for example. In a similar way to the draftsman, sculptor and photographer Hans Bellmer, Kawakubo chops the body in a Cubist manner and reassembles it in a new way using textile volumes. Thus, in her Comme des Garçons Spring/Summer 1997 collection, *Body Meets Dress* (cf. p. 138), she underlaid close-fitting jersey dresses asymmetrically at the back, shoulder and hip areas with big pads of cotton wadding. The association with Quasimodo as an abnormal deformation—already mentioned previously—was closer than with any erotic exaggeration; by this means, Kawakubo succeeded in a fundamental provocation. In *Body Meets Dress* Kawakubo called for a new perception of the human body. Her intention was to obscure the 'contact zone between the body form and clothing'. Using fictive body forms, she responded to an equally unrealistic ideal figure. Fiction especially is viewed as a postmodernist pretension and element. Rei Kawakubo operates less with erotic but far more with poetic overforming. She questions accepted, traditional notions of fashion repeatedly and rejects the concept of the beautiful, noble and perfect. In 1998, Kawakubo continued to experiment with form by creating a double silhouette of body outlines, bringing her work close to sculptural art. Kawakubo also followed her *Body Meets Dress* concept when designing costumes for the ballet *Scénario* by Merce Cunningham.[24] In the Spring/Summer 2006 collection, Kawakubo

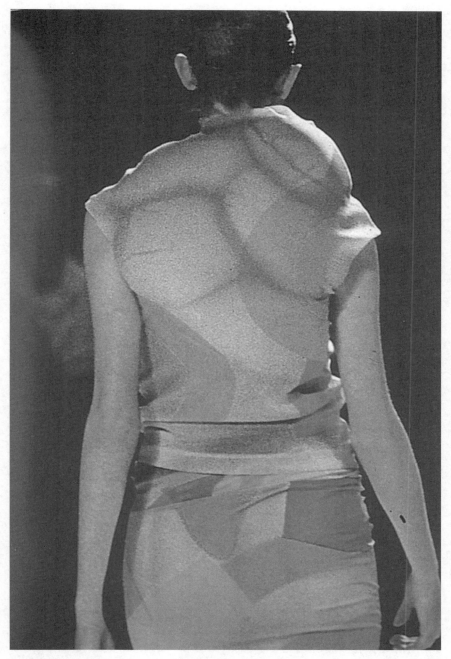

Figure 1   Rei Kawakubo for Comme des Garçons, *Dress Becomes Body Becomes Dress,* 1997. PR Comme des Garçons.

continued the same concept using sashlike drapes around the upper body. Traditional tartans and typical sarong fabrics provided a reference to historical wrapped clothing such as the kilt and sarong. A fragment of a suit jacket was also transformed into an overforming sash.

Figure 2 Bernhard Willhelm, *Molux,* 2005. Photo: Geoffrey Cottenceau & Romain Rousset, *Mode Depesche,* no. 2, 'Luxusmode' (June 2005). www.modedepesche.de.

Bernhard Willhelm's 2005 collection *Molux* was concerned with multiplication and addition. Legs grew out of the head, and several arms from the shoulders, or the head took centre place in a reversal—that is the dress and feet were attached not only at the bottom but once again at the top, a second set of limbs standing up from the head. Willhelm lent textile forms to the 'anatomy of the bodily subconscious'. They are comparable to staged scenes by the artist Erwin Wurm, in which items of clothing become the object of artistic activity. Captured in photographs by Erwin Wurm (among other things in a Palmers advertisement in 1997[25]), they turn into his *One Minute Sculptures,* which represent an extension of the sculptural concept. Similar 'body extensions' can be encountered in Hans Bellmer's *La poupée* torso (1935/1938) as well as in his cephalopod figures, which were already a theme in the work of Hieronymus Bosch. The effect of Bernhard Willhelm's models—like that of Erwin Wurm's *One Minute Sculptures* and Bellmer's sculptures—is scurrilous, witty, amusing, astonishing, and frightening to the point of disgust. Hans Bellmer suggests what lies behind our irritated laughter: 'In most of my works, I deal with situations in which a wide range of fears, ideas, conditioning, neuroses that will always be with us can assert themselves. Apparently that makes some people laugh.'[26]

In the context of clothing as an overforming of the body, the Dutch duo of designers Viktor & Rolf (Viktor Horsting and Rolf Snoeren) overstepped the boundary between applied and free art in their haute couture collection *Russian Doll,* 1999/2000. This impression emerged as the model (the doll, the woman, the diva, the goddess, the person) was overformed with clothing to the point of immobility. As a result, she was made incapable of action, including an inability to continue dressing or undressing. Nonetheless, *Russian Doll* allows associations with historically real fashions, like the stiff Spanish fashion from the second half of the sixteenth century, for example. As in that Spanish fashion, the aura of inapproachability was a theme of *Russian Doll,* an aura that clothing is able to create by means of excessive or even overwhelming volume. (Some aristocratic babies were known to suffocate in the lavish quantities of lace and damask that they were obliged to wear at their baptisms.)

The fashion show *Russian Doll* began with one model—wearing a thigh-length, frayed jute dress by Viktor & Rolf—being led onto a platform and provided with shoes as the first act of dressing. Subsequently, Viktor & Rolf dressed the model in another nine items of clothing, one over the other: a cotton day dress with a belt, lavishly decorated with lace and a ribbon at the hem; a jute dress including shimmering glass fibres; a dress with a layered skirt and puffed sleeves made of jute with isolated embroidery work in the form of half-paisley motifs; a coatdress made of jute with complete, or rather complementary, paisley motifs; an ankle-length dress with big, long puffed sleeves; and a floor-length, sleeveless overdress, the two flower patterns of which interrupted the previous and subsequent brown-gold colouring of the jute dresses. There followed a floor-length coat with a top embellished with flower-pattern lace, a bulging round collar and closing seam, and two armbands with pendulous glass beads and the cross of Christ (several rosaries?), a second coat made of jute with paste

Figure 3 Viktor & Rolf, *Russian Doll,* haute couture 1999/2000. Photo: Peter Tahl. Groninger Museum Collection.

jewels and voluminous trailing sleeves, as well as a final cape—bell-shaped to cover everything, with an oversized rose made from the same jute material on the shoulder. After the model had been 'over'-dressed with ten items of clothing and little more than her face was still visible, she was transformed into a textile object of applied art.

In this way, the everyday activity of dressing—Viktor & Rolf themselves spoke of 'first, second, third . . . and final preparation'—becomes the centre of interest. It is stylised into a ceremony, a ritual—as was once true in the case of kings, religious adoration or a diva. This use of clothing or the textile as an instrument of glorification occurs in many religions and epochs. At the same time, the process of sculpturalising is revealed. The clothing is given a tremendous power of its own and the aspect of wearability is all but lost. The wearer becomes a mannequin, a little man in the original sense of the word, and is merely a carrying frame. The wearer is no more than a doll, a woman in a golden cage of magnificent clothes, like the infanta of Spanish fashion. In Viktor & Rolf's collection, comparison is made to a Russian doll—the *Matryoshka* in the sarafan dress that covers the full body—which can be multiplied and reduced at will. The transformation process of the body/dress volume in space becomes obvious as a result of being clothed in multiple layers. When the change as such is no longer visible, the process of dressing up stays in the memory and so becomes documentation of a sculptural process. However, the emphasis is not on the action of dressing up; the important thing is its objectifying and sculpturalising impact. Ultimately, this is a visualisation of an overforming or deforming process incorporated into the everyday action of dressing. In one of his video works, the Austrian artist Erwin Wurm investigated the process of dressing and undressing in thirteen pullovers in a similar way.[27]

Excessive overforming of the body by means of clothing and embellishments—like the multiplication of shirt collars or bows (*One Woman Show,* Autumn/Winter 2003/2004) or frills (*Black Light,* couture collection, Spring/Summer 1999)—is a recurring theme in the work of Viktor & Rolf. In this context, they emphasise that they are more interested in thematising abstract ideas and emotions such as frustration and fear than in the design principle.[28] Their first official collection, *Detachment* in 1993, was a matter of clothing fragments in the sense of historical leftovers, or pieces that were assembled almost as archaeological work. They called the creations in their haute couture collection *Atomic Bomb* in 1998/1999, for example 'Millennium' or 'party dresses'. The tops of the harlequin suits and dinner jackets were blown up with the help of balloons, the intention being to give the body an 'atomic bomb silhouette', according to Viktor & Rolf—the form of a nuclear mushroom, narrow at the bottom and wide at the top. This illusionary exaggeration burst like firecrackers at carnival time or a bomb filled with confetti, leaving behind the wearable clothing. The idea for this addition recalled their autumn 1994 collection, with the motto *Passive Violent Clothes,* abbreviated to PVC. It is legitimate to refer to such overforms as radical and violent (to perception), but they have had precursors in fashion history, from the wide balloon sleeves of the sixteenth-century man's overcoat (Schaube) to the leg-of-mutton sleeves of the nineteenth-century High Biedermeier period, and the pigeon breast of S-shape dresses around 1900.

In all these multiforms and additions, Viktor & Rolf are also concerned with the revision of perceptions both visual and aural. They irritate by interchanging the top and bottom of an item of clothing (*Upside Down* collection, Spring/Summer

2006; cf. p. 60) or through the monochrome quality of clothing and body (*Black Hole* collection, Autumn/Winter 2001/2002; cf. p. 69). The designer duo also achieved an aural irritation using hundreds of small bells sewn onto their models (*Bells*, haute couture collection, 2000/2001; cf. p. 70), the audio perception of which was intensified by darkness at the start of the catwalk presentation.

Far from any kind of commercialism, Viktor & Rolf's creations go beyond the codification of applied art; however, they must still be regarded as such, since they remain linked to the human body. Their models have been long sought after by museums like the Kyoto Costume Institute and the Museum in Groningen, which have collected Viktor & Rolf since 1999.

By contrast, overforming in the shape of *blow-ups* or *inflatables* seldom goes further than an experimental stage or beyond the avant-garde pretension of sculpturalising. Comparatively speaking, its dimension of experience or memory is brief. This tendency is evidenced by examples such as air-filled trousers (1981) and a coat (1987) by Issey Miyake, photographed by Irving Penn in 1988, a blow-up reversible poncho by Jean-Charles Castelbajac 1976/1977, or a pumped-up bolero collar by Michiko Koshino, Spring/Summer 2000. Although inflatables in furniture design—in the form of blow-up sofas and chairs—have belonged to the category of reasonably priced mass goods for some time now, such ideas by fashion designers and architects are associated with certain elitism. As early as 1972, the Vienna architectural office Coop Himmelb(l)au had designed a 'movable, inflatable and inhabitable cloud', which was adopted in a similar form by Tomas Saraceno in Gallery Pinksummer in Geneva, 2004. In 2006, Rem Kohlhaas and Cecil Balmonds installed a globe-shaped air construction filled with helium (with Thomas Demand's image of a gigantic grotto in the interior) above the Serpentine Gallery in London. Chalayan provided a vestimentary response to the issue of space and control expressed in architectural theory with *Before Minus Now* 2000, in which, among other things, the skirt of a dress was pumped up. Although blow-ups and inflatables remain experiments or catwalk surprises, it is hard to imagine our streets without the overforming of those padded coats and jackets with down stuffing available as mass-produced goods since the 1980s,[29] as well as air-walk, air-bouncing and air-cushioned soles also employed universally for jogging shoes and footwear such as Doc Martens.

Subtraction and Inversion

Hussein Chalayan investigated subtraction and inversion in his Spring/Summer 2003 collection, *Manifest Destiny*[30]. Elastic fabrics were draped to leave openings in the front part of the dresses, from which the 'fabric nets' of discernible parts of clothing (sleeves, collars) swelled like organs from the body. The clothing is inverted and distorted; hollow areas appear to reveal the body in an arbitrary manner. The 'injured' clothing discloses not only the body but also the soul, comparable to a

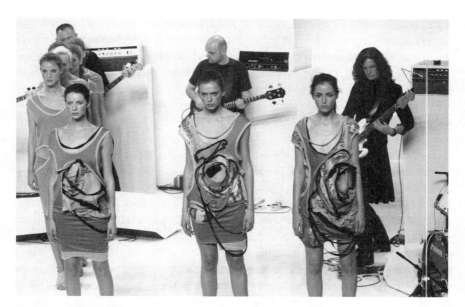

Figure 4   Hussein Chalayan, *Manifest Destiny,* 2003. Photo: Studio Them. www.them.de.

geological intraspection. The hollow areas also transmit a kind of two-dimensional sculpture. On the one hand, Chalayan's symbolic name *Manifest Destiny* (after the nineteenth-century US doctrine that held that the United States had a divine commission to expand, in particular across the borders of North America into the Pacific) intends to highlight the assimilation of Western clothing, but on the other hand it is a pointer to youth culture and its erotic presentation of the body. Our view is certainly directed towards the body.

Organic Form

One credo of fashion is 'culture before nature'. The formal laws of clothing follow classical aesthetics and their postulate of balanced proportions far more than organic and morphological forms. Morphological structures are regarded as rather unnatural, or even as a provocation—as 'mathematically' constructed patterns.[31] The best examples are Isabel Toledo's and Yohji Yamamoto's creations or Raf Simon's coat model from 2006. Yohji Yamamoto's bustier dress with asymmetrical twists—the skirt of the summer 1999 collection as a hyperstructured super-organ—is comparable to Frank O. Gehry's wave-shaped, steel-clad buildings like the Guggenheim Museum in Bilbao. The aesthetics of both designs function as a space-consuming work of art, whereby the wave-shape in Gehry's architecture is equivalent to the organic dynamics resulting from the body's movement in Yamamoto's dress. Display and window mannequins moved by motors would be required to accentuate the ambivalence of rigidity and motion as the key difference between painting, object art (with the exception of mobiles) and architecture on the one hand, and fashion on the other. Almost as a visual supplement or an aid to the rigidly exhibited dress, videos of the fashion show are often shown. The static and the dynamic form of one and the same dress are sometimes as diverse as Isabel Toledo's *Packing Dress* of 1988, which, laid out flat, has a circular geometric form, but when worn it is transformed into the organic shape of a cocoon.

Japanese designers in particular—like Rei Kawakubo, Junya Watanabe and Yohji Yamamoto—devote their work to the interaction of surface and form. In their creations the development process, the overlapping and interlocking of materials or the loss of knitted stitches cause open loops and holes, which result in innovative forms. They are not ornamental like the intentionally cut-in holes and slits in the Gucci jeans of 2004, for example, but an organic pattern. Kawakubo's 'holes' are something negative or missing, and yet also a positive element that lends structure. They are part of the development phase and part of the experiment and not (commercially) calculated strategy or fake ultrarealism as in the Gucci case, or the socially critical, 'no-future' identity of the punks with their torn clothing, including its commercial marketing. In Yamamoto's work, seams do not have the simple function of holding things together; they energise the power of the materials, thus allowing the emergence of seemingly arbitrary indentations, asymmetrical points of cloth or patterns.

By using techniques of folding similar to origami, Junya Watanabe arrives at bizarre overforming that provokes very little due to its charm, although it generates a new dress-body with an abstract morphology. Yoshiki Hishinuma also produced some extraordinary 'sculpture dresses' in Autumn/Winter 2001/2002 by employing folding techniques, doubling and moulding the material into basic geometric forms.

Eroticism: Construction and Deconstruction

Eroticism is a form of communication based on the intellectual-psychic development of sexuality. It means being sexually attractive; it can be perceived as mankind's courtship ritual. The most effective communication of eroticism—besides body posture, speech melody, mimicry and gesture—takes place through partial covering of the body.[32] On the one hand, the wrapping up or enclosure of the body in clothing creates an intimate sphere for the body, and on the other hand, it generates the attraction of something unknown and new. Eroticism focuses on the transitions between dress and body. Clothing overforms, models and presents the body simultaneously. Due to the 'melting together' of the clothing and the body, underclothes worn directly on the body are turned into a fetish and so into a substitute for the body. This connotation of the body and the dress as a single erotic entity or of clothing as a substitute for the body is an important theme in painting in particular (eg in Surrealism).

Throughout the course of fashion history, erotic zones changed continually, inasmuch as clothing receded to reveal parts of the body in turn. These then functioned as 'eye-catchers': décolleté, shoulder, back, bottom, legs or navel. The so-called erotic zone influences our perception of the entire female or male body. While 'free sexuality' was a matter of self-image and its staging in the fashion of the hippies during the 1960s, the dark and often brutal side of sexuality is a theme examined in creations by Alexander McQueen—and to some extent by Gianni Versace, Jean-Paul Gaultier and Jean Colonna—in the 1990s.

Eroticism requires an association with the body. Clothing represents the decisive medium for the articulation of corporeality. The most erotic of models—by Azzedine Alaïa, for example—does not have the desired effect on a coat hanger. Nor does it succeed on a window dummy, although a dummy as a substitute body may trigger an erotic idea or association in the memory. By contrast, a drawing can achieve an erotic aura with its inclusion of body and pose; commercial graphic art certainly makes enough use of this.

The artist Isabelle Steiner exemplified the way in which clothing, especially lingerie, flourishes due to its connection with the naked body. She had an amateur model dress in clothing layer by layer, but in reverse order (2003). In other words, a knitted cardigan was first put onto her naked skin, pullover and skirt over that, then a petticoat, then tights, and finally bra and slip. She documented these individual stages of dressing in photographs. The paradoxical inversion of the *dessous* (bra and slip) to *dessus* does not trigger any erotic association in the observer; quite the opposite, one is tempted to say. Instead, the erotic aura was attributed to the cardigan on naked skin.

Vivienne Westwood deconstructs the eroticism of clothing in a playful or ironic way when she has a fig leaf sewn over the pubic area of a flesh-coloured pair of tights (1990). However, a flesh-coloured slip with a penis painted on it in her collection *Pagan V* (Spring/Summer 1990) was regarded as provocation; American buyers left the show.[33] As early as her *Buffalo* collection (Autumn/Winter 1982/1983), Westwood also had bras made of satin put on over the rest of the clothing, in a similar way to Rei Kawakubo in her Autumn/Winter collection for Comme des Garçons in 2001/2002, *Beyond Taboo*. As opposed to the aforementioned example by Isabelle Steiner, in Westwood's and Rei Kawakubo's work the bra is on top, but the rest of the clothing is put on in the customary order. The suggested eroticism of the fig leaf or the bra is a citation. However, in her Autumn 2008/2009 collection Rei Kawakubo exaggerated erotic symbols to 'as much kitsch as kitsch can': oversized cut-out lips and hearts framed in lace frills form part of her coats and dresses. Tops and pants are held together by straps made of silk frills or even consist entirely of such frills.

Jean-Paul Gaultier adopted a contrasting approach; he shaped over Madonna's torso in 1990 for her 'Blond Ambition World Tour' in 1990 using a demonstrably aggressive-looking corsage. Although covered, Madonna's body proved hyperpresent, precisely because the sharp-pointed breasts of the striking extended casing completely covered what was actually worth seeing—her own breasts. Madonna developed an erotic aura from sexual gestures, dramatisation and exaggeration and this erotic hyperstylisation through Jean-Paul Gaultier's corset. In his collection *Barbés* (Autumn/Winter 1984/1985; named after a Parisian arrondisement), Gaultier had already triggered a sensation with his smoked velvet dresses incorporating utterly unnatural, sharp-pointed, grenade-like breasts (cf. p. 42).

Since the Baroque period, the corset has been viewed as the item of clothing with the most powerful erotic aura, for it shapes the female body according to each age's ideal image and presents the erogenous zones of bosom, hips and slender waist. The extreme breast breathing caused by the tightly laced corset makes the bosom 'quake'; the outcome is a heightened awareness of one's body and 'self-eroticising'. At the same time, the tight lacing suggests a sadomasochistic tone, while a loosening of the laces signifies seduction and defloration. In 2001, in *Des Robes qui se Dérobent*, Jean-Paul Gaultier designed a corset dress that was laced all the way down the back to the floor-length hemline and supplemented it with long, also fully laced gloves. For her leather corset *Statue of Liberty*, Vivienne Westwood—again with irony—added the lacing as 'decoration' in the region of the décolleté. In her Autumn/Winter 1998/1999 collection, A. F. Vandevorst presented a suit with morning coat and a leather corset as a belt that was designed as a riding saddle at the back. The connotation of female–male, of riding and being ridden, is evident. John Galliano deconstructed the corset in 2006 by assembling a patchwork from corset parts, set

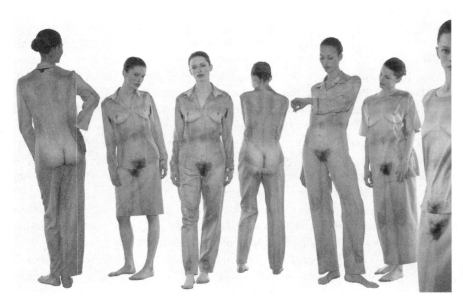

Figure 5   Alba d'Urbano, *Il sarto immortale*, 1995. © Alba d'Urbano.

in an irregular diagonal pattern and with misplaced laces. Galliano shows how these remnants of the corset cause the cultural memory to switch to eroticism, while he employs it as a metaphor for the French Revolution—also the title of his haute couture collection for Christian Dior (cf. p. 188).

In addition to the corset, animal prints, fur on naked skin, the Lingerie Look and the Girlie Lolita Look have become classics in the creation of erotic significance, representative of schemata ranging from the untamed animal to the innocent young child.

But what if the body dressed depicts the body naked; does eroticism become a metaphor? The artist and philosopher Alba d'Urbano picks up nudity as a fashionable scenario and a demand for scrutiny, examining the ambivalence of 'clothed nudity'. In *hautnah* (1995) and in her cycle *Il sarto immortale* ('The Immortal Tailor', 1997)[34] she exhibited her own naked, 'average body', photographed from front and back and subsequently printed onto fabric made into blouses, dresses, coats, skirts and trousers. In the clothing in two parts (skirt or trousers and top), Alba d'Urbano consciously accepted the shifts in the printed naked body that resulted from movement. These clothes, nontransparent yet presenting a naked body, express something strangely shameless. D'Urbano provokes voyeurism with her actions (comparable to those of Vanessa Beecroft). The models who wore the clothing at the performance 'Catwalk' at Art Cologne 1997 confirmed this assumption, saying that they had actually felt naked apart from a few moments.[35] It was possible to buy d'Urbano's dresses and so put on a strange naked body—namely hers—over one's own.[36]

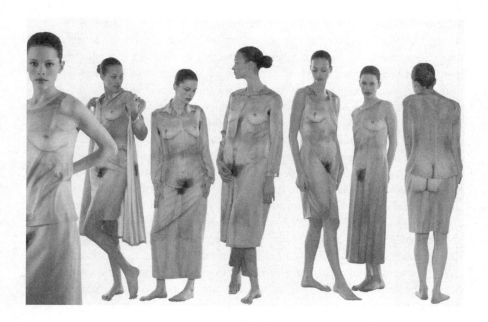

Gender-erotic-crossing turns into provocation when a woman wears a transparent blouse with male chest hair woven into it (*Distraction,* 1992, by Jana Sterbak), or if a man puts on a T-shirt printed with the image of a naked female torso. Gaultier's dresses with outsize, grenade-like breasts dating from 1984/1985 are also intended for wear as travesty or the exaggeration of supranormal attractions—by everybody, also by men. In one of his self-portraits, photographer Paolo Roversi wears the dress with the grenade-shaped bosom from the *Barbés* collection (Autumn/Winter 1984/1985) (cf. p. 52). Metaphorically, clothing stands for a specific gender. Arbitrary dressing and undressing with male or female sexual characteristics is a metaphor of slipping into the opposite sex—into the 'skin' of the other. Clothing that depicts sexual characteristics is more than a simple covering; when it represents the identity of another person's naked body, this covering has an obscene effect. The resulting incompatibility between image world and physical reality leads to an interface of fashion-art-gender-crossing. In particular, the eroticism of gender crossing (cf. p. 115) lies in crossing into a taboo zone, and in ambiguity. The eroticism of the body and the dress merge, or the dress represents a memory of the body in paintings by René Magritte, such as *Homage à Mack Sennett, The Red Dress* and *Philosophy in the Boudoir,* and *Night and Day Clothes of the Body* (1936) by Salvador Dalí. In a comparable way, among other things, Gaultier created bodysuits (1993) with naked bodies printed or stitched onto them, although the allusion was recognisable only at second glance.

The prime interest in Alexander McQueen's collection *Joan* (Autumn/Winter 1998/1999) was eroticism as a symbol of power; Joan of Arc appeared wearing a mini-length plate-armour dress or as a Greek warrior with half-bared breast. His Spring/Summer 2005 collection was devoted to the representation of supposedly weak or strong women; the schoolgirl, the governess, the farmer's wife, the Japanese doll, the cyber woman, the dominatrix, and the liberated woman as a football player with helmet and breast protector. They were intended as a new symbolic transformation of the thirty-six chess pieces, but McQueen was more concerned with a deconstruction of eroticism. In his first collection (Autumn/Winter 1995/1996), given the motto *Highland Rape,* Alexander McQueen had blood-smeared models in torn lace dresses stagger over the catwalk. This looked very much like provocation but had a concrete social and even political background, practising criticism. *Highland Rape* was a reference to the rape—often little heeded—of women, but also to the political rape perpetrated on the Scots by the English. (From 1747 to 1782, the British parliament banned 'the highland dress'—kilts, plaids and tartans—as a symbol of Scottish patriotism.) Destruction of clothing is regarded as an attack on a person's dignity, intimate sphere and personality.[37] The choreography of the presentation of *Highland Rape* with its flayed female bodies disgusts and fascinates equally as a result of its ingenuity and anarchistic-erotic reality. McQueen's pictorial language is part of the aestheticising of the subconscious (cf. p. 39). It thematises traumata in addition to the dialectics of pleasure and pain, eroticism and death, man and machine, love and brutality, victim and aggressor, as well as examining power and threat, desire and vulnerability.

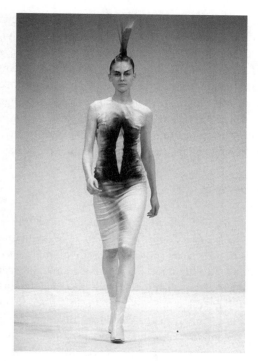

Figure 6   McQueen, *Vulva Dress,* 1996. Photo: Chris Moore.

In *The Hunger* (Spring/Summer 1996), McQueen introduced his *Vulva Dress* to the catwalk, thus continuing the theme of rape and defilement. An oversized, abstract painted vulva on the front of the dress appears almost as a shield, as an apotropaic charm against evil, an aspect that McQueen connects with the voyeurism of fashion and the catwalk presentation. McQueen's world of ideas focuses not on eroticism, but on the same sexuality and violence as the literary work of the Marquis de Sade, for example, or Antonin Artaud's production style in his *Theatre of Cruelty,* in which the body demonstrates aggression and desires. On the other hand, McQueen's flat, two-dimensional dress depiction (like that of his first, extremely low-fitting bumster trousers in 1996) triggers an association with drawings by Egon Schiele and Hans Bellmer. By contrast, the three-dimensional overforming of Vivienne Westwood's creations recalls the eroticism in painting by Goya, François Boucher and Peter Paul Rubens.

A performance by Yoko Ono also examined the subject of defloration and eroticism. The artist celebrated the exact opposite of Viktor & Rolf's collection *Russian Doll* and its 'sublime dressing' (cf. p. 46) in her performance *Cut Piece* in the Yamaichi Concert Hall in Kyoto in 1964 (restaged by the artist herself in Paris, 2003). While

Ono sat in a quiet, almost meditative position onstage, the audience was asked to walk onstage one by one and cut pieces out of the artist's clothing. After hours of silent suffering, Ono was almost completely undressed. Every piece of fabric cut off triggered a sense of defloration and of being exposed. Self-debasement, intimacy and sexuality are concepts Yoko Ono presents to the viewer as self-reflection. In this way, it becomes clear that clothing represents an aspect of a person's dignity.

Today, inventions in the eroticism of men's clothing revert powerfully to the body itself, taking the form of tattoos und piercings. Historically, there have also been erotic connotations in high collars, ties and sharp-pointed shoe forms.[38]

Eroticism of Accessories

While the eroticism of the belt (like that of the fan, the handkerchief, the hat feather, the bust bow or the false beauty spot) plays very little (symbolic) part in today's clothing, the eroticism of the shoe remains. Shoes with high, narrow heels convey a powerful erotic aura, since high heels give women a rocking, sensual walk. High heels also cause a hollow back, pushing out both bosom and bottom. Sex idols and film stars rely on the inevitable impact of high heels.[39] Even in antiquity, footwear was attributed a sexual symbolism that has been retained in fertility rites up to the present day. As a container, the shoe symbolises femininity. By contrast, the foot itself is compared to the male genitals and stands for virility. There is obvious reference to this in old folk tales and legends, as there is to the ritual of the bride's or maiden's shoe. Taking off the bride's shoe—a symbol of virginity—is a symbolic act of defloration. The sexual symbolism of the shoe is also evidenced by its continuing role as a fetish desired by men. The shoe fetishist equates the shoe, as a vessel, with the female sexual organ. High-heeled shoes are much in demand as a fetish. They have to be tight-fitting and are often laced up as a result; masochist ideas of pain and being kicked or stepped on by a woman are combined with desire. There is an obvious reason for the dominatrix's appearance in high, sharp-pointed boots. The shoe fetish is a substitute for the person desired.[40]

Aestheticising of the Subconscious

Fashion is the displayed stylisation of one's own experience.

Jürgen Habermas

Alexander McQueen realises man's original fears—not only in the sphere of sexuality—using an aesthetic vestimentary language. His themes are traumata such as isolation and loneliness (*The Overlook*, Autumn/Winter 1999/2000), as well as the dialectics of pleasure and pain, eroticism and death, man and machine, love and brutality, and victim and aggressor. Thus, he succeeds in holding up a mirror to reality and in achieving distance and transcendence. 'There's beauty in anger, and anger for me is passion'[41] are the words with which Alexander McQueen expresses his basic attitude, which he visualised successfully in a single dress: one with a top made of glass microscope slides and a skirt of ostrich feathers in his collection *Voss* (Spring/Summer 2001). The top consists of two thousand microscope slides sewn by hand onto gauze, each painted differently in blood red to suggest biological examination under a microscope.[42] The thin segments of glass could break at any time, their sharp edges cutting into flesh and so revealing the blood and arteries inside. While the soft feathers of the voluminous skirt attract us with their tactile erotic charm, this affinity is destabilised by the glass top. The visual and the tactile, distance and proximity, play a part in shaping our aesthetic perception. When McQueen uses microscope slides, he aims to express scientific research's power over the body, its control over life and death. In a way similar to that of the work of the artist Bellmer, this is a matter of the anatomy of the physically subconscious as opposed to the psychologically subconscious in Sigmund Freud's theory. However, the dress was given a different connotation when it was worn—just once—by the musician Björk onstage at a concert. Her dancing movements caused the glass slides to rattle against each other, and this gentle jingling was integrated as a component of Björk's music. The 'blood plasma slides' mutated into percussion instruments.

In his collection *The Dance of the Twisted Bull* in 2002, McQueen appeared to be concerned with the issues of victim or aggressor, power or impotence, and gesture and myth. The eroticism of the bullfight, the power of the matador, the fear in the eyes of the bull, the confident flamenco dancer who becomes a victim herself when a lance 'skewers' body and dress—McQueen succeeds in expressing all this with clothes, make-up and performance. The fear of martyrdom and torture in *Dante* (Autumn/Winter 1996/1997) is expressed creatively in photo prints of soldiers with machine guns on the tops of dresses, by metal splinters on the face and barbed-wire jewellery (by Shaun Leane) around the arms, by a skeleton hand on the face and a black eye mask with Christ crucified at its centre. This is apparently thematised in a similar way in *Untitled* (Spring/Summer 1998); a skeleton is used as a corset and the bottom jaw of a skull as a chin clasp, both made of silvery metal. These are off-putting as external body jewellery (by Shaun Leane), but they are accepted as medical 'replacement parts' for inward use.

Alexander McQueen's collections are postmodern, destructive and conceptual. Although they seem like pure provocation at first glance, they have deeper meanings. British fashion designer working in Paris and one-time 'bad boy', Alexander McQueen has long since demonstrated his genius. His shocking provocation aims for a cathartic (although controversial) moment in the recipient and functions as liberation from inner conflicts and suppressed emotions. He incorporates the reflective level into his catwalk presentations, a level normally introduced by fashion photography and advertising. Single unusual creations, like the aforementioned dress in *Voss,* are made only for the catwalk. They demonstrate the designer's tremendous imagination and the technical tailoring skills of the fashion house or production team; their design and realisation are pure luxury. But besides them, every collection consists of many wearable pieces (sometimes accentuated by styling to create a sensation), which are ordered and ultimately go into production.

Deviation

Used in the sense of anomaly, reversal or twist, deviation can be a positive word—in contrast to perversion—and encompasses qualities of paradox (cf. p. 106), subversion and play. After the rigid art concept was suspended in the early twentieth century, deviation became a socially legitimised concept in art. Since the Dadaists, the ludic principle has set out to expand creative thought patterns. Play functions as an intelligent, subversive strategy, a sphere of possibility for experimental thought, and a field of discovery for creative potential. As a result of the social demand for wearability made on fashion, deviation in the vestimentary field is (still) largely rejected, apart from witty prints on T-shirts. Only a few designers, such as Bernhard Willhelm, van Beirendonck, Moschino, Hermann Hiller and Sisi Wasabi, each in his or her own way, integrate deviational and ludic structures into their designs.

Subversion, parody, play and triviality permit designers like Willhelm, van Beirendonck, Moschino, or Hiller to disclose secrets, create new worlds or slip into different roles. Subversion serves to promote the positive destruction of conventions, notions of prestige and accepted matters of course. A corrective can be found behind caricature and comedy. In this context, the astonishingly similar structures of subversion, art and play are revealed. Art and play are considered free (without conscious purpose, for pleasure or relaxation), not necessarily reasonable and not obligated to any definable truth. Play and art function as self-regulating systems and according to self-defined rules and regulations.

Life is a circus, the theme of a collection by Alexander McQueen in 2001/2002, expresses the ambivalence of the cheerful and the melancholy and the fascination of clowns, circus, fairgrounds and roundabouts, in addition to that of dressing up and thus of fashion. Fashion designers like Elsa Schiaparelli in 1937, Galliano for Dior in 1997 and Bernhard Willhelm in 2003 and Autumn/Winter 2005/2006 made the circus into their creations' theme, applying new, extremely different principles of design.

The name Moschino stands for the perversion of fashion and the whole fashion system, including fashion shows and particularly the cult of brands, in which he ingeniously plays his part. The Moschino line (since the death of Franco Moschino in 1994, the label has been continued by a team of designers) saw the origin of a new fashion in the questioning of traditional fashion design. Of course, it could be maintained that this label creates fashion at the expense of others. One famous example of this is Moschino's T-shirt printed with the words "Channel N°5" set in a stylised

TV screen, which involved him in a court case with the House of Chanel. The effect of one of his jackets was similarly provocative; it imitated a jacket by Chanel using a photographic print. But Moschino does not copy, he perverts. His creations are quality products, made of expensive fabrics. Moschino playfully reverses the signs and functions of fashion—such as with trompe l'oeil effects à la Surrealism, when borders, padded edges, folds or ribbons are not carefully sewn on but rather drawn or printed on with equal care; the same applies to accessories like buttons or belts. In this trompe l'oeil manner, a simple coat becomes a trench coat, and a simple suit with a straight skirt turns into a bordered jacket with pleated skirt.

Bernhard Willhelm (cf. p. 44) made use of deviation when—in a similar way to Tommy Hilfiger—he created a pullover bearing the US flag and one knitted with 'USA' in big letters. However, the flag and 'USA' are upside down in Willhelm's work. While the American flag is a statement for Tommy Hilfiger, in Willhelm's work it is transformed into a question mark. 'I was interested in the way that a certain symbolism alters when it is used differently,'[43] Willhelm explains. Uncertainty and irritation represent the foundation of his creative aesthetics. He finds mainstream— that is 'being on the safe side'—merely tedious. 'As I see it, this safety conscious-ness conceals some very real dangers.'[44] He regards kitsch and narrow-mindedness as design elements, from which he develops his own new aesthetics. He finds kitsch not only in garden gnomes, cuckoo clocks and illuminated Venetian gondolas for the mantelpiece, but also in historical fashions and fairy-tale or comic figures. His imag-ination is sparked by everything: by folklorist elements, Pop Art and graffiti, comics, dinosaurs, kangaroos, mangas, and the bourgeois and trivial. Willhelm scratches at the surface of this brave new world without destroying it. He is not interested in pure aesthetics; the ambiguous and deviations are more interesting. In his own words: 'I find bad taste interesting. Through a twist or a different perspective, it can just as easily be considered good taste . . . I love to change the context of things: my current [2006] Superman collection, for example, makes a girl into a new type of Supergirl.'[45]

Walter van Beirendonck reveals a cosmos fluctuating between real and unreal in the world of the comics, computer games and toys that he loves, but also in fabled creatures and figures of gods from different cultures. He calls them 'relics of the future', and they influence the design of his collections for men in particular. In a kind of neo-Rococo style, the justaucorps (the knee-length coat of the aristocratic eighteenth-century male) is perverted into both men's and women's jackets, em-broidered with dinosaurs and elves (of today), and butterflies and flowers (from that time). This is the 'world in-between'—an interface—harmless and aggressive, dreamy and down-to-earth to equal degrees. Beirendonck is inspired by represen-tatives of cultures that have been absorbed by other cultures: the kachinas (gods, spirits and ancestors) of the Hopi Indians, and the Moai statues on Easter Island. Something that seems amusing, such as a little globe-man, represents the maltreated world together with the message 'stop terrorizing our world'. These words—in

Gothic, Japanese and Arab script—are turned into the clothing's décor. Not only political terror, but also aesthetic terror becomes the subject of Beirendonck's criticism. His labels have been called 'aestheticterrorists' as well as 'kiss the future'.

Hermann Hiller takes things word for word, applying the technique of deconstruction in a way similar to that of the Dadaists; however, what he deconstructs is not language, but the significance of its denotations. Hiller uses materials usually judged for their utility value alone but gives them a new, additional message by realising them in a different medium, like clothing, and also employing the medium of narrative. Hiller transforms materials like construction nets, measuring tapes or throwaway gloves into the substance of clothing and so alters their meaning. He makes a made-to-measure suit from yellow measuring tapes, a beach dress from beach mats, a house dress from builder's tarpaulins, a day suit from daily newspapers and a work overall from rubber gloves. Hiller triggers an alienation effect by destroying concepts of value; in this case it is the destruction of the banal. Hermann Hiller's clothing objects occupy a border area between art, object design and fashion design.

Viktor & Rolf achieved an aesthetic inversion (deviation) in their collection *Upside Down* (Spring/Summer 2006). Viktor & Rolf triggered the greatest possible irritation by interchanging top and bottom (the hem became the neckline, sleeves became trouser legs), right and left (the overlap of the women's jacket was from left to right; the neckline of shirt and dinner jacket slipped down to the armpits), beginning and end (the fashion show began with the designers' bow). Although their parts were inverted, the models were wearable; they simply did not correspond to the conventions of clothing design. By exchanging the top and the bottom in a way comparable to that of Georg Baselitz's paintings, Viktor & Rolf liberated their clothing from the body and gave it independence.

Idea—Concept—Process

The idea is an intellectual concept, a leading thought, imagination as an inner image. It is possible to encourage and modify ideas by force of will, using imaginative techniques (cf. p. 33). Intellectual debate and subsequent practical application become a single entity in the creative process.

The characteristic feature of conceptual art, which developed from minimalist art in the mid 1960s and was shaped by the American artist Sol LeWitt, is a turning away from the experimentally creative in favour of (clearly) defined statements or comment on and fixation of processes. In fashion, the designers Martin Margiela and Hussein Chalayan—although not until the end of the twentieth century—repeatedly produced collections approaching the conceptual.

Martin Margiela succeeded in representing the processual nature of both the production and transience of clothing in numerous collections and models: by redesigning

Figure 7   Viktor & Rolf, *Upside Down* (twisted tuxedo), 2006. Photo: Studio Them. www.them.de.

a fifties dress and documenting this process in 1995/1996; by burying, allowing to decay, and digging up his first collection in 1989; and by smearing his models with mould bacteria, which was staged as an open-air exhibition in Rotterdam in 1997. This last example in particular visualised dematerialisation—typical of conceptual art—so that only verbally or photographically produced documentation of the idea and its realisation remain.

Working in London, Hussein Chalayan is considered a consistent concept designer. He explodes all the conventions of clothing design and clothing aesthetics, as well as the interrelations of body and clothing. Chalayan crosses the borders between fashion, art and philosophy. He overcomes the absence of words and history in his models and presentations.

His own statement—that he designs ideas rather than produces fashion—is quite true. Stylistically, his creations operate in a field between minimalism and deconstructivism, whereby both the decorative and the functional character of a dress is part of its structure. He does not necessarily develop new creations on a seasonal basis; he takes up his own ideas repeatedly and continues to develop them. In this way, he meets the constant pressure for innovation in fashion with something constant and consistent: his creations are timeless. As a concept designer, Chalayan is devoted to the wearable as well as the aim to realise abstract theses and ideas. However, many of his creations are not intended for everyday wear or for sale; they are the realisations of ideas.

Frequently, Chalayan starts out from a clearly defined statement, analysing clothing and fashion and the conditions under which they exist. This intention means that he succeeds in innovation without the individual items of clothing necessarily being innovative in their cut, material, colour or pattern. In the vestimentary field, he lends design to a questioning of religions, cultures and morality in their relations to the body and face, and the safeguarding of individuality. His intention in the collection *Between* (Spring/Summer 1998)[46], for example, was to demonstrate the 'in-between quality' and separation of religions and cultures—particularly those of Islam and Christianity—in ideas ranging from complete veiling to nudity. The first model was naked and wore only a face mask, the *batula* (yashmak). The next models came onto the catwalk in different lengths of chadors, from waist- to calf-length, but with their eyes uncovered. What protects a person's individuality more from view—*batula* or chador? Who is staring at whom, the wearer at the audience, or the audience at the wearer; who is the voyeur? In the same collection, one model appeared in a red dress that left her hands uncovered but encapsulated her arms, thus robbing them of their freedom. The head was concealed under an egg-shaped wooden helmet with a small slit for the eyes. This wooden capsule concealed and simultaneously protected the wearer's individuality. The face of a different model was framed by a rectangular mirror so that the viewers saw not only the model's face but also their own faces as a reflection. Both these creations, although very different, are concerned with voyeurism. In a similar way, the ancient Arabian architecture with its perforated, carved wooden facades enabled undisturbed observation. (Architect Jean Nouvel adopted this typical pseudo-facade for the Arab World Institute in Paris, constructed from 1981 to 1987.) The artist Vanessa Beecroft also adopted the theme of voyeurism in her installations of (almost) naked female figures, besides an investigation of nakedness as a fiction and a uniform.

As a deconstruction of the Muslim understanding of veiling and to symbolise a lack of freedom, in his clothing Chalayan negates limbs (whereby the elastic materials permit limited movement). Two side seams of a dress are left open, as in the *Tabard Dress* (1997, based on the Renaissance coat with open sides which is retained in the herald's costume) and thus reveals the side of the body as a panorama view. The unusual nature of this view is sufficient to create an erotic-voyeuristic effect (*Panoramic*, 1998/1999). At the same time, the models were condemned to keep quiet by covering their lips, entirely in the spirit of Ludwig Wittgenstein's statement 'Whereof one cannot speak thereof one must be silent.'[47] That of which language is incapable—that is precisely what Chalayan attempts to express in design, using visual, haptic and physical perception. In addition, in 1998 he worked on the idea of a kinetic dress with fine, golden rubber threads linking the back to the arms so that arm movement was possible but restricted; at the same time (intentionally?), any alteration of the threads led to a fluctuating Fluxus Image.

Religious rites, especially those of the Catholic Church, were the focus of Chalayan's *Kinship Journeys* collection (Autumn/Winter 2003/2004). On the catwalk there was a trampoline, a confessional box and a boat resembling a coffin. Behind these items: hope of reaching the heavenly and divine with the aid of the trampoline; sins that control life but—with the aid of confession—can plant the seeds of a better life; and finally the boat that may signify either death or rescue on the river of forgetfulness. The possibility of rescue is integrated into the dresses as inflatable 'cushions'—'lifejackets'—in the skirts. At the same time, the irregular arrangement of inflatables gives the skirts new, space-consuming forms.

The theme of travel appears repeatedly in Chalayan's collections, with numerous abstractions, including life as a journey (process) between birth and death, the journey from A to B as a symbol of modern life, modern technology and flexibility (*Geotropics*, 1999; *Echoform*, 1999/2000; *Before Minus Now*, 2000), but also migration and exile, and the process of self-alienation and self-finding—also through clothing. His collection *Afterwords* (Autumn/Winter 2000/2001), made in collaboration with the product designer Paul Topen, examined the issue of multifunctionality and the mobility of mankind. Furniture metamorphosed into clothing, in the sense of context crossovers (cf. p. 105). Chalayan's aesthetic vision was to completely integrate clothing into space. Clothing and space were to be merged into one, forming a single unit. Step by step, a living room with four upholstered chairs and a low, round table constructed from a series of wooden hoops inserted into each other was transformed into clothing by five models. The reversible armchair covers could be removed and put on as dresses. These dresses were designed to include many pockets (openings) so that possessions such as pictures and vases could also be carried along. Personal, social and political identity was retained as a result. The wooden chairs could be dismantled and assembled into suitcases. One model removed a round lid at the centre of the table, climbed in and pulled out the table into a hoop skirt; the table legs could be folded away using a simple mechanism. The room disappeared into the models' bodies, becoming a part of their wardrobe that could be carried away with them. It was Chalayan's idea to make the everyday objects that mean a lot to people transportable; in this way, people could take their familiar surroundings with them wherever they went.

The idea is representative of wartime conditions, when people are forced to leave their homes with just a few minutes' notice and yet want to take as much as possible with them, often without this even being noticed. The fashion performance beginning with the appearance of a typical family—grandmother, parents and children—thus took on a political dimension, which included autobiographical aspects for the Turkish-Cypriot Chalayan, remembering the division of Cyprus in 1974. In addition, he wished to transform the extreme situation of flight into a positive experience and utilise the advantages of mobility. Chalayan employs clothing as a component of formed space, intending to reflect the function of protection, individuality, mobility and flexibility. As a rule, qualities like mobility and flexibility cannot be found in architecture. The idea was presented in Sadler's Wells Theatre in London and not as a défilé on the catwalk.[48]

Experiment

The experiment is an empirical method in both scientific and artistic fields. Also, it builds upon the already existent by deconstructing and thus studying and changing its substances or conditions. It is an attempt at renewal with an open outcome, based on the possibility of trial and error.

The design of clothes and accessories, like a bag for example, becomes an experiment at the moment when it no longer has any pretension to practical function (e.g. to carry food).[49] An eighteenth-century hoop skirt is an experiment in form, just like Issey Miyake's blow-up coat, as well as useless, merely decorative breast pocket or collar and lapels on a jacket, which no longer can be turned up as protection against the cold. The latter are the expression and design of a ritual. However, the question arises as to whether something loses its experimental character when it is established and has turned into a convention. Once it has been accepted, is an experiment no longer an experiment, becoming available for further experimentation? Collar and lapels remain on the jacket even when they have become relics without any purpose. As a monstrous overshaping of the female hips, the crinoline asserted itself as an object to create social distance and generate a resource of attention; the inflatable, muscled male torso for *Wild and Lethal Trash* by Walter van Beirendonck in 1986 failed to do so. Instead, unhealthy anabolic steroids were taken in order to achieve a

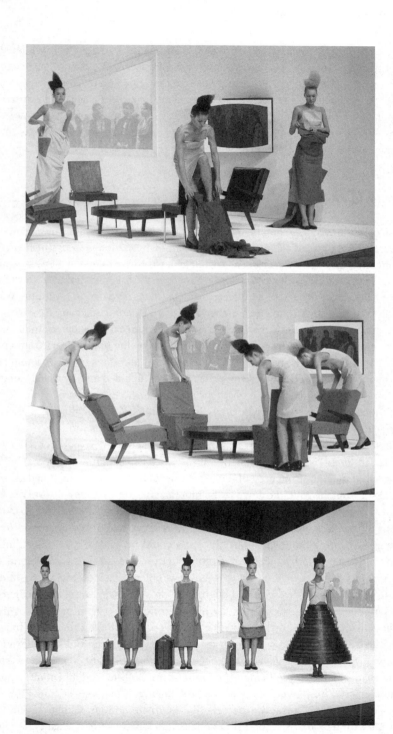

Figure 8 Hussein Chalayan, *Afterwords,* 2000/2001. Photo: Chris Moore.

muscular body, as the natural can be produced artificially. In the same way, something that is practical for any journey, like Hussein Chalayan's dress with an integrated chair consisting of head and armrests and a seat, presented in the collection *Geotropics* (1999), retained the character of an experiment. The acceptance of an experiment is dependent on its realisation—that is the step from an invention to an innovation (cf. p. 87)—its marketing, and its subsequent adoption by society. This is further evidence of the social definition of when clothes become fashion (cf. p. 133).

Transformables

Transformation refers to the alteration of a figure, form or structure into something different without loss of substance. The aim of transformation is to tap fresh energies (in a creative-artistic sense as well), stimulate new processes and achieve new aims.

The design of types of vestimentary transformables is expanding with the mobility of the target group. In a collection titled *Urban Protection* (Autumn/Winter 1999/2000), the C. P. Company launched a coat with a hood that can be transformed into a hammock. Lucy Orta invented the *Habitent,* a rain cape that can be transformed into a tent, in 1992. The *Shape Memory Shirt* (2000) by the Italian brand Corpo Nove adapts its shape to the body due to a special material and stays in this form until the next time it is washed. Blow-ups (cf. p. 48) are also included among transformables, for example a jacket designed by Moreno Ferrari for C. P. Company, which can be transformed into a recliner when inflated (Spring/Summer 2000). Other ideas are based on magnets sewn onto a dress, making it redesignable in various forms.

Hussein Chalayan caused a sensation with a series of experimental dresses moulded in fibreglass. In the collection *Geotropics* (Spring/Summer 1999), a dress was screwed together from grey fibreglass elements for the first time. It had a narrow vertical slit from the neckline down to the hips, an unusual—modern—form of décolleté. In *Echoform,* the subsequent Autumn/Winter collection of 1999/2000, individual parts of a fibreglass dress could be made to slide apart, and a season later in *Before Minus Now* (Spring/Summer 2000), the parts could be folded out. This sliding or folding out was done by means of remote control. The dresses were reminiscent of aeroplanes adjusting their airbrakes and thus entered fashion history as 'remote control' or 'aeroplane dresses'. Although these dresses shape over the female body in an entirely rigid way, they are not without erotic aura. The attraction lies in the openings that are caused by the movement of the parts or the turning up of the skirt at the sides and above the bottom, from which a tulle skirt unfolded, for example. In *Before Minus Now,* Chalayan was concerned with intelligent controlling systems and mechanisms like those being tested in modern, high-tech architecture. He used design elements from aviation as well as the high-tech material of fibreglass. The quality of his dresses' plastic surface is like futuristic armour, which permits connotations with the body's second skin nonetheless—because of a sensitive, delicate pink in the contours. The model's unwearability develops into an elegant, mobile form. Chalayan's designs express the body's reference and relationship to many rational events and experiences as well as to irrational, intangible atmospheres like flight, gravity, speed or radio frequencies. Chalayan uses his designs to transfer information between the wearer and his or her environment and so repeatedly points to the affinity between the human body and surrounding space. In his own words, Chalayan designed the 'remote control' dress not to investigate the relations between technology and the body, but to experiment with the way in which the contour of the silhouette can develop in a spatial relationship with its surroundings. Chalayan designs body spaces. By means of their architectonic structure or graphic motifs, his models convey symbolic values like technical and scientific development and progress; they proffer safety and security for the human body in the postmodern world. Communication functions as a tool. His integration of the clothes into technological systems opens up new processes and possibilities, which abolish many of the borders separating the constructed and formed body from its architectonic environment.

Chalayan's collections *One Hundred and Eleven* of Spring/Summer 2007[50] and *Airborne,* Autumn/Winter 2007/2008, were no less spectacular. Chalayan believes that technology points the way for the future and, in cooperation with the company 2D:3D, he had mini-motors built into some dresses. These served the purpose of historical morphing, presented as a vestimentary time lapse in front of a sort of clock with rapidly turning hands in the background. A model wearing a floor-length, high-necked dress, lavishly decorated with frills and flounces in the style of the Belle Epoque, appears on the catwalk; quietly and gently—as if by magic—it opens up and the hem of the dress beneath is raised. The tulip-shaped skirt of a second dress lifts, and fringes fall down from the flounces. Both dresses are then transformed into knee-length sack dresses from the 1920s. The fashion of one decade transforms into that of the next. A third dress is swallowed up entirely by a wide-brimmed hat, undressing the model.

Another example of transformation is provided by Hamburg designer John Ribbe as he alters the silhouette of his dress and coat models using fastenings, straps, ribbons and clasps, which also give the clothes variable ornamentation.

Ultimately, clothing itself consists of a transformation, from a one-dimensional thread via a two-dimensional piece of cloth to a three-dimensional covering that is either draped around the body every time one dresses or put on as a premanufactured sheath (cf. p. 18).

Light, Colour, Pattern, Ornament

Light is a means used to achieve colours and patterns not only in architecture, but also in experimental clothing. LEDs (light-emitting or luminescent diodes), some integrated into clothes, others draped around the body as decorative necklaces or bracelets or as a light-projection surface, as well as fluorescing fabrics attract the desired attention

Figure 9   Hussein Chalayan, *Airborne* LEDs Combined with Swarovski Crystals, 2007/2008. Photo: Studio Them. www.them.de.

at catwalk presentations in particular. In his Autumn/Winter 2007/2008 collection, Hussein Chalayan made his hats and dresses glow by means of integrated LEDs and increased the intensity of light by sewing on Swarovski crystals. The glowing winter hat and the automatically shining party dress radiate an aura of sensuality and emotions.[51] In *Readings* (2008) by Hussein Chalayan, dresses with fitted laser lamps symbolise worshipping the sun. Although in this collection Chalayan was concerned with the historical development from sun worship to glorification of individual personalities, these dresses that glowed by means of laser could also be interpreted as a visualisation of the energy radiated by the wearer, the rays of which may be blinding.

Viktor & Rolf carried out an experiment with light and colour by presenting their 2001/2002 prêt-à-porter collection *Black Hole* in black light (UV light). Black appeared not only as the colour of the clothes, but also as a symbol of the black hole that swallows up everything, the place of silence and the unearthly. The models' visible skin was covered in coal-black make-up, and only their eyeballs shone a striking white in the dark room. Even the bride was black.

In the near future, there will be an increase in the use of so-called performance-fabrics. Lumalive, a textile-emitting light created by means of integrated LEDs and produced by Philips[52], can be made into T-shirts or seat covers; images or texts can then be played onto it using a remote control device, mobile telephone or SMS. It becomes a light-projection surface for advertising or brand symbols, as required. Since the 1990s T-shirts have been available that visualise the temperature of the body zones and so develop a slightly fluctuating pattern of colours—from dark red to light blue. Others reveal their pattern only when exposed to the sun's rays.

Microprocessors repeatedly inspire designers to create futuristic patterns, such as Jean-Paul Gaultier, who had this type of pattern embroidered onto leather jackets in 1981, and Alexander McQueen, who designed bodysuits with luminescent computer-switching circuits for Givenchy in Autumn/Winter 1999/2000. In their 2002/2003 *Bluescreen* collection, Viktor & Rolf used the film industry's blue-box process and had landscapes, street traffic or sky and clouds projected onto their clothing while the models walked along the catwalk. The creations seemed dematerialised as projection surfaces, but the variability of these 'life patterns' as well as the disintegration of the clothes into the background projection was fascinating. Susumi Tachi, professor at the University of Tokyo, achieved a similar effect with his 'transparent' coat made of retro-reflective material, which is similar to a projection screen that enables one to see a three-dimensional image. Tachi had the scene behind the wearer filmed and simultaneously projected onto the front of a coat. The coat therefore appeared transparent, since one could see what was happening behind it on the front. Other experiments originate in the chemistry laboratory, like fungi that form coloured patterns on (cf. p. 76).

Alexander McQueen employs the ornament (cf. p. 197) to eroticise the body when he sews pieces of crochet work onto gauze—loose, frayed, hanging and apparently arbitrarily draped regardless of erogenous zones. The ornament itself thus questions

Figure 10 Susumu Tachi, *Invisible Coat,* 2003. Photo and © Tachi Laboratory, University of Tokyo, Japan.

whether it is truly necessary and exists merely for the sake of its attractions (*Hunger,* Spring/Summer 1996).

Sound

Wrapped in thick fog, the creations for Viktor & Rolf's haute couture collection *Bells* in 2000/2001 could be only heard and not seen as they glided over the catwalk: a collection for the ear. This represented a challenge to the senses and was irritating for those who can see and are not accustomed to concentrating on the audio, an irritation of our expectations regarding fashion and vision. Hundreds of different-sized golden bells were sewn onto coats, jackets, tops and belts. Only towards the end of the show were spotlights shone onto them, and thus the eye was satisfied as well. Exhibited in a museum, the creations leave an inadequate impression, for their special quality is the sound.

Material

There is no form without material, and no style without form. The chemical compound and structure of fibres, and the layering and finishing of materials belong to the field of highly complex technologies (cf. p. 33).[53] It is the task of the textile engineer to investigate this subject. At present, the highest rate of innovation is in the field of nonwovens. While they provide valuable service with respect to comfort—as biomimetic almost-skin fabrics for swimsuits (by Speedo) and especially for all types of protective clothing—there still seems to be relatively little interest in establishing them in visionary designs for fashionable clothing. The blinking dress, the jacket that changes its colour, and the like exist in the experimental field—as high-tech couture—but they are still far from serial production.

Electronic finishing of textiles is still in a trial phase. In cooperation with the British company Eleksen, the semiconductor producer Infineon is developing control elements to be woven into fabrics. These consist of five layers of isolation, semiconductor, and carbon fibre material. They are only 0.6 millimetres thick and insensitive to folding and water when washed. The sensors can be integrated into any part of the clothing (cf. p. 122).

With very few exceptions, vestimentary experiments with inappropriate materials can be traced back to the delight in experimentation of fashion designer Paco Rabanne. As early as 1966, he presented twelve experimental dresses made of materials such as hard plastic and metal, which had been created using pliers and welding irons instead of scissors and sewing needles. Rabanne knitted metal threads into an 'aluminium jersey'. He created paper dresses as day and evening wear, which may be interpreted as contrasting counterparts to his indestructible metal dresses, but these were also characteristic of the contemporary conviction that there was a future in throwaway fashion. In 1967 he made his first dresses from metal moulded into body shapes, which he replaced with acrylic glass incorporating holograms in 1988. In 1992, Rabanne created dresses with drinking glasses hanging on chains—his own form of recycling fashion—and in 1996 he assembled a minidress out of slide frames. Yves Saint Laurent also used bizarre materials such as wooden beads, Yohji Yamamoto designed a dress from wooden rods and hinges, Andrew Groves used razor blades, Alexander McQueen made dresses from microscope slides (cf. p. 57) and shells. In his Spring/Summer 2000 collection, Junya Watanabe presented dresses and capes that mutated into dresses made of the water-resistant fabric NanoTex in order to make rain protection superfluous. And for summer 2005, Watanabe created big collars and belts from zip fasteners. In 1995, Helmut Lang had Chantilly lace melted onto rubber, from which he produced a minimalist-style sheath dress described as 'hard-core glamour'. Especially popular in the experimental field is Tyvek, a textile similar to paper which can be wiped clean. Materials are also manipulated to the point where they become unrecognisable using acids, bacteria, steel brushing and burning. The production of heatable clothing has also been a subject of experiment since the First World War.

The (mass) production of ecologically defensible or unobjectionable materials has become an enduring topic. Eco-fashion is an important issue, and not only for specialist providers; international fashion houses have become more aware of 'green luxury'. The nonprofit environmental group Earth Pledge opened New York Fashion Week in Autumn 2008 with *FutureFashion* (founded in 2005), and in the same context houses including Yves Saint Laurent, Givenchy, Maison Martin Margiela, Marni and Jil Sander presented clothes made of organic wool and hemp, as well as biological materials produced on a maize basis. Spanish-Majorcan designer Miguel Adrover, who also works in New York, presented a collection for the German eco-clothing company Hess Natur in an art gallery in Chelsea. It came under the category of free design, close to art, and included the dress *Philodendron,* made of brown ecological wool with natural batik work reminiscent of a huge autumn leaf as a gesture to ecology.

Handling an ordinary (ecologic) material in an extremely unusual way, applying it to an innovative creative design and so achieving something quite extraordinary was the idea behind Jula-Anna Reindell's master collection *Inside Out* (2008) at London University of the Arts. The collection made vestimentary use of hair as ornamentation under transparent materials, as stuffing for a padded jacket, as a fetish object, for fringes, for a cloak and a tie and even for something as conventional as a long skirt and trousers. The theme of hair was explored as a metaphor of male strength and female eroticism as well as a recurrent element in Surrealist art.

Another constant topic of experiment is clothing without seams, and a particular textile-technical or chemical challenge is presented by the production of extremely flexible materials like the spandex bodystockings of the 1980s. Bras moulded by warmth and pressure have existed since fashion designer Rudi Gernreich suggested the one-size bra or 'no-bra' bra. In 1968, Pierre Cardin embellished dresses using convexly moulded mini cuboids. Gianni Versace caused a sensation in 1984 with his evening dresses made of light aluminium metal-mesh, which was cut and soldered using lasers. In addition to these, there are many experimental processes of pleating, felting and matting, machine and hand knitting, and crocheting.

On the basis of endless knitted tubes, Issey Miyake—together with Dai Fujiwara—developed the clothing concept *A-POC* (A Piece of Cloth) in 1997, introducing it as a collection in 1999. *A-POC* consists of three-dimensional tubes produced using a knitting computer, from which each customer can create those items of clothing that he or she wants by cutting along perforated lines. Without sewing or hemming, they can be made into an individual outfit, bag or cap. Miyake and Fujiwara thus revolutionised the conventional clothes-production process including the production of fabrics, pattern construction, sizing and sewing. It is only the cost of all this that makes it unsuitable for mass production—as yet.

During the 1990s, natural and technical materials were combined, but since the beginning of the twenty-first century there has been a clear separation. On the one hand, since 2004 Manel Torres has been experimenting with spray-on garments made of FabriCan, a fine, liquid dust of cotton fibres. Several layers ranging from thin and transparent to opaque, folds and patterns can be sprayed onto the skin,

Figure 11   Jula-Anna Reindell, *Inside Out,* 2008. Photo: Nikolas Ventourakis. © Jula-Anna Reindell.

Figure 12 Nicolas Ghesquière for Balenciaga, model 2008/2009. Photo: Studio Them. www.them.de.

or decor and jewellery can be oversprayed. It would be possible for the wearer to redesign his or her clothes from the spray can (with logo) individually and in a new way every day.

On the other hand, surface coatings such as metallization and digital prints allow for new optics and haptics, changing materials to the point where they are no longer conclusively identifiable. Therefore, even the material itself is the subject of a simulation and becomes illusiveness and a false front. It becomes impossible to classify the visual and the tactile; cognition works only by decoding forms and ornaments: 'On account of the high-gloss surfaces that reflect the light, or matting structures that swallow the light, the materials used can render our familiar perception of spatiality inoperative.'[54] In this way, Nicolas Ghesquière's Autumn/Winter 2008/2009 collection for Balenciaga depicts modern, richly chiselled armour consisting of a cuirass and shirt-robe made from apparently rigid material with prints of a simulated nature. The models represent a defensive attitude and, in the designer's own words, they are intended to radiate 'seriousness'. Not least, tattoos also resemble visual armour for the skin. They are ornaments, individual statements, and something enduring in the short-lived consumer world—at least in the eyes of their adherents. When skin is tattooed, it seems as if the first and second skins merge into one.

Second Skin

The key phrase 'second skin'[55] embodies a vision for the future in which a synthetic material similar to human skin is integrated into the skin, repairing itself and growing back, and producing colours or logos on the skin itself—according to how the material has been processed. Today, some new types of material already react to light, heat, touch and mechanical strain. Flexible membranes can be digitally networked, folded, stretched and inflated with air to create a second skin in place of textile clothing.

Skinthetic is a hybrid of material, pattern and brand logo by Peter Allen and Carla Murray from the company KnoWear in Cataumet, Massachusetts, USA. On their homepage, the project is described in the following way:

> Skinthetic is a two-part project that first focuses on how large corporate companies will continue to sell and distribute their brand names in the future.
>
> The first aspect of the Skinthetic proposal trades on the idea of branding once removed. Given that in the next twenty years as implant and explant technology becomes more sophisticated and branding more intertwined into our commodity driven culture, labels and bodies will become one. Where in 2000 we as consumers put labels on our bodies through the act of clothing by 2020 we will be implanting designed body parts that are not only genetically coded but also will bear the signs and identities of the couture and product house that have created them.

The second aspect of Skinthetic suggests a form of distribution for these brands. The form of distribution for these labels would be through interactive street level web based billboards. Each billboard/advertisement works like a web page that one interacts with on their home computer; but instead of using your mouse to browse through pages, these interactive billboards are touch and voice activated. One can gather information on products, find out the nearest distribution point, or pay for merchandise right on the street.

The Skinthetic Proposal Uses Three Brands as Case Studies:

MasterCard: fingernail implant allows user to purchase merchandise through digital DNA.

Nike: air bladder implant allows the user to push their physical performance.

Chanel: quilt implant allows the user to have a 'designer' body.[56]

Another vision is based on the biological design of textiles using fungi. In 2006, Donna Franklin presented the material Fibre Reactive, which alters its surface and colour as a consequence of micro fungi. These fungi are kept alive by humidity. There are ideas to apply the fungi not only to fabrics, but also directly onto the skin, thus stimulating changes in the skin surface itself. The result would be a symbiosis of skin and textile, of first and second skin; clothing as such could become superfluous. Increasingly, therefore, the object of design could be man himself—a continuation and enhancement of his own being into a 'bio-machine ready for adaptation'[57] (cf. p. 15). In the imagined age of Fibre Reactive, clones, cyborgs and BANG-design (see next section), perhaps the association of naked skin and eroticism will no longer be applicable, or things will turn out quite differently to the way that we can imagine the future today. The question certainly arises as to whether people will be able to complete this 'anthropological quantum leap',[58] as Peter Sloterdijk calls it, or whether a knowing-doing gap will continue to exist, quite apart from the ethical problems involved.

Neurocomputing and BANG-Design

According to the old European philosophy of the duality of body and spirit, the spirit forms the body using materials not immanent to the body. At the same time, the body provides a covering for the spirit, soul or psyche. Since the end of the twentieth century, research has followed the opposite path, considering how the spirit may be formed or expanded: another as yet fictive anthropological quantum leap. It is conceivable that the brain could be provided with access to further knowledge and information by means of wearables or brain implants (brain chips).[59] Wearables are digital systems integrated into clothing, which are worn on the body but do not become a unit with it (cf. p. 122). Attempts to network the brain and a computer directly in the form of neurocomputing are more efficient. In other words, a brain chip could be used to increase hugely the calculation and storage capacity of the brain, or the other way around—highly intelligent computer systems could be taught the human brain's dynamic way of functioning. Or body jewellery like piercings could function as a brain-computer-interface. Brain chips could be worn like piercings, taking the form of small bumps on the forehead like those designed as 'face jewellery' by fashion designer Walter van Beirendonck in his *Avatar* collection 1997/1998. Outgrowths of the skull might also be possible and could be designed fashionably with bobbles and little chains (as in an advertisement for '25 Years of Greenpeace' in 2006) or using tattoos. And the efficiency, competitiveness and value of these advanced cyborgs—human beings with a second skin and a second brain—could be judged by means of benchmarking. The US evaluation concept of benchmarking is a globally utilised process for the evaluation and improvement of a company's products, services and working processes, and in addition has been used to test the effect of political guidelines. Is this an invention that could actually be realised, or is it a utopia?

Perspectives and visions for design in the future are oriented on BANG-design, made up of bits, atoms, neurons and genes. In his 2006 manifesto, the design theorist Norbert Bolz declared that BANG-design was the basic component of culture and the economy in the twenty-first century. The fact that these four elements 'can be grasped as a unit today, is inseparably connected with research into the magical dimension: ten to the power of minus nine metres . . . On this nano scale, the difference between the natural and the artificial is disappearing. Nature itself becomes a design object'.[60]

Fashion for the Virtual 'I'

'There has always been a dream of separating the human body from its spirit. It is quasi the metaphysical aspect of our notion of the perfect existence. Now the computer age enables us to believe that this dream could come true: the dream of separating body and spirit. A life as pure spiritual energy—never feeling bad, never becoming ill, never dying?'[61] In Christianity, angels represent pure spiritual energy; however, so that the human brain can imagine the angels, they are given a human shape, some human qualities, and human if not fashionable clothing. In a similar way, Hindu gods appear in human or animal shapes, known as avatars, so that they are perceivable and recognisable to man.

Conversely, a person's spiritual form on the Internet is known as his avatar. In other words, this term has been transferred to mean an artificial person or the virtual representative of a person in virtual reality. The avatar—the virtual 'I'—in virtual space is usually composed from a sampling of different historical and contemporary body images. Anthropological and anthropometric body schemata are combined with art historical image patterns, deriving from sources including Vitruvius, Leonardo da

Vinci and Albrecht Dürer. The sampling of a virtual 'I' may also include other contemporary artistic and cinematic visions of the future such as cyborgs and androids.

Christiane Luible's and Alexander Lindt's ideas in their diploma *Extended Body* 1999/2000 at the University of Applied Sciences in Pforzheim went a step further in artistic experiment. They created virtual body designs for identification of the 'I' without a body. Although clothes as such ought not to play a role in virtual reality, since the virtual person is not tied to any body structure, the idea was directed at a body design with which different virtual identities could be conveyed. Fashion for the 'I'—in the absence of a body—was designed at the computer. Apart from this, it is not unrealistic that there may be a need for protective clothing in virtual space as well, as a defence against computer viruses, for example. Could some kind of clothing, embellishment, accessory or tool give the virtual body a certain life quality—especially as there are no boundaries, time zones or rooms in virtual space? This consideration led Luible and Lindt to create different body coverings at the computer. An oversized pair of pants plays loosely around the body as a spatial covering which—since it exists in a vacuum—can never leave or impede the figure. Every movement of the virtual 'I' causes a change in the pants; in other words, the virtual 'I' becomes visible only as a result of the change in the pants. In the case of another avatar figure, the clothes—which are visible only as fragments—wander up

Figure 13 Christiane Luible and Alexander Lindt, *Extended Body,* computer animation 1999/2000. © Luible/Lindt.

and down the body, capturing the viewer's attention. A skirt only floats around the body, for it has no need of physical ties. The virtual body is not bound to any real motoricity, either; it also floats freely in space. Another garment is located inside, below the skin. The body is fat, as the clothing is worn inside the body, and only a collar is outwardly visible. We see quasi into the interior of the virtual body, which wears a kind of inner fur clothing. Another garment flows into the virtual space around it; the wearer is alienated from the image of his real world, and the 'material' is replaced by a film projection that slowly fades into the body. The border between clothing and body disintegrates. Ultimately, the clothing dissolves completely into total abstraction and the figure is recognisable only as an imprint. Yet another garment consists of only the tiniest robots or nanocomponents, of pure energy that whirs over the surface of the skin. Their sound is communication. The textile is pure design material for the body. Clothing has developed dynamics of its own; it plays with the body and stimulates it, in an erotic sense as well. The clothing is part of the new quality of life. Another example shows that externals are the spirit's way of expressing itself, for example communication as a language of pure colour or light. Thus the body is surrounded by an aura of rays, which can be more or less concentrated according to the level of heat or chill. The movement adopts a grid system—environment, textile—plays with it, and lets it go again. This means that the dark grid network is taken up arbitrarily by the figure while walking and carried further along. We continue to see a figure in script language. The virtual body emerges from the blue script and intermingles with it. In the metaphorical sense, the spirit becomes a person only through the writing, and so communication is the clothing of the body and of the 'I'. One figure walks in its programming language, another draws all the desktops into its movement, remaining only sketchily discernible in itself. As a further step, the figure could dissolve completely and its portrayal and communication could take place through entirely different means such as light, sound or colours.

Christiane Luible wrote about her work *Extended Body* five years later (2005), when she was working at Miralab in Geneva: 'It is interesting for me to see that today, 5 years after our diploma many developments have not arrived as quickly as we thought they would. I can still remember that when we wrote our diploma everyone was talking about 3D websites, which would of course utilise three-dimensional virtual representatives. That has still not really been established. Working on our diploma, we also assumed that people were fascinated by a reproduction of the real world first, but that they would then abstract it. I think our work here aims in a parallel direction instead. The clothing industry is interested in real reproduction, 1 to 1, so that prototypes of clothes can be realised in a virtual sphere and save costs. That is exactly where a lot of research is funded. Museums and other institutions are more interested in (abstract) visualisation and are often very open to new approaches.'[62]

In an age of chat rooms, bloggers, Skype, Second Life etc. and the like it has become appropriate to design clothing as virtual reality and virtual body design, in order to offer the possibility of conveying virtual identities for the 'I'. In future, the virtual human image will admit completely new iconographic interpretations.

Avant-garde fashion designers have also discovered the virtual world as a depictive form for their creations and have integrated it into catwalk presentations.

Performative Invention

In order to bring across the intellectual message or the allure of a fashionable creation or to mediate diverse creations in a visual way as a collection, the designer employs performative realisation. This is the only, the final opportunity for a designer to present the character of his or her clothing from the creator's viewpoint. Afterwards, the creations are released—on the one hand for photographic production as advertising and in the media, and on the other hand as order goods, whether for multiplication and distribution, as unique garments for a single wearer, or as exhibition pieces for a museum. Designers' vestimentary inventions are not empty coverings for a body, but the manifestation of design ideas and processes. For that reason, they search not only for creative product inventions, but also for inventive presentations that do justice to their philosophy of design and fashion *and* to the message of their clothing (cf. p. 143).

In his shows, Alexander McQueen repeatedly questions duality by bringing together (apparently) diametric contexts like subject–object or organic–inorganic. He examines a crossing of the contexts man–machine in the sense of both the autarkic cyborg and the remote-controlled human being. The presentation of McQueen's Spring/Summer 1999 collection *#13* concluded with the appearance of model Shalom Harlow, who spun on a turntable like a music-box figure to music from P. I. Tchaikovsky's *Swan Lake*. Her white dress was sprayed with green, yellow and black paint by two wildly spinning paint-spraying robots like those used in the car industry. Associations are awakened, such as the original meaning of the word *mannequin,* which is a modelling and tailoring dummy devoid of will—martyred but nonetheless important. These are personified forms of alienation, the abstract and a fetishisation of functional commodities.[63]

In a photo sequence by Nick Knight that thematised 'The Beauty of Imperfection—A Dubious Beauty Cult' for the magazine *Dazed & Confused* (September 1998), McQueen dressed the model Aimee Mullens—whose legs have been amputated—in a hoop petticoat, a bolero made of filigree wooden fans (Givenchy haute couture, 1998) and a velour leather top. Her wooden leg prostheses came from an historical window-display dummy. The trauma of a leg amputation is turned into a beautiful, doll-like creature; E.T.A. Hoffmann's Olympia (Jacques Offenbach, *Hoffmanns Erzählungen,* 1881), Hans Bellmer's *La Poupée* (1934), a marionette, an automaton doll, an angel, or a cyborg? In several of his films, including *Drawing Restraint 9* (2005), the media artist Matthew Barney also examined the prosthesis as an aesthetic option, as well as the ethical philosophy that valuable experience may be arrived at through loss.

McQueen supplements his creations with performative concepts that aestheticise the subconscious (cf. p. 57). In his collection *Bellmer's La Poupée* (Spring/Summer 1997) the focus is on the proximity of life and death and its shattering effect when his models wade through water—the life-giving element, but apparently signifying doom for one model whose limbs are constrained. (However, the association with Bellmer's *La Poupée* was much clearer in the above-mentioned photo shoot.) At the end of the fashion show *Voss* (Spring/Summer 2001), McQueen presented life in a glass test tube; a young, voluptuous female figure, depicted as a faunlike creature, was artificially fed and ventilated through tubes. The test-tube cube burst, scattering thousands of moths. In addition, fashion shows like *Voss* (Spring/Summer 2001; cf. p. 57) or *The Overlook* (Autumn/Winter 1999/2000) by Alexander McQueen proffer a new level of realisation that goes beyond the tradition of a performance.

The high point of Alexander McQueen's fashion show *Widows of Culloden* (Autumn/Winter 2006/2007, named after a battle that Scottish rebels lost near Culloden in 1746) was a holographic image of the model Kate Moss, who danced as a perfect, floating illusion—as a widow and bride of the wind—in a dress with flying flounces. The catwalk was transformed into a form of virtual reality; a real staging outside the field of media art. The viewer was energised more than ever before, torn from the peace and quiet of mere observation. Such moving images on a high intellectual plane have little in common with the character of the classic défilé.

In Hussein Chalayan's presentation *Ventriloquy* (Spring/Summer 2001), the real reflected the virtual. The virtual world of computer animation showed one figure blowing out another, which then disintegrated into a thousand small geometric symbols. A poppy emerged from those symbols and then developed into two human figures. The second of these wore a fragile dress with lines of construction running through it; again, this exploded into thousands of pieces. The first figure made itself another dress from the pieces as they flew past. This sequence was followed by real models in real dresses, but with a similar appearance to the ones in the computer animation. The show's conclusion echoed the beginning, so to speak, when models appeared wearing dresses of crystallised sugar, and the dresses were destroyed by other models wielding hammers. The pattern of some dresses was like graph paper, intending to symbolise the design process; other dresses were assembled as patchwork, which stood for newly emerging values. Some others had poppies, the first flowers that bloom on battlefields attached as ornaments. The sugar clothes represent the unreal aspect of real fashion, which is shattered again and again. Chalayan explains this: 'The garments in the animation were also part of the real show, and they were destroyed on the stage, as they were in the film. The real clothes are an alter ego for the virtual clothes, similar to a ventriloquist who is two beings in one. The real clothes then destroy their virtual twins. On a more abstract level it is about how values disappear completely in times of war and catastrophes.'[64]

Figure 14 Viktor & Rolf, *Fashion Show,* 2007/2008. Photo: Studio Them. www.them.de.

As said already, Hussein Chalayan is famous for presentations beyond the conventional catwalk and his intellectual staging of creations, which explode the boundaries between fashion, design, performance and art. His collections and shows are concerned with issues like expulsion, identity, isolation, oppression, morality, the Muslim veil and the fate of refugees (cf. p. 62). To some extent, these topics have autobiographical traits—identity, the home country and the associated human emotions are decisive for the Turkish-Cypriot designer.

In their 2007/2008 collection *Fashion Show*, Viktor & Rolf appeared to be concerned with a heightening and fetishising of the utility commodity, clothing. A scaffold with mounted spotlights was attached to the body of each model, so that the creation he or she was presenting was illuminated individually while the model walked along the catwalk. The clothes were thus given an aura, or rather a ring of light, which recalled the aura, nimbus or halo of Christian figures or a baldachin, brought down to the level of profane technology in crude spotlights. The dresses themselves were designed as a reference to Holland, including their pattern, which was intended to suggest Delft porcelain.

John Galliano's magnificent spectacles (for both his own label and the House of Dior) are directed solely at the image of fashion, at its being and semblance; regardless of whether he cites the clothes of ancient Egypt or the fin de siècle, the idea of global fashion as conglomerated ethnic items of clothing or the circus as an illusionary setting. Galliano is even concerned primarily with fashion when—in place of beautifully proportioned models—he sends people beyond the customary norm along the catwalk: extremely fat, thin, old and ugly people, dwarves and giants of both sexes (Spring/Summer 2006). Here, too, Galliano was concerned with proportions, not only of clothing (even a small marionette wore the same dress as the tallest model) but also of bodies and facial features. It was a matter of characterising and typifying human beings, but never without the light touch of irony. Galliano granted positive aesthetics to people who were exceptional in appearance and character. The catwalk presentation was intended not as a caricature or mockery of the physically different, but rather as a call to think carefully, about beauty mania, the adulation of models and catwalk voyeurism, but also about people's right to designer clothing regardless of their figures.

Martin Margiela seeks to deconstruct not only the clothes, but also their presentation: no star models, no catwalk, and no bows. In his collection *Blow Ups* (Spring/Summer 2000), he showed clothing that had been considerably enlarged—by 148 percent, 150 per cent or 200 per cent—demonstrating new proportions, although the clothing was far too big for the models. The collection was presented in a sports hall on oversized circular tables, around which the audience sat, then appearing quite diminutive. Each model was led onto a table in the dark by stagehands or tailors in white overalls and then spotlighted so that the tables functioned as a stage. The resulting associations range from 'table dance' to Alice in Wonderland.

Margiela rejects any form of celebrity hype and denies it to his models as well. He conceals their faces by combing their hair forward, or using material to protect or not

Figure 15   Martin Margiela, *Papillon,* haute couture 2006/2007. Photo: Marina Faust for Maison Martin Margiela.

reveal their personal identity and to investigate the whole question of who is watching whom—the model or the audience (basically, this question is also relevant to the veiling of Muslim women). Sometimes, Margiela works without models altogether, and assistants present his creations on coat hangers. In an extremely ingenious way, he had each creation of his haute couture Autumn/Winter 2006/2007 collection projected onto a silhouette photo of a model (without a face). In this way, Margiela succeeded in arriving at a surreal type of presentation that is similar to a peep show, although oriented not on the body but on the clothing. The clothing—as an external covering or an intimate message of inner feelings—is exposed to discursive evaluation in a way reminiscent of the painting *Night and Day Clothes of the Body* (1936) by Salvador Dalí. At the end of the presentation the clothing hangs on busts, so lacking any form of intimacy or eroticism.

Walter van Beirendonck takes away his models' superficial identity and gives them acrylic glass visors or stereotyped frizzy hairstyles. As a final consequence, the German fashion designer Frank Leder presented his models to blind people, who were not permitted to touch the creations. Tellingly, he entitled this collection *The Blind Leading the Blind* (Spring/Summer 2005).

In *Ghosts,* Bernhard Willhelm experimented with the presentation of his Spring/Summer 2004 collection as a feature film. The film was directed by Swiss artist Olaf Breuning, who lives in New York. It is set in the visions of a young man: a horde of ghosts reminiscent of the Ku Klux Klan—wearing white hoods and capes—fall upon young girls in a riotous manner, then embrace, annoy and abduct them. What starts out as fun becomes a threat and develops almost into rape. On the one hand, Bernhard Willhelm's ghosts are dressed conventionally in white linen (bed sheets), but they are humanised and individualised on the other hand by means of painted-on expressions ranging from friendly smiles to threatening leers. Their sexually neutral masks offer a protection and freedom comparable to Alemannic Mardi Gras costumes. Do Bernhard Willhelm and Olaf Breuning also question the apparent contradiction between the protection and freedom offered by civil and military uniforms in exceptional circumstances? Bernhard Willhelm is unwilling to confirm such interpretations; his primary concern is to blur the boundary between dramatic action and concept.

These exemplary, innovative fashion performances represent simulation and an abolition of the boundaries to fiction. Their aim is only partially to reproduce the designers' creations. Nonetheless, they always combine creations that are wearable in the traditional sense with imaginary and visionary highlights. Occasionally, however, the highly symbolic message of these shows makes an understanding of the actual fashion creations more difficult.

–7–

When Is Innovation?

Only those who accept change are able to grow.

Paul Wilson

'If we allow the old to persist, it will defend itself forcefully against the new.'[1] This is the classic theory of creative destruction, still recognised today, which is seen as the key message of the theory of innovation propounded by economist Joseph Alois Schumpeter in 1911. Schumpeter appealed to 'creative destruction'[2] as the ability to assert innovations successfully in face of objective, social and/or psychical opposition. As an economist and social scientist, Schumpeter saw innovations as possible only when the different departments within a business cooperate. He was concerned not with innovation as such, in a creative-artistic context, but far more with the possibility of realising inventions, that is with effecting innovations 'feasible for the everyday'. As a general rule, he saw innovations as subject to 'structurally linked processes of change'[3], which are not limited to a single part-system. They are bound to productive-technical and economic possibilities and to social structures. Innovation requires the fulfilment of contradictory demands; change and stabilisation.

Some people believe that the tyranny of the existent must be overcome, others that the new is always founded on the old. Fashion provides suitable verification for both theses (cf. pp. 42, 11). Breaking with the past in order to arrive at the new is based on the capacity and will to forget. But radical creative destruction is related to the old as well, albeit from the perspective of nihilism. The Romanist Hans Robert Jauß already sees a radical demand for the new and a devaluation of the old in the emergence of Christianity, which was exemplary in its impact on European culture as a whole.[4] Especially in urban development, the postulate of creative destruction has always been asserted radically.

Continuity—as in the case of an evolution—can also lead to something completely new. The quality of the past lies in evidence; the 'stored symbols' indicating why, what and how things functioned; and this also applies in creativity for the— unknown—future (cf. p. 98). Philosopher and media theorist Boris Groys establishes: 'Contemporary criticism, quite correctly, doubts that man is capable of creating the new from nothing or even from sources directly accessible to him. Various theories of intertextuality, therefore, have shown that the new always consists of the old—of citations, references to tradition, modifications and interpretations of the already existing.[5] Even the invention of the wheel was an interpretation of something that already existed, like a round stone. The wrong conclusion is often drawn from this, namely that there is nothing new whatsoever in culture, and no true authors. But according to Groys, the intellectual capacity to cross boundaries is typical of man alone; in other words, only man has mastered the logic of crossing contexts (cf. p. 105)—round stone–wheel—as a strategy of innovation.[6] The new emerges with the aid of the imagination, the capacity to conceive something as a supplement to what exists in the sense of complementing it. Innovation creates a possibility that demands an action. Innovation means deviation, and as such it is free of evaluation, but change is different, for it can lead to either the positive or the negative.

The new cannot be grasped without the referential concept and evaluation 'old'. 'The new can only be defined in relation to the already canonised old',[7] or rather, it must be recombined. Thinking (grasping, evaluating etc.) is also based on recombinations of the synaptic links in the brain. This statement not only indicates the helpfulness of investigation into history, it also explains the urge to interpret the new by means of historical comparison.

Research and Development

Since Schumpeter, innovations have been understood as inventions that have asserted themselves. This implies two completely different processes—the process of inventing and that of realisation. The innovation, the newly created, presupposes inventiveness, that is the 'invention' (cf. p. 31). The association and lack of terminological differentiation between invention and innovation is frequently detrimental to stringent analysis, and the generic term *innovation* degenerates into a nebulous catchword.

Innovation research operates in a wide field of application including products, technologies, organisation, services among others. Correspondingly, a distinction must be made in analysis between creative, interpretative and economic innovations. Concepts, technical feasibility, value assessment, safety, usefulness—including efficiency and feasibility for the user (cf. p. 79)—and costs are all checked, as well as the possibility of realising an invention to a point when it is ready for the market, which also includes distribution. In addition, it is a matter of assertion involving advertising and the acceptance of the innovation, which is difficult to influence. It is the aim of innovation research to reduce future uncertainties by means of anticipatory thinking and action. Possible scenarios, diverse alternatives and imponderables are played through in theory, almost as 'thinking ahead' or 'corporate foresight'. Operations occur in a triangle of scientific forethought, discursive brainstorming and design prototypes.

The fashion business does not prioritise funds for investment in innovations by any means. A world company like Siemens spent until 2008 approximately 500,000 euros per hour on research and development; in the Organisation for Economic Cooperation and Development (OECD) and its thirty, mainly Western industrial countries, the total is well over one billion dollars per day. More than 70 per cent of this sum is expended in the research and development (R&D) departments of industry. Only a relatively small part (ca. 5–10 per cent) of the total R&D budget serves nonspecific, basic research; the rest is for specific innovations.[8] Innovation investments in the fashion field, however, are made only in the areas of textiles and clothing physiology. That is why creative freedom is generated or retained in industry—like design laboratories in the car industry or haute couture in the fashion world. Correspondingly, Bernard Arnault, president of the luxury concern LVMH, which also includes the House of Dior, sees haute couture as the 'research and development laboratory of Paris style . . . Research and development in any enterprise is a cost centre and not a profit centre'[9]. The normal, the average, the masses pay for experiments in innovation in all fields, from cars to fashion. Nor is the fashion world in first place when it comes to striving for acceleration. This extended into an industrywide phenomenon long ago and is manifest in the electronics field in particular. The next generation of products is already being developed and announced even before the previous one is on the market, and certainly before it has become established. In February 1995, the Japanese electronics company NEC announced the production of the first experimental storage chip with one gigabyte capacity. Only two days later, its competitor Hitachi published the same announcement. In the electronics field, the time intervals for the introduction of completely new product lines have been reduced to less than two years in recent years. By contrast, fashion still requires six months between the generative idea and a collection that is ready for the market, plus another six months for ordering and delivery; only copying is faster.

Innovation means progress, but progress is not necessarily positive. Quite apart from this, current design—including fashion design—is defined less by the world of progress and far more by the cyclic world of revival (cf. p. 102). All fields of knowledge and creativity are not always involved to the same extent in innovation. While one of the most progressive scientific disciplines up until and into the nineteenth century was geography, since the end of the twentieth century it has been digital communication. In fashion to date, the most innovative periods were the seventeenth century and more recently, the 1920s and 1960s.

When Is Innovation? When Is Something New?

Innovation is no more than the fact that today we have something that did not exist yesterday, for example the iPod or baggy pants. However, this quite evident statement implies a basic knowledge of what comprises the old and what has entered the world in the way of the new, as well as the extent to which the new may be regarded as truly new and not merely as a variation of the old (cf. pp. 100, 101). That is why the degree of innovation is evaluated, for example in the sense of an innovation that is fundamental, an improvement or an adaptation within every artistic, technical, organisational, institutional or social system. In addition, a distinction is made between an objective innovation, one that no one in the world was aware of previously— namely a 'world innovation'—and a subjective innovation, which appears new to an individual or a group of people alone. For the new becomes new inasmuch as it stands out against our expectations, because it differs from what is expected. The new compels us to select. It is the observer whom we credit with expert qualification who decides on the objective innovation and quasi selects it. In our eyes, the new is dependent on his evaluation; is it considered a usable innovation or a utopia, a fiction, and therefore pushed into the niche of the nonusable or—as something enthralling—into the sphere of art, like the remote-control dresses by Hussein Chalayan (cf. p. 66)? Around 1900, if someone had taken a walk in subfreezing temperatures clad only in a thin jumper and a thin anorak and (thanks to their high-tech materials of the twenty-first century) had done so without freezing, it would have been interpreted as science fiction, and in the late Middles Ages it would probably have been regarded as witchcraft. As a definition of value, evaluation is controversial, since it considerably restricts freedom and vision as the foundations of invention.

The new differs from expectations; it is the unusual (for one has not yet become used to it) and the unstable. For that reason, in the historical context the new was seen—particularly by the Catholic Church—as undesirable and a distraction from God and truth until the late Middle Ages. Around 400 AD, theologist and philosopher Augustine of Hippo condemned *curiositas* because it was related to superficialities and defined by risk due to a surplus of stimuli. However, such warnings evidence the fact that there was also curiosity at that time, in the sense of a fundamental desire for the new.[10] From the twelfth century onwards, clothing or dress regulations—above and beyond the existing sumptuary laws—evidence efforts to attract attention by means of new clothing and thus underline one's social—rather than individual –status (cf. p. 19). One high point of such endeavours was demonstrated by the fashion in Burgundy during the late fourteenth and fifteenth centuries. It was not until the Renaissance that the new was favoured as something remarkable in art and art philosophy, especially when it was something that did not exist in the natural world. From that time onwards, effort was directed towards the extraordinary, the deviant, the unexpected and the completely artificial. People began to derive individuality from innovation.

The brain's self-organisation paves the way for the new (cf. p. 33). The speed of any understanding is dependent on already existing knowledge. The brain's neuronal networks could not learn anything new without apparently chaotic neuronal activity. The effect of this is the human being's infinite capacity for creativity. Innovations and diversity are possible as a result of the regulated chaos of recombining (cf. p. 34) and not of established orders. Every life should be viewed as a balance between order and chaos, and neither order nor chaos alone can bring about an evolution. The discovery that all processes essential to life take place in a nonlinear manner substantiates the thesis that the new is possible in principle. Without innovation, a culture becomes rigid and ultimately extinct. Innovation works in favour of its preservation and is part of an evolution. The behavioural scientist Irenäus Eibl-Eibesfeldt sees innovations as 'evolution continuing to the present day and beyond' and 'for that reason alone, we should not wish to be without the new'.[11] However, evolution—because of flexible biological strategies of adaptation—is not possible to plan or, since it is always part of the future, in any way foreseeable.

Perception and Cognition

We bring forth the world through the process of living itself.

Humberto Maturana

As explained already, innovation is not merely a matter of developing something new as an invention (by the creator) and realising it as an innovation; it is equally necessary to perceive the new and to recognise it as such (cf. p. 8). The new is an intellectual or real product that must be recognised as such, evaluated and finally asserted. Recognising the new is the obligation of experts. In fashion, these include fashion theorists, fashion journalists, manufacturers and dealers. The foundation of recognition is perception; sociologist Erving Goffman emphasised that 'perceiving presupposes an active permeation and interpretation of the world, as well as applying the correct frame of analysis'[12]. That is, knowledge determines our ability to discern the new (cf. also p. 34) in a decisive manner.

Neurobiology explains the new as 'a pattern of stimulus' that is 'all the more "powerful", the more it extends to other areas of the brain and becomes capable of overlaying the patterns of stimulus usually generated there . . . For this to happen, the sensory impression must be particularly unexpected, incisive or innovative . . .'[13] The new presents itself as exciting, stimulating and/or disturbing in a cognitive sense. 'The "new" always emerges before the background of the "already known", which delineates the horizon of the new. With every piece of "knowledge", our "non-knowledge" grows as well.'[14] Perception is the process of assimilating information, but it is directly linked to the processing of knowledge, to cognition. 'All perceiving is also thinking, all reasoning is also intuition, all observation is also invention.'[15] Cognition influences our constructed reality through expectations, experiences, values, emotions and concrete needs. Accordingly, an essential characteristic of the new is its dependence on knowledge, inasmuch as one both thinks or acts differently and recognises the new as such and evaluates it—as the valuable other—on the basis of historical or current comparisons.

Equally, *individual taste* does not develop without resort to the traditional—like the influence of one's parents, the culture in which one grows up or freely chosen role models. In addition, there is a synergy-parameter, which makes the new appear comparatively better, more attractive, more useful within its context and develops into the principle of comparative advantage. After this, the evaluation 'new' is valid until refuted by fresh knowledge, which is a reason why opinions concerning innovations are often revised or even withdrawn altogether. The continually changing view of the beautiful is also subject to comparative judgement and exists in comparison to the old. 'Beauty is made up of an eternal and invariable element, which is extremely difficult to determine, and of a relative circumstantial element, which one might say is represented parallel or in turn by the epochs of fashion, intellectual life and passion.'[16] This complies with the findings of ethnologist Helge Gerndt on the creation of tradition: 'However, "new" is not a value concept, but a *referential concept,* which means nothing without a precise point of reference.'[17] The knowledgeable observer recognises and decides whether he is dealing with an objective innovation (world innovation) or a subjective innovation (for an individual).

Culture

Culture is a constant, practical process of negotiating the rules according to which people live, revealed in a society's or community's execution of its practical existence. Among other things, both language and clothes may serve as indicators and codes of cultural processes, but they are essentially involved in their creation as well, making it easier to determine one's own identity (cf. p. 160). Culture is generated through communication (also simplified to clichés) and is thus subject to a process of constant change.

Innovation is opposed to the (apparently) valid, that is to the conventions and traditions, in short to the culture which represents the identity of a people or of a social group. Our identification lies in these conventions and traditions, which is why people are often unwilling to accept the new. 'Scientific discoveries, technical inventions and artistic designs are always embedded in a cultural context, which simultaneously specifies the possibility and limits the feasibility of new insights.'[18] They are more or less bound to political and/or religious systems, to the free expression of opinion and environmental conditions. The cultural historian Egon Friedell discerns a 'creative periphery':[19] the centres are stable, the peripheries are more flexible. Cultural innovations take place wherever conventions and tradition are not restricted rigidly, as in so-called open cultures or on the social edges (known as subcultures today). Examples are the Roman Empire, which crumbled at the borders first, and the 'invention' of Christianity, which took place in the colonies. History shows that the majority of inventions originate from social or national outsiders. Usually, vestimentary inventions also come from the high end or from the low end, in other words, from either the creative genius or the street. Certainly, the stylistic elements of subcultures emerge in their own social surroundings, whereas their aesthetic form is often incorporated into what the creative industries offer.

Artists and designers are predestined—due to their disposition, including lateral and associative thinking (cf. p. 37), among other things, and their training—to pay little respect to the traditions that have been passed down to them. In addition, the generative moment is more demanding in extremely turbulent environments like the fashion world. In order to turn the new into reality, there is a need for social enthusiasm. This applies to certain examples like the 'invention' of the miniskirt by Mary Quant. As early as 1958/1959, Quant created the first thigh-length short sack dress, which was only a limited success in sales terms. The social and cultural circumstances alone—youth revolts, the Beatles, the contraceptive pill, and so on—made the mini into a fashion as from 1964. Mary Quant's radical new stylistic starting point for clothing was based on her idea for a new image of female youth, the outcome of dissatisfaction with the social and cultural as-is state.

'It is a . . . principally insoluble question whether man creates his conditions or the conditions make man. Similarly questionable is the role of the individual as a creator or as the creation of culture, science, economics and technology.'[20] Related to fashion, it is equally impossible to decide whether fashion shapes the zeitgeist or the zeitgeist shapes fashion. One should assume a reciprocal influence, starting out from the invention and the cultural context via communication. Key innovations like book printing, the steam engine, antibiotics, the contraceptive pill and finally digital data processing have altered societies all over the world. However, history makes clear that democratic forms of government, or rather 'the open society'[21], as Karl Popper termed it, permit a much greater degree of innovation than absolutist or communist state forms. Individual freedom and the will to renew seem to be evidence of this.

Fashion is and always has been an aspect of culture. It is historically incorrect to believe that '[i]t is only now that fashion has become analyzed within a framework of cultural thought'.[22] Early fashion journals from the late eighteenth and nineteenth centuries in particular, as well as the first books of costume theory from the second half of the eighteenth century, viewed fashion as part of culture, together with interior design, music, literature and all the other beautiful things of life. But from the middle of the nineteenth century, fashion experienced a field of conflict between mass production and commercialisation on the one hand and haute couture on the other. Fashion became part of industrialisation, and its creative, hand-fashioned quality was forced to adopt a special, elitist status.

One way to innovation is to question cultural conventions. To achieve this, it is necessary to perceive our own culture as we perceive other cultures, that is from the outside. The important thing is 'the relativisation of any one culture, the perception that it is not an absolute but just one approach among many to the shared human project of civilization'.[23] Then—if society permits it and more than a few individuals want it—it will be possible to go without wearing a tie. 'The origin of an innovative fashion creation [Groys: work of art] does not lie in rebellion against cultural tradition', but in the strategic 'combination of positive and negative adaptation to tradition . . . the aim being to create a significant of the present'.[24] In time, the thrill of an innovation fades; it is valorised and put into the archives, making space for a new innovation.

Value

'The new is not simply the other, it is the valuable other—which has been judged valuable enough to be kept, investigated, commented and criticised, and not to disappear again the next moment.'[25] Among all cultural and profane commodities, including fashion, a hierarchy of values determines what is worth remembering or collecting (archive and museum value). The following question ensues: does an assumed or anticipated historical value determine the value of the new? Many works of fine art were worthless when new and have achieved their value only by means of the future, at least in retrospect. But how much of value has been forgotten? Conversely, many new things have been treated as top-quality innovations but soon forgotten. Values are connected to the individual cultural epoch; their persistence is explained by memory and forgetfulness.

In current evaluation it is a mistake, according to Groys, to accept every difference as culturally valuable and worthy of archiving. 'Indeed', we have 'no legitimising concepts available other than identity and difference . . . Under these circumstances, if there are no criteria and no independent instance to define the cultural value of a work, the outcome will be direct competition among different cultural starting points and works, as already occurs in the field of mass culture.'[26] The principle on which this competition is based, according to Groys, is that of tautology—in the sense of one and the same, but with different appellations. In this situation, understanding of the new 'can only emerge by comparison with the already existing'.[27] However, if too much cultural rubbish exists, the level of the culturally valuable sinks further and further, and the level of comparison with it. The British fashion expert Colin McDowell has referred to this development significantly as 'the death of taste'. The new—irrespective of whether it is innovative or only marginally different—is usually employed as a driving force of consumerism, and as such, it should not necessarily be judged as a socially positive value, or at least it should certainly be evaluated critically.

Authenticity is (particularly in Germany) often incorrectly understood as the culturally valuable, the traditional and the original. Around 1999, this term experienced a revival as a (commercially effective) journalistic word-creation referring to sportswear like 'cult' jogging shoes of Adidas and Nike brands. The appellation 'authentic' says little about the clothing itself, but all the more about the zeitgeist when this term became modern, at the end of the brand-cult era of the 1990s and of the New Economy. That is—the brand, and its originality, was turned into an icon. The timelessly modern and classic was set against the fashionable (fakes). This is reminiscent of the comparison between old and new money, inasmuch as there was once a time when the old moneyed classes' money was also new.

Aesthetics

In design itself, the exclusive aim is neither technology nor functionalism but rather the aesthetics of the product as such. 'The aesthetic emerges as an organising pattern, the construction of which is defined according to our perception. Since we have no access to the processes of our perception, all that remains are the products, whose patterns can be altered through reflection. We experience the "aesthesis", the sensual perception, as a standardised phenomenon. To perceive an object, an event, an action or a situation as it is, as opposed to all the associations that point beyond it, constitutes an aesthetic moment.'[28]

Tension

Tension is guaranteed by the interrelation of values: historical or avant-garde, artistic or profane, innovative or traditional. The collection mentioned in the preceding chapter, *Body Meets Dress* (1997; cf. p. 42) by Rei Kawakubo, may be considered exemplary of extreme tension, altering the conventions of the human body image by means of overforming and so questioning aesthetic habits. But if models recall a tradition already valorised as high art or as high-end fashion, like the little black dress, no tension will be arrived at a priori, unless it is through a distinctive variation, a famous wearer, or an outstanding social or spatial context (cf. p. 140).

Assertion

Innovations are not established overnight but are subject to a temporal process of assertion. This takes place in a communicative interplay of system (e.g. fashion) and environment (e.g. society).

In the field of clothing, the assertion of an (innovative) collection is bound up with aspects of production technology, economics and society. First and foremost, fashion designers intend their models to be accepted, that is to be worn, and not to lend impulses of expansion to a company. In today's fashion, the process of assertion—despite quick response—takes one or two years. This duration is less dependent on possibilities of production technology, communication or distribution, but is far more a matter of the processes of perception and acceptance by society, a community or target groups (cf. p. 97). From the moment of generative innovation—that is an invention like the minidresses by Mary Quant in 1958/1959—to the assertion of the mini as a line, which began in 1963, the process of universal acceptance took a further three years. Alexander McQueen's jumper knitted in XL loops from the 1999/2000 season took the route of adaptation by New York designer Donna Karan, and from there it became cheap, ready-to-wear clothing in winter 2002. During this time span, the old and the new exist parallel to one another. The new does not necessarily push aside the old; both can exist side by side, especially when the new has a limited target group. At the beginning of the twentieth century, for example, there were still horse-drawn carriages on the roads for a long time after the car had been invented and began to be seen in the streets.

'The shock of the new'[29] triggers communication. In order to explain the new plausibly, one suitable method is the use of *metaphors*. 'A successful metaphor transforms a false equation into a fitting analogy. To this extent, metaphor assures the possibility of connecting with the familiar and is capable of generating popular labels.'[30] For instance, one of the most frequently cited trends—the term cocooning, coined by US trend expert Faith Popcorn in the 1980s—is pure metaphor. Analogies, as cognitive scientists have established, appear more compelling when the metaphor behind them is more vivid. It is an attempt to express the new, the unusual or the difficult to grasp by combining familiar concepts. Metaphor often begins with an obvious discrepancy and ends with the recognition of similarities. The associations work because man is obsessive in his search for meaning. 'The process of understanding is regarded as an attempt to transform something not understood (strange) into something understood (one's own). The unfamiliar other is traced back (reduced) to one's own, familiar figures of thought and in this way—falsified! Or as Nietzsche would have said: "distorted to fit".'[31] However, in the public sphere of the media, it is more a matter of the novelty than of the new.

Economist and innovation researcher Franz Liebl sees a key driving force behind change and progress in criticism and contradiction. Criticism promotes analysis of the positives and negatives and thus an understanding of what has been produced. Equally, criticism and contradiction permit us to recognise unexpected side effects like misuse and so promote lasting improvement. Misuses may emerge in both the physical field and the symbolic field of image and aesthetics. When Calvin Klein put his name on the waistband of simple, fine-rib underpants in 1982, he did so in the spirit of brand advertising. But hip-hop kids found it cool to shock people in underpants with a visible logo under their low-slung baggy pants.[32] The luxury brand Calvin Klein Underwear was copied in its millions and became a sought-after mass commodity.

Deviation creates the original; the norm creates copies. (A signature even revaluates serial consumer products into an original, as in the case of Readymades and Pop Art in the art world.) Products, structures and systems produced by society (communicatively) are always an image of society itself. Deviants—in no matter what political system—have more chance of creating the unique than the noncontradictory and indistinguishable. The only thing that remains for adapters is to occupy unknown territory (in terms of social status as well) and to copy the original. It is a matter, therefore, of the degree of innovation still accepted by an audience (cf. p. 98). Wolfgang Amadeus Mozart never wished to meet the desire for popular music alone. His father was horrified by this: 'I beg of you, in your work you should think not only of musical listeners, but also of those lacking musical discernment—you know there are 100 ignorant souls for every 10 who are truly knowledgeable,—do not, therefore, forget the so-called popular music that delights even the longest ear.'[33]

Considerations of growth mean that deviations and the quality of difference are rejected or offered only at an extremely high price. Mass production norms, standardises and smoothes over the differences that exist in real life. As early as 1905, the programmatic text of the Wiener Werkstätte already regretted '[t]he infinite harm caused . . . by poor-quality mass-production'. And this 'is a powerful current permeating the whole world . . . To swim against this current would be madness . . . Nevertheless . . . we wish to create close links between the public, designers and craftsmen'.[34]

Acceptance

Acceptance expresses an evaluation of agreement as opposed to rejection. Acceptance is linked to sensations. Generally, these are sensory impressions and are triggered by perception or memory. In the process of acceptance or rejection, interplay develops between an impression stemming from the environment—a sign, a form, a colour—which is accepted at face value, and an individual subjective memory. This means that it is possible to be deceived in a perception but not in the case of sensation, as this is always subjective. As a consequence, every form of acceptance remains bound to the individual. Acceptance can be influenced from outside, certainly—by persuasion that addresses sensation or an argument that addresses reason—but this cannot be assumed a priori.

As the process of acceptance is tied to a person, it presupposes his or her free will. (In this context, there is also the possibility that a person has acted under coercion, although he has never accepted something for himself.) In this sense, in the wearing of fashion as well, a duality may evolve between social adaptation and individual pleasure: 'I did wear it, but I never really liked it.' Acceptance can be traced to synergy parameters that make the new appear comparatively better, more attractive and more useful within its contexts. In principle, comparative advantages like those in the case of the mini fashion may depend on two different factors; on the one hand, the new itself as a bonus of attraction; and on the other, its association and relation to the social environment. The purchase of the new (seldom the innovative in the sense of different) is not dependent—in the industrial countries—on the existential need of 'having nothing to wear', but rather on superfluity as a resource of attention, in order to continue being talked about as an addressor (competitor or co-applicant).

The assertion of product innovations is linked to acceptance. It comes about via a step-by-step process of dissemination or respectively adaptation, which can be described as primary (fashion insiders, freaks), secondary (pop stars, celebrities as leading figures), tertiary (start of actual distribution; people of the scene and young-sters), and quartiary (the fashion-conscious masses). As the distribution of a new fashion is dependent on the social process of acceptance (see the mode of experi-ence, p. 145), its temporal duration (see time, pp. 133, 142)—regardless of any kind of market acceleration—is also determined by this process and in today's age of acceleration it can take an astonishingly long time. Hedi Slimane, chief designer for the Dior men's collection 2001–2007, says of this: Fashion 'is actually a very slow medium. Everything is decoded, analysed and processed by fashion. It takes such a long time until fashion has digested what reality has to offer it'.[35] One example: in-novations like frayed seams and open edges were first seen on creations by Japanese designers like Rei Kawakubo and Yohji Yamamoto in Paris in 1981/1982, but they made it into universal fashion only around 2002, where they were still a top fashion in 2006. Hipsters, the extreme bumster trousers by Alexander McQueen, triggered a shock effect in 1996, became a matter of course among young people as from around 2002, and arrived at the extreme of bumsters in youth ready-made fashions only in 2005. Once a basic innovation has asserted itself, or, in other words, once it has arrived at the tertiary stage or expansion phase, there is a relatively dense concentra-tion of the new fashion image. During a depression—generally to be observed in the secondary and tertiary field in particular—the search increases for alternatives, and a relatively large number of apparent innovations are imitated by the manufacturers, sometimes indiscriminately, for fear of a 'black hole'. Shortly before the point of satiation, anomalies, or, rather, exaggerations often arise; for example the height of platform soles became dizzying around 1973, and twinsets became especially tight at the beginning of the 1960s. These excrescences indicate the start of a period of crisis. The result is the spread of ad hoc programmes or revivals, which are perceived incorrectly as something new.

Future

> For philosophers, the burning interest in fashion lies in its extraordinary anticipations.
>
> Walter Benjamin

The new is not foreseeable, either as new knowledge, as innovation or as evolution, because it would already be familiar otherwise.[36] The new develops through recom-binations with the passage of time, and not before. For the change itself can occur only in the *present*. Everything that happens happens in the present, even memory and prophecy. And the present itself is not recognised until it is recognised in retro-spect.

Figure 16   *Used Look,* 2003. © Ingrid Loschek.

Nevertheless, innovation is always oriented towards the future, even though the planning of the future always takes place in the present. If an innovation is perceived by an outsider, this happens in the future that occurs after the invention. To be absolutely sure that an invention will assert itself, we would have to know today what is going to happen tomorrow. Early warning systems, as we know, are successful because the warning means that danger can be counteracted in time—that is, in the present—and so the feared catastrophe does not happen (the warning therefore makes itself superfluous, self-fulfilling). On the other hand, something that is massively advertised has good chances of becoming reality in the near future. In this way, influence is taken on the future in the present. 'The present is preparation for the future and less a result of the past. The role of the past is not to guarantee continuity in time—there is no linear history—, but to create conditions for a future!'[37] However, this does not mean that we know the future, only that we have some concept of it. Future perspectives are no more or less than worlds of pure imagination, which the communicators create from their audience's interests. It is not possible to achieve innovative concepts by asking the consumers what they want. Far more, it is a matter of offering the customer something that he would like to have, although he is not aware that he is searching for it, and about which, when he finally gets it, he will say that he has always wanted it. Inventions from the car to the mobile telephone, from the bikini by Louis Réard in 1946 to the city rucksack by Miuccia Prada, make this very obvious. Future design, therefore, does not signify simple reaction or adaptation. Emotional intelligence and empathy are important; as the British musician Brian Eno said in 1992, '[I]f there is any unit of cultural intelligence, it's empathy.'[38] The inventing of themes and the subsequent test of their plausibility is certainly a conceivable way to anticipate needs or—in the language of marketing—to orient the customer.

Particularly the economy is dependent on prognoses so that investments can be justified. Prognoses are diagrams of probability founded on past and present; they are efforts to construct, building on dimensions of experience, and they serve to make decisions that will set the course for the future. The future remains the great unknown, for an infinite number of incalculable factors are involved in it.

The future always develops from what we do in the present. In the present we manufacture clothing, which we hope will become fashion in the future. The idea of the future always corresponds to the current zeitgeist, whether the vestimentary creations of Italian Futurism in 1910 or the astronaut look from 1964 to 1966. Yet it has been not space, but media technology that has made decisive progress since then, thus defining a future that is now the past.

Fashion and Innovation

Innovations are possible at several levels in the fashion system: at the stylistic, idealistic and conceptual levels as well as in production and cutting technology or in materials. As far as innovation is concerned, the reward is not the journey but the end product; this alone is the measure of judgement.

The journey to the reward of innovation can take two possible routes—either creative destruction in the sense of breaking down old ideas in one's mind, forgetting what already exists, breaking rules and creating spaces; or deriving the new from continuity (cf. p. 87). Both may lead to success, as is shown by the examples of Prada and Louis Vuitton. In 1978, Miuccia Prada took over the family business, founded in 1913, which produced select handcrafted leather goods. Having studied politics, she had no relation—not even a negative one—to fashion. At the beginning of the 1980s, the one thing that she invented was a mid-sized black rucksack with outside pockets made of light, water-resistant nylon; it was unlined, light and practical. Without any logo or monogram initially, it was produced industrially in a parachute factory. Her city rucksack was the absolute antithesis of the company's former craftsmanship, and philosophy become product. Only after the impossible idea had begun to assert itself did she add the original metal triangular label of the early Prada suitcases and use the high-tech material Pocone. The one-time hiking rucksack and backpack became a symbol of urban mobility and—as a result of the logo—a gender-free prestige object.[39] After this, Miuccia Prada developed the company into a luxury fashion concern.

Innovation can also be developed further as a continuum. With equal success, Prada competitor Louis Vuitton took the route of continuity from luggage packer and manufacturer at the court of Napoleon III to a global fashion company. Julien McDonald frequently readopts his own experimental techniques for the production of lace, Jean-Paul Gaultier varies bustier dresses in a highly innovative way, and Hussein Chalayan conceived a series of new, innovative solutions for his 'aeroplane dresses' made of fibreglass. The continuum is comparable to the situation in painting when a painter interrupts work on a picture and then takes up work on it again some years later.

The current addiction to novelty, from which the status of fashion never develops, raises a question: Should the new clothing that thousands of designers create per season, to which billions of photographs are devoted, filling hundreds of fashion journals, be anchored in the cultural memory at all, and most importantly, how can it be archived? Do we need an economic administration to separate the innovation-garbage, to deal with all the new fashion design presented on a seasonal basis? Or do billions of copies lead to this vestimentary garbage pollution? Boris Groys throws open these questions with respect to art, and in his book *On the New* he postulates a cultural economy. The problem lies not with designer fashion, which is too easygoing, flighty, shocking or emotional, but with ready-to-wear fashion that is oriented too much on consumerism. The social and ecological consequences of the latter are far more negative than fashionable exaggerations in designer and avant-garde fashion. We should be advocating designer fashion rather than mass fashion.

Viktor & Rolf responded with a resounding *NO* to the creative pressure of the fashion world's seasonal rhythm (although they still uphold it) in their Autumn/ Winter 2008/2009 collection of the same name. The word *NO* in large felt letters became part of a collar or sleeve on jackets and coats. In addition, (apparently) arbitrarily puckered seams and hemlines—which simultaneously created an ingenious decoration—are intended to visualise the demand for rapid production. However, only a few designers, like Azzedine Alaïa, have succeeded in evading the creative and economic pressure or rather the expectant attitude of journalism, trade and society to present new models each season.

The framework of relations or reference for a vestimentary innovation comprises both the old fashion—that is the fashion that a group or community agrees to classify as 'out'—and new fashion.

The New without Innovation

In fashion, the present-day is questioned not only due to innovation, but also due to a fashion beyond the beautiful, to the classical, or to a search for the past in a revival.

Fashion beyond the beautiful is the aesthetically ugly or an aesthetic anarchy, which finds acceptance in subcultural fashions like punk and goth. Here, the vestimentary focus is on freedom from the mainstream and self-realisation of design. In fine art, the classical is a revaluation of the ideal of beauty in antiquity now anchored in our cultural memory. In fashion, the classical is the symmetrical form that encases the body without exaggerations, for it aims to be as simple, stable and consistent—in other words, as harmonious—as possible. A quintessential example is the classic suit, which developed from the English costume or *tailleur* in the late nineteenth century. The functional demand of Modernism led the ladies' tailored suit to develop from the ladies' riding costume, which had always been made by a men's tailor. It is the tailored costume for which, applying the classical postulate of symmetry and balance, tailoring technique is employed to counteract the nature of the body, that is its irregularities and asymmetry. This classical (in reality by no means functional, particularly due to the narrow waist) costume was readopted by Christian Dior in 1949, with a narrower cut. Because the classical—due to its recurrent up-to-date design—is organic rather than a rigid tradition, as fashion it remains capable of communication; in general terms, it never becomes old-fashioned or is always up-to-date. The Italian fashion designer Giorgio Armani, for example, modernised the classical as purist in the 1990s. In addition, the concept of classic clothing is a wider one today, to include even jeans and a white T-shirt, which are also termed basics. Basics enter the market seasonally, as 'new' without innovation. The best example is the twinset, which simply continues to reinvent itself by means of colour and embellishments, guaranteeing continuity as a classic.

Revival versus Innovation

'Life is an idiosyncratic repertoire of repetitions', as Robert Pogue Harrison declared in his lecture on 'Juvenescence'.[40] We can assume that in the future there will continue to be repetitions of the past. One-to-one copies of the past have no independent value (either as a product or as a symbolic statement), and at best, they are nostalgic looks back and cultural memories. Nostalgia is oriented on a past that never was that way and never will be. Ultimately, it is reactionary to put the past in place of the future. But if repetitions are no more than references back to the past so that they can be used to construct something new, quasi-aesthetic tools for new compositions, they focus the future and thus come into the category of redesigning (cf. p. 111).

In general, however, repetitions are helpless attempts to bring the past back into present time, even when they occur not as nostalgia but as a bringing back to life, a revival, as citations of history for a new generation. Photography is an important medium in this, constituting the visual reproducibility of the past. It separates the past from time, as a fragment. As part of the picture of an epoch, clothes remain present in this way. And the fact that fashion is passed down to us in images means that its history will survive; it inspires retro looks and facilitates their decoding and perception as a retrospective image. In this way, the past may seem familiar even though we have not experienced it ourselves. When a stylistic epoch is thematised, the media operate as a potential style archive. By this means, the photographed, drawn or painted world causes the image or appearance of past times to appear consistently present and available. This basis for debate with and inspiration by past fashions is in our memory as an inalterable, constantly returning concept of time. The authentic is nothing more than retro, only with a different name.

For Walter Benjamin, retros were an expression of redeemed demands from the past; for Karl Marx they were merely a burden, a falsification of the new revolutionary repertoire of forms. Avant-garde ideas also remain tied to ideas of the past in the past, regardless of whether they are classified as thoroughly modern. This applies, for example, to the leaning tower of steps as *Monument of the Third International 0 10* by the Russian constructivist Vladimir Tatlin from 1919, or to Oskar Schlemmer's visionary *Triadic Ballet* (actually performed) from 1922.

However, present-day postmodernism is misunderstood if it is interpreted only as an art of historical revival. (cf. p. 182). It is comparable to a DJ's experimentation; the process and outcome of his sampling, mixing and scratching of past sounds correspond utterly to the present.

The meaning of any product, in clothing as well, can be sought and analysed exclusively in the *present.* However, fashion makes something come true that is otherwise only possible in the imagination: time travel. Karl Lagerfeld has mastered time travel, because he applies sufficient imagination to it: 'Lagerfeld has always believed in Goethe's axiom about 'making a better future by developing elements from the past',[41] Suzy Menkes wrote in the *International Herald Tribune.* However, time travel in the 1960s led to an ideal future, while at the beginning of the twenty-first century it leads us to an optimistic past. Its 'looking backwards' resembles a look forward without a future. Western culture today is a present-day culture, after the future turned out to be a 'no-future' in the late 1970s.

Avant-Garde

Avant-garde should be understood not only as a stylistic concept, like that of Italian futurism or Russian constructivism, but—in this context—as a supratemporal theoretical concept. 'The avant-garde suggests a temporal positioning beyond one's own present, which includes the possibility of influencing the present in order to prepare the future.'[42] Indeed, the avant-garde is not temporal, but an ideal positioning of aesthetic experiments developed from the present. The attractiveness of the avant-garde lies in the fact that it presents the possibility and framework to permit interruptions in everyday awareness, to make radical demands, and to promote social visions. If there is one thing that the avant-garde ought to do, then that is to provoke.

Avant-garde fashion creates projection surfaces for a socially relevant visualisation of individuality. The avant-garde is attributed a pioneering role in the broadest sense, one that can be assessed only in the respective historical or present context. The common understanding of the avant-gardist is as a person who practices lateral thinking, questions conventions, abandons traditions and triggers new developments to point the way in the future. He is accredited with a kind of foresight or first contact with the enemy. In postmodernism, the concept of the avant-garde lost significance due to its own defeat of the belief in progress; today it is experiencing a revival under the premises of post-postmodernism in the sense of 'many avant-gardes'.

The concepts of avant-garde fashion are based on creative destruction (cf. p. 87): They are directed not towards its functional or commodity value, but towards aesthetic, conceptual and emotional values. Avant-garde designers formulate their aesthetic positions at their fashion shows. In current avant-garde fashion, an attempt is being made to evade reproducibility (cf. p. 127). In addition, the contemporary avant-garde is characterised by a pronounced relation to technology, both as a critical position (McQueen, cf. p. 57) and also as avocation (Chalayan, cf. p. 66). For this reason, avant-garde fashion today has become a subject for museums far more than for the fashion market.

How Does the New Enter Fashion?

Nothing new can emerge without change. Even a slight alteration in perspective may bring about a dramatic change in the whole sometimes.

Rei Kawakubo

In April 1981, Yohji Yamamoto and Rei Kawakubo, working for Comme des Garçons, showed their collections together for the first time in Paris. Little note was taken of this small show in the Hotel Intercontinental. Their intention was to gain more attention in Japan and the USA, which could be achieved at the time only with a presence in Paris, by maintaining that they had already shown in Paris. It took the journalists' breath away but their voices even more so: most daily papers and international fashion journals refused to comment on their textile impertinences.

In October 1982, the Japanese designers were placed on the Chambre Syndicale's official list, Kawakubo opened her first shop in Paris, and the first buyers came. It was not until the show in October 1982 that the print media commented, some with feeble descriptions and evaluations like 'Hiroshima chic', 'postatomic ragged look' or 'somehow apocalyptic'. This was not a new beginning for Kawakubo but a continuation of the style she had been developing for more than ten years. Peter Bäldle, fashion correspondent of the *Süddeutsche Zeitung,* was one of the few journalists to recognise the innovative quality of her autumn fashion show 1982: 'Japan's avant-garde astonished the international audience with a completely new understanding of fashion, a kind of intellectual rejection of fashion, which echoed neither past decades nor kimono-bliss nor samurai glory. What some have met blunderingly as 'apocalyptic end-time fashion' emerged as modification rich in ideas . . . produced in apparently poor materials like creased linen or crinkle-cotton . . . Rei Kawakubo . . . became known for holes (in knitting), her cave-look presented on wildly dishevelled girls, their faces entirely without make-up. She ripped skirts into flapping strips, tore things and knotted them together, and removed the back from jackets below the yoke seam. And in all this, she surprised us with a great number of new ideas for cross-wrapped dresses.'[43] The reputation of the Japanese increased, although they were not yet understood in Europe and the USA. In November 1982, the Yamamoto show in Tokyo filled a huge stadium: 'It was filled with young people and the runway ran clear across the stadium. One by one the models came out. Everyone was quiet. When it was over he came out and the place erupted. The kids yelled and carried on as if he were a rock star. They waited for him after the show to see him, to touch him.'[44]

The literary and cultural scientist Barbara Vinken explains the style of the Japanese, like that of the Antwerp School with Ann Demeulemeester and Martin Margiela later on, as 'fashion after fashion'.[45] It is a fashion that makes transience and traces of wear visible, beyond the demand for eternal youth and beauty, a fashion that does not feign the illusion of eroticism or elegance in the old European sense. The style of Comme des Garçons, like that of Yohji Yamamoto, proved one of the most enduring trends: twenty-five years later, frayed seams, open edges and pointed hems have arrived in the ready-made clothes of the masses. Mass, ready-made fashion as such offers no innovative designs, since it is restricted to simple reaction or adaptation.

Clothing is convincing when it echoes the zeitgeist and mood of the times. When—in the late 1950s—women were becoming increasingly independent and forcing their way into the world of work, Coco Chanel offered an uncomplicated tailored suit, suitable for any occasion. In the 1980s, Giorgio Armani acted comparably when he introduced typically male items from men's fashion into the women's collection, with soft feminine forms, for women who were rising to the management level of companies more and more often. Radical designers like Issey Miyake and Jean-Paul Gaultier or intellectual designers like Martin Margiela and Hussein Chalayan use clothes to communicate their views on fundamental matters like cultural and gender identity or design possibilities, and sooner or later this influences commercial clothing (cf. also p. 107).

Context Crossings—Hybrids

Context crossings are based not necessarily on genuine ideas, but far more on associative thinking. They represent an ability to construct relations between unconnected ideas or structures, that is to see inspiring links between separate phenomena.

Context crossings are a technique promoting, for example cultural innovations and lead to a revaluation in the sense of identity switching. The reassessment of values represents a new outcome, but it is not the trigger of change (cf. p. 94). Context crossings in the sense of fusion, adaptation, revaluation, increased valuation, anachronism and paradoxes are among its tried and trusted strategies. Here, iconic and emotional logic plays a decisive role; it is more important than mathematical logic.

Paco Rabanne deprives material of its logic when he adapts metal platelets, pieces of glass or wooden balls in place of soft-to-the-touch textiles for his dress creations, so arriving at innovations. Coco Chanel transferred the regional identity of an alpine 'farmer's jacket' to the international haute couture of a Chanel jacket. The anorak developed from the clothing of the Inuit into a global functional garment and sportswear, and finally universal street wear. By devaluating the clothing's original function—that is its origins, tradition, environment, functional task, material and so forth—the original reference is questioned and the garment is made 'free', or, in other words, globally available. Such revaluations of context and particularly the ensuing availability are also seen as a precondition to globalisation. It is precisely the global strength of fashion and its self-referential system (its autopoiesis; cf. p. 24) that is expressed in this lack of respect for cultural independence and social conventions. In the crossing of borders, the borderline experience becomes an activity, a constructive self-benefit.

As far as design is concerned, this means being bold enough and assimilating everything. Depending on the context, we may regard this as frivolous when religious values are used, as the misappropriation of cultural values in the ethno look, as a social encroachment in the case of jeans or as a linking of ideas in the sense of lateral thinking (cf. p. 37). Whether a society succeeds in asserting itself in global competition is dependent not least on whether it not only tolerates lateral thinkers, but even promotes their way of thinking.

In his treatise *On the New,* Boris Groys comes to the conclusion that in general, innovations must be understood as the result of context crossing.[46] As examples in art, he cites all those things that were previously outside the art context, like Marcel Duchamp's bottle dryer, the black square by Kasimir Malevich and the everyday objects in the art of Andy Warhol. The artist explodes traditions—that is, he crosses boundaries.

In the revaluation of values, the original ('authentic') values are led to a fresh outcome. The commonplace becomes noble; the outlawed becomes establishment. In Gianni Versace's fetishist *Bondage* prêt-à-porter collection of 1991/1992, the sadomasochist (SM) connotations lost their aggressiveness and were perverted into luxury fashion. The Moschino label plays with an inversion of the signs and functions of fashion. Franco Moschino made a pair of jeans into a jacket by adapting the waist into a neckline and creating a kind of lapel using belt loops and a wide, gold-studded leather belt. A sailor shirt made in black leather by Jean-Paul Gaultier is both a proper-naive sailor shirt and hard-rocker clothing, or it is neither/nor. In Chalayan's collection *Afterwords* (cf. p. 65) a context crossing takes place via the defunctionalising of a room into the functional quality of clothing, thus leading to a revaluation. In design it is a matter of an affirmative, meaningful language, whereas in fine art it is about self-reflection and analysis. It becomes clear that these two languages, or rather contexts—design and fine art—are connected in Hussein Chalayan's collections *Afterwords* and *Before Minus Now.* Chalayan is an idea and concept artist, who—perhaps quite by chance—has chosen clothing as his form and medium.

Polyvalence develops when sport fashion is accepted, or even desired as a fusion of functional and fashionable clothing. In the case of trainers, therefore, high-performance models from the upper price range function as symbols of affiliation for certain subcultures and give the wearer entry into specific music clubs. The sportswear manufacturer Nike admits that 80 per cent of products are not used according to their actual purpose.

An anachronism occurs, for example, when Gianni Versace combines a denim jacket with a silk crinoline-like skirt with a Renaissance-style pattern in his *Neo-Baroque Composition* from the Spring/Summer 1992 collection.

Paradox is viewed as the fusion of contradictions to arrive at something new. Contradiction succeeds by exploding conventions, leading—according to the convention—to paradox. For instance, such a contradiction may emerge as a consequence of the negation of self-referentiality: the slip as trousers or the corset as an upper garment; it is true when it is false and false when it is true (according to the Greek philosopher and logician Eubulides of Miletus, ca. 400 BC). The paradox of customary concepts of morality lies in the fact that the slip or underpants cover our shame but have to be covered in their turn. This moral notion exists in all monotheist religions in contrast to natural religions, in the areas of which the loincloth covers the pubic area and is therefore an outer garment.[47] Apart from the latter, the underwear (particularly so-called sexy underwear) belongs to the intimate sphere and is therefore a part of the body rather than the clothing, or it is an interface between the body and clothes.[48]

Context crossing in the sense of paradox also permits the (supposedly) incompatible (the nonsticky sticky stuff). The new via the incompatible means that a thin, light material (e.g. the synthetic fleece Polar-Tec) is nonetheless warm; a new pair of jeans is nonetheless full of holes, frayed and expensive (like those by Gucci, 2001). The latter can be seen as a fashionable innovation but not as a product innovation, for old, holey jeans are familiar to us. This fake ultrarealism is the basis of today's so-called authentic articles.

Context crossings lead to hybrids (crosses, fusions) like traditional costume fashions, trekking sandals or cargo pants. Military combat pants were perverted at the end of the twentieth century into fashionable urban trousers known as cargo pants. Helmut Lang introduced the trimming (with a galloon, a satin ribbon) from the outside leg seams of dress-suit trousers to both avant-garde business wear and everyday sportswear as minimalist ornamentation for men's pants in avant-garde fashion.

Art Crossing

Art crossing is understood as the inclusion of free art and its techniques in the design of clothing. Elsa Schiaparelli made use of fine art by transforming the surreal sculpture of *Venus de Milo* with drawers by Salvador Dalí (1936) into the *Desk Costume*. Clothing as a picture carrier or the picture as a pattern on fabric is viewed as art crossing. Jean-Charles de Castelbajac created picture dresses echoing Pop Art, which were painted with a cola bottle, a toothpaste tube, the US flag, *Time* magazine or a flip chart. He commissioned contemporary artists such as Jean-Charles Blais (1982) or Hervé di Rosa (1984) for these *robes tableaux,* all unique pieces. His picture dresses also include *robes hommages* with portraits of famous personalities painted on them. In 1966, Yves Saint Laurent designed dresses with Pop Art motifs like Tom Wesselmann's *Nudes,* a Mondrian collection in 1965, and models with Cubist motifs in 1980. Stella McCartney worked together with the artist Jeff Koons in 2006 and used his paintings *Cake* and *Pink Bow* as models for fabric patterns.

Border Crossing

Fashion has proved itself an extremely successful cultural melting pot. In fashion design there is talk of sampling, redesigning or mapping the world. In this context, the global design is oriented on local traditions; it assimilates everything—whether Romanian peasant blouse, Mongolian waistcoat, Japanese labourer's pants or Hawaiian shirt—and puts it together in a new way to create a new whole that is available across the globe.[49]

The foreign as something of equal value—in the sense of 'cross the border, close the gap'—first came into fashion with the hippies in the mid 1960s but soon degenerated into a levelling consumer commodity with the ethno look. The adoption of ethnic clothing by hippies symbolised their sense of belonging to the group; triggered by a political belief in 'one world', it was not due to an interest in innovation and commercial profit at first, but it then developed into an arbitrarily available fashion. Since then, designer fashion has presented a multicultural world without borders. Designers bring together different types of things to create a new symbolism. They dare to disregard the local traditions and identities of national costumes—not according to the superficial slogan 'anything goes', but from curiosity and openness to ambivalence and diversity. Entirely in the spirit of postmodernism, they confront common sense with a vision.

Ethnic crossing had already been invented and perfected by Kenzo in the 1970s. He always borrowed from diverse ethnic garments and combined them into an unconventional, varied and colourful folklore fashion. Blue padded jackets based on Japanese coolie jackets were worn with brightly coloured, wide Peruvian skirts, wrap-around skirts over narrow pants, and Norwegian jumpers with Turkish harem pants, often with a wide sash around the waist. Antonio Marras, leading designer in the House of Kenzo since 2004, remains true to this style and mixes Western clothing with folklorist aspects and patchwork.

In his *Tribal-Styles* (1996), Jean-Paul Gaultier wrapped and draped Mongolian coats that left one breast free like an Amazon over Indian dhoti pants or knitted leggings and adopted Red Indian jewellery as accessories. In his Hussar creations of 2002/2003, he cited the wide hanging sleeves of the Hungarian coat, the *mente*; in *Les Rabbins chics* (1993/1994) he adopted elements of Jewish clothing; and for summer 2005 he presented a skilful mix of European regional costumes. John Galliano called his Autumn/Winter 2004/2005 collection *Mapping the World*. He combined elements of Eastern European costumes with items of clothing from the Yemen, Peru and Vietnam into a super sampling mix based on the notion of a vagabond globetrotter.

By contrast, the ethnic borrowings of Dries van Noten owe much to elegance. Vivienne Westwood repeatedly refers to England and Scotland, whether she is inspired by the paintings of British artists or by Scottish tartans. Rei Kawakubo made the British available when—in her Comme des Garçons Spring/Summer 2006 collection—she wrapped tartan fabrics around the upper body and set crowns on the models' heads.

Today, ethnic crossing is also common practice in the design creations of non-Western cultures as well, for example in the embroidery and patchwork work of Ashish Gupta and Manish Arora.[50]

In Bernhard Willhelm's work, border crossing begins within his own country, under the premise that it is often more difficult to perceive one's own than to explore the foreign. Willhelm, who comes from southern Germany, believes that 'in every valley there are impressive costumes that look as if they have come from outer space, especially the hats'[51]. He discovers traditional handicrafts like cross-stitching and folklorist embroidery motifs, which might also pass as Romanian, Spanish or Mexican. Ironically, the question is raised here whether the image of an ever-cheerful folklore is no more than a standardising, tourist perception of ethnic characteristics. His use of the foreign does not stop at Japanese labourers' pants, African wraparound shawls, Arabian galabeya, or clerical Christian or Buddhist robes. The world is his inspiration when producing the new. Based in Berlin, the label Sissi Wasabi develops Bavarian dress conventions into a style that crosses over borders and appeals to a young clientele.

Eva Gronbach questions political correctness as a social construct. She breaches taboos concerning the limits of politics, depoliticising the national—the German—and making it freely accessible. The German designer takes the German national colours and heraldic animal, the eagle, and employs them in the fashion context. Gronbach sees this as a fashionable declaration of love to Germany and called her 2001 collection *déclaration d'amour à l'allemagne*. The design of the clothes is youthful, up-to-date. For her collection *mutter erde vater land* (mother earth father

Figure 17 John Galliano, *Mapping the World,* 2004/2005. Photo: Studio Them. www.them.de.

land, 2003), she designed pullovers with stylised eagle's wings in gold (yellow) on black or red or with black wings on yellow. Although Germany is not the only issue, Eva Gronbach is a committed designer who skilfully integrates political statements into her work (cf. p. 121). In her collection *the sacrosanct* for Autumn/Winter 2006/2007 she dealt with global violations of human rights, for example in the US prison camp Guantanamo Bay in Cuba. Classics like trench coat, parka, blouson and hoody shirt bear the silhouette of a crouching prisoner and above this a text from the bill of human rights.

Historical Context

In all cultural fields, border crossing is one of the oldest means leading to innovation, its foundation being trade and conquests. The exotic, the alien, the unknown, the distant become a resource of the new in border crossings, in high cultures as well as among primitive peoples. In the course of political, economic, cultural and religious assimilation, the unfamiliar, rare and difficult-to-obtain became desirable and turned into something promoting prestige: a luxury commodity. 'The Ionic materials and styles of Asia Minor infiltrated into Greece, the Greek into Rome, and so became fashions in foreign territories. In other words, they became characteristic features of a higher level of society, which—by demonstrating its acquaintance with foreign cultures—laid claim to an advantage in contrast to the *misera plebs.*'[52] The traders of the silk route brought the desired textile to Europe, the crusaders introduced piked shoes *(poulaines)* and hennin from the Orient to the fashion of Burgundy; in the eighteenth century, chintz and cashmere shawls came from India, sable furs from Russia and pearls from Japan. Diverse forms of behaviour developed among different peoples and social communities, for example personality cult or demonstrative consumption in order to gain prestige.

Fashion Crossing—Redesigning

Innovation researcher Karl H. Müller suggests the following possibilities as operative forces in recombination: adding—the addition of new components; deleting—the removal of components; replacing; duplicating; inverting; swapping; crossing over and merging (integrating).[53] Equally, free quotation of stylistic details or those concerned with the technique of cutting (not only in the sense of deconstructivism or eclecticism) can lead to innovative aesthetic design. This is made clear by details in Rei Kawakubo's Comme des Garçons Autumn/Winter 2004/2005 collection, like the dress-suit shawl collar that embellishes a double-breasted, high-necked costume or the gathered puffed sleeves that seem to have slipped halfway down the upper arm. Olivier Theyskens sees his creations for the House of Rochas as a citation of elegance and drama, features that were a matter of course in the haute couture of the 1950s

Figure 18   Eva Gronbach, *mutter erde, vater land,* 2003. © Eva Gronbach, PR.

and early 1960s. In 2006, Theyskens quoted the elegance of the tent dress (1958) by Yves Saint Laurent for Dior or the cape jacket (1963) by Cristóbal Balenciaga—only the insider recognises such reminiscences. In addition, he uses materials such as lace, brocade, satin and velvet, which are not necessarily considered up-to-date. Nonetheless, Prada interpreted them new in 2008/2009. In his Autumn/Winter 2004/2005 collection, Helmut Lang combined the design idea of intricate pleating—an echo of Madame Grès—with the diaphanous lightness of a gauze dress. A pleated length of material formed an apronlike skirt, which was combined with bast flounces on the hips to awaken associations with native African clothing. In 1991, Martin Margiela redesigned a T-shirt, wide-cut jeans and a ball dress from the 1950s to create a new ensemble. The wide trousers became a skirt and the ball dress was cut up the front to become an ankle-length waistcoat. Margiela reflects fashion by dismantling and reshaping it. Vivienne Westwood's creative ideas are much closer to eclecticism, like her redesigning of voluminous eighteenth-century 'Watteau-robes' (1996) and her revival of sixteenth-century English fashion in the collection *Five Centuries Ago* in 1997, which she had photographed as stylised versions of famous paintings; among others, there was a photo of the designer herself in the role of Queen Elizabeth I.

The intention of Miguel Adrover, a New York fashion designer with Spanish roots, was not to copy but to pervert the authentic. Adrover bought original examples of the brand-protected Burberry trench coat in second-hand shops and converted them into dresses, often by turning out the significant check lining and the brand label that is hidden inside in the originals. The House of Burberry sued him for denigration; Adrover's response was that he understood his work as redesigning—that is as something new and not as an illegal fake or denigration.[54]

Second-hand and vintage fashion without redesigning means that the old is the new and the new is the old, without any kind of innovation. However, the disposal of mass commodities may mean that former mass fashion becomes unique pieces today, and what has been individually used and worn will experience a reindividualisation in the hands of a new user. These were the reasons that prompted Hennes & Mauritz to introduce a vintage corner in selected H&M shops in 2006 (or perhaps it represented a stimulus to buy new things after all?). Old clothes can be bought there at fixed prices, but they are absolutely nonreturnable.

New or Simply Different

The new can be distinguished from the simply different inasmuch as it creates a new interpretation that does not already exist in the cultural memory, in other words within the history of fashion. By contrast, a dress that differs only in colour and/or material from another, without a cultural, that is fashionable, significance—is simply different: it is different from or self-similar to a hundred other dresses but by no means new in the sense of being innovative. It is different from, but alike. A horizontally striped shirt can be innovative, if the concept of horizontal stripes and shirt is new as such. To produce jeans full of holes and sell them as new is an innovation in the sense of a faked ultrarealism, whereas holey jeans per se are not an innovation.

Because of its recognition value or capacity to connect with the familiar, the simply different has better chances of asserting itself than the completely new. Its effectiveness lies in a combination of memory, emotion and functionalism. One reason why the tweed suit, which was scorned for many years as a petit-bourgeois, old-lady style (and perpetuated only in Chanel haute couture) became world fashion again was the introduction of unconventional—anti-bourgeois—elements like frayed seams and open edges in 2004/2005. Neither the Chanel tweed suit (created by Gabrielle Chanel in 1954), nor the frayed seams that appeared for the first time in intellectual Japanese fashion at the beginning of the 1980s, were new, but the combination of the two facilitated their assertion in ready-made fashions. In summer 2004, Karl Lagerfeld invented a Chanel trench coat, a design model that he described in the following way: 'I don't know why I didn't think of it before, a simple idea, to add the braid in a specially made cotton, on to the trench coat and as soon as you wear it, you know it is Chanel.'[55] Other things are reactivated after being forgotten for a long time, like the nineteenth-century men's frock coat, which was made feminine in 2005/2006 by ethnic embroidery and successfully adapted for women in that way. An aesthetic crossover occurred with the frayed tweed suit and the Chanel trench coat; in the case of the frock coat it was a matter of gender crossing (cf. p. 115).

The Valuable Other

'The different' is a concept of indifferent value—in the sense of being simply different—but as a new interpretation it may also create a new work and so become culturally significant. Such works develop the dimension of permanence and remain in existence as a style or an artefact. In music, a new interpretation can be protected by copyright laws. The evaluation of the new has moved on from discourse on authenticity to discourse on being different.

Helmut Lang gave dresses and tops with a simple cut something special by means of structuring elements. He underlay a transparent white top with an asymmetrically arranged, coloured bandeau or with an arbitrarily placed narrow ribbon, or he made the seams visible through the delicate fabric. These are minimal details that are not necessarily visible at first glance but give the item of clothing a new kind of ornamental effect. Here, the ornamental is to be understood not as a forceful pattern but as structure and division. As such, the variation is a creative act. The eclectic interpretations of fashion by Vivienne Westwood (cf. p. 113) are equally innovative.

Gender Crossing

The significance of being a man or a woman has always played a natural, definitive role in fashion. This became obvious when the implied association was violated by a gender-crossing fashion that had a provocative effect (cf. p. 54). It was primarily on the basis of clothing that the significance of gender was established, and what freedoms and development possibilities were available. In the (fashion) journals as well, the roles of the sexes and the relations between man and woman continue to be understood as a fundamental aspect of the social order; they are mediated as such to the present day. The introduction of the concept of gender in 1955, however, made it clear that there is a social, cultural sex (gender) by contrast to biological sex (cf. p. 162).

Literary theorist Barbara Vinken highlighted an exciting vestimentary gender crossing in a model by Yohji Yamamoto shown on a famous photo by Nick Knight from 1986. Yamamoto combined an ankle-length men's paletot coat with a bouffant tulle form as a kind of bustle (Cul de Paris). On the photo, the bush of tulle with its intense red colour and apparent three-dimensionality forms a stark contrast to the wearer of the coat—with visored cap and low-heeled shoes—who appears as no more than a black silhouette. Here, the bustle that appears with feminine connotations in the history of fashion can also be associated with a male cockstail. More than this, Vinken points out that *le coq* (French for a cockerel, a male animal) is also the word stem for *coquetterie,* which was attributed to both sexes until the end of the eighteenth century. Yamamoto thus questions the binary attribution of this Western fashion as female or respectively male. A similar gender crossing can be encountered in Alexander McQueen's work, when a patterned silk frockcoat similar to a just-aucorps (man's eighteenth-century frockcoat) is combined with a lavishly flounced dress in his 2006/2007 collection, but also in Emanuel Ungaro's 2002 collection, in which he combines the torero's bolero and flamenco skirts.

Historical Context

Early women's-rights movements, such as the women's suffrage movement in England around 1900, attempted in vain to influence the women's clothing of the era, pleading for women to forgo their corsets. Paul Poiret's suggestion of overalls as day, sports and evening wear for women in 1911 was the only negation of the categorisation of pants as a male item of clothing and represented a gender crossing (apart from the bloomers movement circa 1860 and the adoption of knickerbockers and plus fours for cycling and physical exercise). Only in the 1920s, and more recently in the 1960s, did women's claim to equal social rights have a much stronger influence on the appearance of fashion on the streets. At first, the adoption of male clothing (man's suit, beret, pyjamas, etc.) by the *garçonne* in the 1920s appeared to cross into

Figure 19 Alexander McQueen, model 2006/2007. Photo: Studio Them. www.them.de.

a taboo zone. The eroticism of the androgynous developed from this ambiguity of sex. In the clothing of the hippies, by contrast, the dominant aspect was sexual liberation, which resulted in a vestimentary equation of the sexes.

Nevertheless, the adoption of men's clothing by women did not abandon the vestimentary connotation 'female' insofar as the female adoption of male clothing is never a 1:1 copy, but an adaptation. Both the aesthetic and constructive design of a trouser suit for women differs from that of a man's suit, quite apart from the fact that the blouse as opposed to a man's shirt, the necklace versus the tie, shoes, and hairstyle and make-up provide clear gender connotations. A vestimentary equation, by contrast, was arrived at with jeans and T-shirt. While there may still be a constructive (technique of cut) difference between men's and women's jeans in order to do justice to their contrasting body structures, this is not necessary in the case of the T-shirt (apart from the different sizes). The utopia of complete equality—social, ethnic, but also with respect to age and sex—became reality in the (white) T-shirt, even though a differentiation in design is possible by means of statements, logos and so forth, thus providing pointers to the identity of the wearer.

Future

Because gender crossing took place primarily as context crossing from men's clothing to women's clothing in the twentieth century, in the future the reverse path from women's to men's clothing still remains largely open. Context crossing as the acquisition of women's clothing—above all of the woman's skirt—by men has not (yet) happened. Various models suggested—by Rudi Gernreich in 1970; Gaultier in 1985, 1991 and 1994; Dolce & Gabbana in 1994; Westwood in 1996; Beirendonck in 1999/2000; Yamamoto in 1999 and Galliano in 2000/2001—were all failures. Even the mass fashion provider Hennes & Mauritz—despite selling men's wrap-around skirts in 1999—has failed to assert the half-skirt for men in the Western world. Nor has there been ethnic crossing of the galabeya, sarong or kilt, apart from a few holiday integrations and memories. The answer to the question 'When will the man's skirt be fashion?' lies exclusively with society's communicative negotiation and not with the designers' innovative ideas. The total vestimentary equality of the sexes is thus left to the future; until then, it is true to say that fashion is prescribed by the concept of men's clothing, for if that was not the case, men would wear women's skirts.

Cross-dressing

Gender crossing should not be confused with cross-dressing, which refers to the wearing of clothing that is usually attributed to the opposite sex within a specific society. This act opposes the implied norms and rules, which—like fashion—are socially constructed. There are various types of cross-dressing, of which drag is one of the best known.[56] The term drag is read as 'dressed as a girl' or also as 'dressed as a guy'.

Multi-crossings: Sportswear, Workwear, Military Wear, Street Wear

As explained in the introduction to context crossing, crossings do not lead to inventions per se, but they may result in new aesthetics or forms of use, in the sense of an innovation that emerges via the fusion or combination of systems—fashion and sport, fashion and work, fashion and music. However, there are also examples whereby an unintentional idea conquers the market or leads to copying, like the Freitag bag, which the Freitag brothers created from a combination of messenger bag, recycled truck tarpaulins and safety belts.[57] A contingent idea (or a practical consideration) initially, hipsters became a radical fashionable reinnovation when pop star Mariah Carey cut off the waistline of her jeans and so popularised McQueen's idea of bumster pants (cf. p. 133).

Sportswear to Street Wear

Excursus: A woman in her mid thirties travelling on the underground is wearing a polar-fleece outdoor jacket of the brand 'active', jogging shoes and a headband, and she is carrying a shopping bag. The body in the sporty outfit is not particularly sporty—rather, it is the opposite. One asks oneself: is the outfit a sham package? Her sportswear outfit makes it clear that her only concern is comfortable clothing. If the argument is continued, it becomes clear that today sport adopts the role that fashion should take, defining lifestyle and clothes. In the twentieth century, sport became a symbol of societal change and social status. Athletes now become stars; sportswear mirrors the zeitgeist. Sportswear represents a global feeling of life (cf. p. 152). People in jogging pants run through the English Garden in Munich and Central Park in New York or across the Square of Heavenly Peace in Beijing. The snowboarder's baggy pants, the leather blousons of motor sport, yachtsmen's windbreaker jackets, football players' shorts, and baseball players' caps define the style on the streets.

Historical Context

Until around the end of the nineteenth century, history was familiar with sport only as a pleasure and pastime pursued by the nobility, such as hunting and riding (with male influences in women's clothing), or the nineteenth-century promenade as a means of passing the time among the bourgeoisie. At the end of the nineteenth century, movement (in the truest sense of the word) entered the life concepts of young people mainly—a movement that is known quite consciously as *Jugendstil* (art nouveau, style liberty). Young ladies and gentlemen from good homes discovered cycling, tennis and golf, and the comfortable knickerbockers and flat cap of the working class rose in society as a result. At the end of the nineteenth century in the industrial countries—led by Great Britain and the USA—an attitude to sport as physical training that was healthy for the body began to spread. This went hand in hand with the liberty style, in Germany the so-called reform clothing movement, which banned the unhealthy corset above all else. Sports clothes, that is 'active wear', became synonymous with natural clothing, which was clothing suitable for the body and its movements. This ranged from the first nonrestricting bathing costumes made of knitted fabric to the first running shoes made of linen with rubber soles rather than stiff leather shoes.

Around 1900, the term sportswear consequently became diversified in the English language: in Great Britain, sportswear stands for the active, functional clothing used to practice a sport: *active wear.* In the USA, by contrast, sportswear is equated with casual clothes—that is with practical daily clothing or even more casual evening wear. Therefore the USA is correctly regarded as the country of origin of both sportswear and street wear. Not least, this is connected with the development of leisure time. Not the free time of the upper class, which had always existed and was the subject of the now famous treatise *Theory of the Leisure Class,* published by the US sociologist Thorstein Veblen in 1899, but the increasing free time of the middle-class citizen as a consequence of the first reductions in working hours (reduced to eight and a half hours on five and a half days in the USA after the First World War and to eight hours on five days after the Second World War). In the 1920s and 1930s, therefore, there was first talk of so-called popular sport (as a precursor to mass sport) as well as physical exercises and physical training (not only in fascist countries). The demand for comfortable clothing influenced the so-called casual look as both daytime and evening wear in the USA by contrast to Europe, where sportswear began to influence street wear at most. The initiator of these innovative impulses was American fashion designer Claire McCardell from the 1940s onwards, with garments including leotards (a kind of leggings) in 1943, jersey dresses in 1946, and hooded dresses in 1952. This tradition still continues today in creations by Geoffrey Beene, Calvin Klein and Donna Karan.

At the beginning of the 1980s, in the USA sportswear also became street style as it is still understood today; through aerobics on the one hand and break-dancing on the other. From the beginning, these two completely new forms of sport—and this is essential for the success of sportswear as a whole—were practised in two completely different social milieus and differentiated by gender to a great extent. Aerobics (from aero-bicycling, invented as a sporting programme for astronauts) became an upper-class fitness sport practised mainly by women (powerfully promoted by the US actress Jane Fonda after 1982), break-dancing was identified with lower-class, if not the lowest-class, male African American youth. Both outfits—aerobic leggings and baggy pants (cf. p. 133)—became normal street wear (leggings in the 1980s, at least) within the social group and developed their own brands. Almost from one day to the next, therefore, sportswear stood for youth and youthfulness, for fitness, power, and an active lifestyle; it was a symbol of status or differentiation and, above all, ease of wear; in other words, of the comfortable. This active sports clothing (active wear) was modified into fashionable sportswear and as such into actual street wear, into a street style. More than 80 per cent of trainers are sold as street shoes, which have to fulfil a high demand, providing what they promise for professional sport. In the same way, sportswear is closely connected with the development of high-tech materials, which were developed and tested for professional sport but are valued equally in everyday clothing: windproof materials, membrane fabrics that absorb sweat and synthetics that dry quickly.

In addition, sportsmen and sportswomen became fashionable leading figures, not least due to tremendous media presence and the character of sports events—similar to pop events—like the Hahnenkamm Race in Kitzbühel, Austria. Sportsmen like Dennis Rodman, Stefan Kretzschmar and David Beckham have become pop stars. Today, sportswear also conveys status and differentiation, whether it is designer sportswear by Boss or Escada or worn by big-time rappers and DJs like Kani Kool and Puff Daddy.

A direct fusion of sportswear and designer fashion evolved through collaboration on a collection between the Japanese designer Yohji Yamamoto and the German sports article manufacturer Adidas in 2003. Sport couture was the name given to Yamamoto's wide, ankle-length skirts, soft hooded shirts with the typical three white stripes, or jogging shoes with the Y-3 logo. Adidas places emphasis on a diverse line of products. The successful street-style collection *Respect Me* for rapper girls is promoted and styled by rriot-girl Missy Elliott. Since 2008, Hussein Chalayan has been creative director of Puma. All-round designer Philipp Starck has been designing his own shoe collection for Puma since 2004; the optical impression lies somewhere between comfortable slip-ons and sporting jogging shoes. The sport brand Chiemsee has been known in street style since 1984—with jumping kangaroos as a print pattern—and with its famous logo of a cliff jumper since 1987.

Workwear to Street Style

Workwear should be understood as working clothes like an overall, but also as a specific labourer's clothes such as those of a lumberjack. Often their transformation into street wear is connected to marketing as a youth fashion brand or designer fashion. However, the transformation does not necessarily lead to the improved social standing of the wearer group.

Famous examples are gold-digger jeans and their adoption as leisure or everyday pants ranging from mass goods to luxury brands; the Canadian lumberjack's jacket which became the thick, checked jacket of everyday wear or cord trousers that were worn by labourers in the nineteenth century. The process from workwear to street style was first noticeable in the USA (among other things, because of the lower urban concentration) at the beginning of the twentieth century and followed in Europe only from the 1950s onwards.

The German designer Eva Gronbach intended a conscious takeover of authentic working clothes (cf. p. 111). In her collections *Glück auf* (a traditional miner's greeting in the sense of 'good luck', 2005) and *Glück auf 2006* she transferred the value of working clothes to that of leisure and street clothes. The initial basis was old, used miner's clothing from the redundant coal pit Sophia Jacoba near Aachen. Gronbach left oil stains, roughly darned holes and the personnel number of the miners as proof of the clothes' unique quality. Gronbach altered these items of clothing, which did not have to be made to look old, into casual urban clothing. Designed in an up-to-date, fashionable way with white satin ribbon trims and printed by hand with 'Glück auf' or a sand-coloured German national eagle, here a piece of industrial history became fashion history.

Sportswear, Workwear and Military Wear into Subculture and Club Wear

As the preceding heading indicates, interweaving and reciprocal influences are multiple; they can be cited only by means of examples. In general, the fusion of sportswear, workwear and street wear develops to a greater extent when the functional, comfortable and practical are demanded in both everyday and high-end fashion. This demand corresponds to a flexible, extremely mobile lifestyle. The German health shoe Dr. Maertens from 1945 became the English working shoe DocMartens and later evolved into a cult subculture shoe and finally a global youth shoe, the Doc's. The leather blouson motorbike jacket Perfecto dating from 1927 became the padded US fighter pilot's jacket and later a jacket favoured by teenage street gangs. The bomber jacket of quilted satin, first worn by boxers, became the ghetto-glamour street wear of hip hoppers. The camouflage pattern of military battledress developed into a fashionable pattern, whereby the original purpose of camouflage during military deployment became its opposite as a fashionable pattern in a civilian environment—in other words it was a means to be noticed. Camouflage became suitable for the streets. By means of social application, camouflage clothing items developed into fashion by progressing from an antiestablishment signal via careful carelessness to the eroticism of power. Originally, they evolved into what they are—from informal to formal subculture and club wear, from the local to the global—*without* the specific influence of design and marketing.

Social Crossing

As opposed to all other systems, in fashion it is possible—despite all distinctions—to negate social barriers or at least to abolish them as far as external appearance is concerned. As early as the eighteenth century, a social equation with the rural peasantry was quite common, as documented by the female nobility's *costume à la bergère* ('shepherdess'), and in the nineteenth century, dirndl and lederhosen were worn by urban summer visitors (including the Austrian and Bavarian courts). The worker's flat cap succeeded as the sporting cap of the aristocracy, the sailor's polo neck became intellectual businessmen's or artists' clothing, while the jacket of the Chanel suit was inspired by the rural *janker* of alpine locals (cf. p. 106). Social crossing is not restricted to one social direction. Workmen's increasing self-confidence was also documented by their clothing in the nineteenth century; outside of working hours, they strove for a bourgeois appearance. Even to the present day, workmen—and not only they—have old, used jeans for work and new, going-out jeans in up-to-date, fashionable styles.

As a creative challenge, avant-garde fashion today combines the social contrasts of punk and the aristocracy (Vivienne Westwood), hippies and the nobility, or Ivy League preppies and ghetto rappers (Tommy Hilfiger). A psychological strategy lies behind this: by assimilating something, one can take away its power.

Technical Crossing

Wearables—Clothes and Technology

The integration of electronics, new technologies and fashion signals the start of a new era in the clothing and textile industry, in which visions are giving way to products now ready for the market. In the future (not forgetting that 'future' is a factor of uncertainty) electronic equipment will be part of clothing. A microphone will be hidden in the collar and connected to a mini speech-recognition PC in the breast pocket. This PC will have a face recognition programme, and any new person in front of us will be transmitted to this via an integrated camera. On the mini display integrated into our glasses or a headset with screen (augmented reality), data and background information can be read to provide telling arguments in conferences, or the description of functions. If things become stressful, our body-function control will report a dangerous overfunction of stress; a weight-watching system will warn against every superfluous mouthful at a business lunch. Not least, the energy-power shoes we are wearing will provide the necessary electricity in order to keep these apparatuses working. Is this a horror vision or a new, positive life quality?

The terms *wearables, wearable computing, wearable technologies, smart clothes, smart fashion, interactive wear* and *e-(electronic) dresses* refer to functional electronic objects integrated into clothing.[58] Portables become wearables and clothing becomes a user surface—in other words, an electronic interface.

The high-tech GEOX jacket of today is similar to the classical blouson. Conventional designs are combined with new technologies and high-tech materials. It is not so much their fashionable design or unusual form that attracts attention, but far more their innovative inner workings such as the integration of touch pads, Bluetooth, MP3 players, navigation systems and solar cells/photovoltaics to provide energy. Already existent high-tech textiles (smart textiles) are capable of conducting electricity. Manufacturers in the various fields are striving for intelligent clothing, from pure electronics producers like db electronics and mobile device providers like Sagem and Venzero to system integrators like Eleksen and Interactive Wear and clothing manufacturers like O'Neill, Bogner, Lodenfrey and Urban Tool. Different companies in Germany (Interactive Wear) and worldwide (Philips, Xybernaut) are testing wearables. Wearables technology is presented at fairs like the Cebit in Hannover and Avantex in Frankfurt, and also at the sports equipment fair Ispo in Munich.

The declared aims of intelligent clothing are to maximise function and performance or—where appropriate—to offer functions largely independent of the user and his surroundings. An integrated navigation system should not require input of the user's present location, but should ascertain this independently and then lead the user to his chosen destination, paying attention to weather conditions and personal preferences. (If it rains, rain-protection gear on the bicycle is automatically activated.) In this way, a man-computer-clothing symbiosis develops and is able to offer hybrid realities. The start was made by pioneers like Steve Mann from the Massachusetts Institute of Technology: as early as the 1980s, Mann invented a shoe computer, and in the early 1990s a headset and NetCam for a wide range of augmented realities. These have been reduced in size since to the dimensions of sunglasses and to the WearCam. Wearable electronics are realised, tested and utilised in the military field. Among other things, the companies Interactive Wear and GPSoverIP GmbH in Schweinfurt developed the Know Where Jacket for civilian serial production in 2006; a small series is produced by Loden Frey Service GmbH in Munich. As well as an MP3 player, headphones and microphone, a waterproof and shockproof sleeve keyboard and an emergency button, the Know Where Jacket includes the complete integrated electronics of a machine known as GPS-eye that detects and transmits position data specifically for the location of human beings. It not only facilitates the location of the jacket's wearer with the precision of GPS, but—thanks to GPSoverIP—the wearer can also be located in real time, sometimes even inside buildings. The range of use for Know Where solutions is almost unlimited, ranging from sport and leisure time uses (e.g. mountain climbing, mountain biking, sailing) to work and protective clothing and finally security and medical technology.

One major field of use for intelligent clothing is represented by so-called Life Shirts for the supervision of the sick, precautionary health measures and fitness surveillance. Sensors are integrated into the textiles of Life Shirts that continually measure the vital functions such as pulse, blood pressure, blood sugar, heart rhythm and fat-burning rate and the pH value of the skin, and then signal corresponding warnings or take counteraction automatically. A dress with integrated massage sensors—which can be activated during train journeys, for example—is intended to improve general well-being.

The research project Solartex[59] develops and tests the possibility of integrating flexible *solar cells;* the company Solarion in Leipzig has developed flexible, thin-layer solar cells (only 7.5 micrometers thick and almost weightless). These are integrated into clothing to provide energy for small mobile apparatuses via a USB interface. The Institute of Clothing Physiology Hohenstein e.V. in Baden-Württemberg plays a decisive role in this context; here, jackets are also being tested that produce energy by means of solar cells or from body heat (the human body produces energy of about 10 watts, so that body heat could give up its energy to high-tech textiles) and sport shoes that create energy from motion (the prototype is a smart sneaker by Nike, developed by Thad Starner, MIT). This idea is also being pursued by the project Sustain, whereby energy won by kinetic, static and solar-technical means is stored in textiles.[60] In many cases, researchers are working with individual layers of fabric that communicate by means of Bluetooth: one layer functions as a store, another is sensitive to light or sounds, and a third registers changes of location using acceleration sensors.

At the Geneva Institute Miralab, research is being carried out into possibilities for *virtual feeling of materials,* using the name Haptex, in the form of physical parameters in the virtual simulation of fabrics. The Hug Shirt by CuteCircuit has already been tested as interaction design and received numerous awards.[61] Hug Shirts convey the physical feeling of being hugged, including intensity, warmth and heartbeat. The impulse for this 'hug' is sent by one partner to the other via mobile telephone.

In a similar way to brand clothing, in the future the wearing of electronic fashion could become a means of distinction. At first (in the initial phase of acceptance) the attraction would be wearing an intelligent outfit, such as an audio jacket with integrated headphones in the hood and a control panel on the sleeve. But it would be pointless to be the only person wearing this electronic fashion, since the aim is to exchange data with others. Data suits are useless without some form of compatibility. And so the wearables will need to become a matter of course for specific groups and perhaps even develop into basics. Afterwards—in a similar way to designer fashion—distinctive features will develop: the wearer may draw attention to himself with a 'wrong' (in other words uncool) device or—to stand out from the rest—brand buttons will provide information about the integrated system, visible printing will show the performance data or processors, or specific colours will light up to indicate the information data symbolically. Desire for prestige and striving for competence will be expressed not by means of material values, but in terms of who owns the most and—above all—most useful and ideologically valuable or perhaps even most attractive information, and how fast it can be accessed. (In the case of Internet groups, there is already a tendency in this direction.)

Today's society is defined by the information that it possesses and passes on. The creative packaging of information could be the design of fashion at the same time. Consequently, wearables will also offer modern and nonmodern systems. There will be flea-market goods and retro aesthetics—perhaps in the form of an 'old-school' processor. This scenario for the future must (still) be set against a wealth of doubts concerning care, emissions and the protection of data. Further technical developments are likely to have a strong influence on fashionable changes.

Cyborgs—Man and Technology

The term cyborg (cybernetic organism) refers to a being who consists of both biological and artificial parts. The cyborg is a mixed being between living organism and machine. It is debatable whether a person who surrounds himself with technology, for instance by moving from A to B using a car, wearing contact lenses or having a heart pacemaker implanted, is already a cyborg. The fashion designer Hussein Chalayan designed a dress that is attached to a chair back and seat so that the body-dress-chair form one unit and the body can use the chair at any time.

People who transform themselves into machines, machines that mutate into human beings (android or humanoid robots) are not a new idea, but they are being constantly perfected as virtual reality by means of computer-generated 3D design. In art, too, one finds the concept of the cyborg. In Hans Bellmer's work, the human skeleton mutates into mechanical rods and roller bearings onto which the genitals and breasts are fixed, moved by the machine man. Degraded into an erotic cyborg, woman could consist of only breasts, like the breast dress by the French-American artist Louise Bourgeois (which, theoretically, can also be worn by a man).

'Perhaps in some years' time . . . everyone will find it disreputable and disgusting to remain in a soft, hairy, sweating body. The body has to be washed, cared for, freed of odours—and yet it still rots. By contrast, with the—new quality of life—you can tack yourself together from the most beautiful masterpieces of engineering art'[62], in the words of the Polish philosopher and science fiction author (of *Solaris,* e.g.) Stanislaw Lem. 'Surely every woman would like silver halogen lamps instead of eyes, breasts that project like a telescope, the wings of an angel, glowing calves and heels that produce melodic sounds at every step?' As a cyborg, man will be brought to perfection and the possible conclusion is that those who still display some fault will become unique (Lem). By contrast, Donna Haraway published a feminist cyborg manifesto.[63]

It is to be expected that expensive replacement parts like the C-Leg by Otto Bock, the first knee-joint system in the world to be operated exclusively by microprocessors, will no longer be concealed below pants or a long skirt. For technology and media have become more and more visible in the course of design history; the time when a television set was hidden away inside a piece of furniture is past, at least since the 1990s. The development could be similar with respect to high-tech prostheses. Then, Alexander McQueen would have been a pioneer once again with the hand-carved prostheses created for Aimee Mullens (see p. 80) in his Autumn/Winter 1998/1999 collection.

Reality Crossing: Cyberbodies

The computer promotes the fictive and enables entry into a world beyond reality, a world out of space or a Second Life.[64] The Internet leaves the experiment to fiction, removes it from our everyday life and thus makes it easy to tolerate. Computers help us to cross the borders between the probable and the miraculous, between the real and the mythical.

In the novel *Neuromancer* (1984) by science fiction writer William Gibson, the people of the book create cyberspace (cybernetic space). Gibson also refers to it as the Matrix, because the protagonists are linked to it via a neuronal interface on the computers of a special network. The complete immersion into cyberspace that is described here seems to anticipate the immersion of virtual reality. Gibson describes cyberspace as the consensual hallucination of a computer-generated graphic space. Cyberspace appears as a virtualised impression of space that demonstrates no topographical locality. Current socio-scientific approaches to research understand cyberspace as a sensory horizon created through computer media. Those who enter into cyberspace experience a virtualising of their social, objective, spatial and temporal perceptions. Surely the blue box of the old-fashioned film medium is also a reflection of virtual reality?

The Australian performance artist Stelarc experiments with body extensions like a third arm. For him the body is obsolete, so that he incorporates human machine interfaces in his work.

However, most protagonists in common computer animations are still caught in conventional (real) gender and body images. In a study entitled *Sheroes,* Birgit Richard investigates gender role play in virtual space.[65] She calls them Lara's (Croft) Sisters, these heroines from Tomb Raider to Heavy Metal F.A.K.K. The digital beauties embody a myth of femininity; their physical construction resembles a body sampling that makes them into female cyborgs. They are not dematerialised, either as an idea or in their pictorial realisation, and yet they are still unreal. The unreal media body—the heroine without wrinkles and monstrous metamorphoses—becomes the ideal of the female body as such. This affects real self-portrayal and thus the fashion of young women in particular. The clothes of Lara Croft, who was created as a video figure by Toby Gard in 1994, are reduced to the minimum of a tight T-shirt with bare midriff and brief shorts, while—as in the case of the male heroes—the full power lies in her huge belt.[66] At the same time, there are retro heroines dressed as gothic princesses in mediaeval clothing. Although reciprocal influences are leading to a blurring of the distinction between real and unreal, the idea or the possibility of the dematerialisation of a cyberbody is still left. Astonishingly, the clothing generally sticks to forms typical of the times.

The body's infinite formability or hybridisation—man-fighting machine or man-animal—was already a stimulus to crossing over realities in the old media such as painting or photography. Ultimately, the real body is only a medium as well, a medium of culturally and media-encoded perceptions, including those of fashion and art.

When Is a Copy?

The term *copy* appeared in fashion with the first fashion creator who was specifically named and claimed to have created a unique work (product). Thus the 'creator' became synonymous with the 'artist'. When Charles Frederick Worth established haute couture in the mid nineteenth century, a decisive distinction emerged between the unknown tailor who discharged work, as an artisan or guild member, and the haute couturier as a designer whose name was known. The claim to an original brought the copy along with it.

The French philosopher and sociologist Jean Baudrillard saw an 'autotelic aesthetic of repetition'[67] in fashion. Repetition in the sense of a copy is a precondition to fashion. According to the motto 'clothes do not become fashion until they hit the streets', fashion thrives on the copy in the sense of the reproduction of a work. This ranges from the legal copy to sewing patterns, free imitation and even illegal forgery. It is this process that makes designer fashion suitable for the mainstream. It also leads to similarity in the fashion offered during one season: similarity brings security for both producer and consumer. This complies with a comment made by sociologist Georg Simmel in 1911: 'Imitation gives the individual the security of not being alone in his actions'.[68] In the 1950s, even haute couture existed—at least in part—from the sale of its very expensive original models, which could be reproduced once this was sanctioned by the houses of haute couture. Their dissemination lay in the contradiction 'authentic copy'.

As the dissemination of a vestimentary innovation, the copy comes about after this initial creation has been recognised as new and innovative by an observer (dealer) and is commissioned for imitation. Imitation (turning it into ready-made clothing) usually takes place in the form of a defusing (downward declination) of the radical and will include a stylistic adaptation to suit the ideas and taste of the customers (target group, milieu). However, inasmuch as its saleability thus becomes decisive, the model loses the authenticity the designer intended.

According to Alois Schumpeter, the founder of classical innovation theory (cf. p. 87), every inventor is a monopolist, and his status declines only when imitators appear. Schumpeter sees the interplay of invention and imitation as the driving force of competition. As in all other commercial fields, in fashion it is often not the inventor (the provider of ideas or first creator) who is most successful on the market, but clever followers (copiers) who avoid the mistakes of the pioneers, downsize the extreme and wield distribution power.

The great prestige value of a specific product, that is a social rather than an actual fashion component, is the reason for most copies—since it offers the greatest potential for financial profit. Logos and authentic brand labels generate the originality and thus identity of a fashion product. Tens of thousands of illegal copies—forgeries, in other words—are burnt by the container in order to protect the brand and the prestige associated with it and, ultimately, to maintain a high sales price. It is also worthwhile imitating expensive materials, like 'real' cashmere scarves made of English lambswool, 'real' silk blouses made of polyester, or 'real' mink coats made of wovens.

Besides the cut, certain manufacturers, namely brands, epitomise a specific fit and design. The best example is jeans, which—despite their assumed sameness—are extremely different due to the types of quilted seams, studs and pockets. The cult of the original grows along with progress in reproducibility.

A suitable example of the imitation of a style—from the copy to the point of forgery—is the Chanel suit. The original Chanel suit jacket displays specific criteria to characterise its originality: coarse-grained tweed, bordering, cut of the sleeves, processing of the lining, small metal chains to weigh down the hem, logo buttons and label. Some of these criteria are generally missing in copies, because they are too expensive. The House of Chanel sets great store by authenticity and follows up any incorrect use of the name Chanel suit, and even 'à la Chanel' or 'Chanel-style suit' are forbidden. This actually constitutes a partial contradiction of the fact that Coco Chanel—a quotation often cited—was interested in the copying of her fashion, believing that only the important or significant is copied. In its turn, the copy represented a guarantee of success (cf. p. 129).

There are also some items of clothing that remain fashionable for a very short time but are remembered as a result of many hundreds of copies, like the Vichycheck petticoat dress by Jacques Esterel which Brigitte Bardot wore for her marriage to Jacques Charrier in 1959. The wide rage of copies was triggered by a desire to identify with the wearer or rather with her role as a star—and not by the item of clothing itself.

In the current avant-garde, designers attempt to avoid reproducibility and with it the danger of being copied. Hussein Chalayan employed textiles that exhibit an individual patina and traces of use, having been buried in soil; he has had dresses produced from sugar frosting, which did not last or were destroyed deliberately (cf. p. 81). Margiela painted his dresses with bacteria so that they would decay at their own pace (cf. p. 62). Viktor & Rolf used their models as a blue screen and projected environmental scenes such as big-city traffic onto them (cf. p. 69). In this way, their fashion approaches the art of the happening. A refusal to be imitated is also discernible when designers redesign second-hand items: Margiela, for example, reflects on fashion by deconstructing and simultaneously refashioning, redesigning and altering it.

However, copying—at least in the fashion business—is not a one-way street. Designers' ideas are copied by mass producers; ideas from everyday life, whether from youth fashions or ethnic clothing, are copied or redesigned by designers. In each case, it is the quality of the materials that is decisive. The fact that clothing is cheap does not mean that it is uncreative a priori. The imitation, adoption and copying of subcultural styles like hippie or punk by ready-made clothing develops into alienation, since the clothes' original radicalism is altered into a financially 'lucrative, but symbolically emptied fashionable gesture for everybody'.[69] Whenever reference is made to subcultures today, it is usually as a—sales-promoting—argument to differentiate fashion from the so-called mainstream.

Appropriation as an 'Authentic Copy'

Since the late 1960s, in fine art there has been a movement known as appropriation art, which questions the claim to be original in principle. One of its best-known artists is Elaine Sturtevant, who painted (repeated) Pop Art that is easy to copy—from the viewpoint of technical or artistic skill—including Jasper John's *Flag* (1954/1955), frequently giving offence in this way. Sturtevant defended herself against accusations of copying by posing the following questions: Why is it not permissible to copy something once produced? Why is a second artist not allowed to have the same way of painting, the same idea? Who forbids cloning in art? Is art, are ideas tied to specific people? These questions are based on the concept that it is the repetition that is new in appropriation art.

Transferring this to fashion, one should recall that it was always Gabrielle Chanel's wish—according to her biographers—that her fashion be copied, including the little black dress and her Chanel suit; for she regarded the very fact of being copied as a continuing guarantee of success. Her aim was to be copied but not cloned, since it ought to be possible to distinguish the original at all times. Niklas Luhmann referred to this method as zero methodology (cf. p. 28).

Historical Context

During antiquity and the Middle Ages, as well as in historicising epochs, imitation was not understood as simple copying and did not contradict the demands for creativity and inventive talent. In an imitation, the original was not reproduced exactly; it was an attempt to approach ideal forms. It was always a matter of imitating the idea and not the work of a specific person. Seen in this way, therefore, imitation was oriented on an ideal of perfection; it remained autonomous and represented a broadening of the imagination. By this means, insights and availability were increased; a further interpretation of *copia* in the sense of excess.

Part III
When Clothes Become Fashion

–8–

When Is Fashion?

When fashion is clothes, it is expendable. But when fashion is a form helping us to understand everyday life, it is essential.

Yohji Yamamoto

In Western-influenced countries, we are confronted by fashion on a day-to-day basis. But what is fashion? Low-slung hipster pants and the bare midriff top appeared on the international catwalks as designer models in 1996, but it was not until 2001–2006/2007 that they could be seen on the streets as youth fashion. Triggers for this wider impact were style icons of the popular music scene like Mariah Carey, who cut off the waistband of her jeans in 2000. This prompts the following question: Were 'bumsters'—as Alexander McQueen called his extremely low-slung hipsters designed in 1996—a fashion, or were they clothes in 1996, becoming a fashion only in 2001?

This terminological problem arises because in general use, our language makes no distinction between the terms *clothes* and *fashion*. Since the 1960s at the latest (since postmodernism) the word *fashion* encompasses all forms of clothing and accessories without making any statement about their actual fashionable status. In other languages as well, there is the same lack of terminological differentiation today, for example in German *Mode und Kleidung,* in Italian *moda et costumi, abito, vestiario,* in French *la mode et le costume, le vêtement.* Among others, this is one reason that the lack of distinction is not questioned as a deficiency and foreign language communication still functions within the fashion business. In the historical context, however, there is a distinction between *le mode* (Italian *modo*), that is the modality of form (from the Latin *modus,* the stem of all these loan words) and thus of the product—clothing—and *la mode (moda),* which was the custom, habit and taste of the day or times (Latin, *modus vivendi*) and thus of clothes subject to a time limit—of fashion. (In this context, we will not go into the term *fashion* as it is used to define a widespread form, typical of a specific era, outside the sphere of vestimentary products.) By contrast, the term *modern* is derived from the Latin *modo* and means right now, present. In colloquial language today, *modern* is often used incorrectly as a synonym for *fashionable, i*n the sense of 'in accordance with the fashion'.

It is actually this lack of terminological differentiation that implies that fashion changes every year. In fact, we are confronted by a change in clothes (models, prototypes, order goods), which does not necessarily include a change in fashion. Change is not the primary aspect of fashion, for—apparent—change is generated by the economic concept of seasonal renewal in clothing, without this renewal necessarily being accepted by the consumers or a fundamentally new image of fashion being created. The seasonal renewal of clothing, therefore, creates discontinuity as a basis of continuity.

By contrast to clothing, fashion is defined not first and foremost by the 'binding character of the temporary' (Esposito),[1] but rather by the binding character of social validity. It is negotiated on a communicative basis within society. This does not mean that fashion is timeless, but its validity is determined socially and is variable, multilayered and discontinuous as a result. The social limits of toleration are also being continually renegotiated and are therefore subject to constant change, which is why acceptance of innovative creations and ultimately of new fashions develops at all. By contrast, in the industrialised world clothes are defined in economic terms—in their temporally enduring form, but also as far as their seasonal renewal is concerned. The latter has become an independent mechanism, on which not only the production of clothing but also advertising and journalism depend. As opposed to clothes, the fundamental significance of fashion is the social dynamics of 'in' and 'out'.[2] In this way, it affirms the present and permits both local and global self-definition. The entire global sphere arranges and organises hybrid identities, flexible hierarchies and a great number of reciprocal relations. Even mass fashion is multilayered and thus based on the binding quality of social validity to the same extent, thanks to pluralist-liberal democracies.

Clothes, including accessories, are products which are realised by means of a design process. Which of the products are accepted and become fashion is determined by the society, a group within society or a single community. Another important factor is the individual's inner prompting to wear fashion at all—or merely comfortable clothing, typified by the extreme case of tennis socks and Birkenstock sandals. To this extent, the semiotic definition of fashion is subject to a communicatively negotiated, social process. Fashion extends far beyond the objective aspect of the product, clothing. It gives this clothing a social purpose, above and beyond those of function and aesthetics. Clothing is supplemented by semblance and illusion, which are defined as increased value or additional usefulness; in short, as fashion (cf. p. 146).

The first step on the road to fashion takes place when clothes are staged on the catwalk (cf. p. 80) as well as by photography and advertising. This introduces them to a wider audience in magazines, among other things. Real clothing is confronted by an artificial staging. It is significant that we do not refer to a 'clothes show' or 'clothes photography', but to the 'fashion show' and 'fashion photography', for they grant the semblance and illusion of fashion to clothing. Fashion is far more than its appearance; it is function and meaning (cf. p. 139). As early as 1851, the German philosopher Arthur Schopenhauer spoke of the 'fashion of dress, a physiognomy . . . of every epoch',[3] which he described as significant with respect to fashion, viewing clothes as functional and long-term, and defining the two as existing parallel to one another. Friedrich Justin Bertuch, publisher of the early fashion magazine *Journal des Luxus und der Moden,* explained the emergence of fashion in 1786 by 'man's thirst for diversity, his tendency to finery, an inclination to stand out as a consequence of distinguishing features, and the rich fountain of luxury'.[4]

Due to a failure to differentiate between clothing and fashion, sociologist Elena Esposito comes to the wrong conclusions concerning changes in fashion, quoting Godard de Donville: '[S]o fashion is, for example, the creator of a mimicry that leaves space for individual idiosyncrasies.'[5] *Fashion does not create mimicry; it is through mimicry that clothes become fashion.* Mimicry refers to imitation of our fellow men and women—especially of leading figures like pop icons—and their clothing, as well as to the mimicry of images in advertising and fashion journals. Fashion is not the creator of mimicry; fashion is created and disseminated by means of mimicry. As a consequence of imitation, a fashion—accepted by a group of society—will always already present a more or less uniform image.

Richard Dawkins, behaviourist and evolutionary biologist, invented the term *meme* for a cultural prevalence (1976). According to his hypothesis, memes (Greek, 'something imitated') are to cultural evolution what genes are to biological development.[6] Memes (melodies, ideas, keywords, fashions) are spread through mutation and selection in a similar way to genes and, indeed, in such a way that only the strongest survive in social competition (cf. p. 160).

Let us move on to the generative factor. The generative factor of clothes lies with the one or more individuals that create them. In the professional field of creative design, the term *designer* has been used universally since around the 1960s. The designer employs ideas, imagination, fantasies, emotions and his or her ability for realisation to make plausible an infinite generation of the new (cf. pp. 33–38). This means that there will be no end to innovations in clothing. Proof of this is provided by the designer shows that take place every six months in Paris, Milan, London and New York (to name only the most important) with their approximately 50,000 extremely individual models (see Chapter 7, 'When Is Innovation?'). These models by designers are termed—because of their creativity, unusualness, aesthetics or provocation—fashion (which implies unwearability to some extent) as opposed to clothing. This is a further example of the conceptual impurity of the word fashion. The historical term *le mode* would be valid for designer models, whereas forms of design, production and distribution like haute couture, prêt-à-porter or designer fashion have now become stylistic concepts as well. *Le mode* becomes *la mode* when *le mode* reaches the streets.

That is why the question 'When is fashion?' represents a time factor, certainly, but it is actually defined by a creative and social dimension that is dependent on the creation as a prerequisite and usage as a consequence. In her book *Mode und Moderne*

Juliane Bertschik quotes the 'total social phenomenon' of fashion, which has become included in fields of sociology, cultural anthropology, philosophy, ethnology, psychology, communication theory and semiotics.[7]

Interim Summary

Due to the creative and social definition of fashion, it is affirmed as ambivalent. The following, therefore, are referred to as fashion:

A priori, the creatively anticipated, like John Galliano's ideas expressed as models, for example. The creatively anticipated may remain a prototype or unique work, but it can also be copied and so assert itself as a universal fashion, regardless of an apparent unwearable quality—for example the crinoline, corset or high heels.

A posteriori, the clothes that a community decides to wear are in fashion.

By contrast, any garment other than what has been agreed upon as fashion is simply clothing (for example, the huge number of quilted down jackets or jeans). However, this does not mean that clothes cannot be defined socially as fashion for a short or even longer period of time.

This diagnosis of fashion corresponds to the one established in the context of fashion's definition as form and medium within system theory (cf. p. 21). The statement continues to be valid that clothing is dependent on the initiative of the designer, while fashion depends on the acceptance of the observer and the wearer.

Historical Context

In the historical context, the social construction of fashion also explains the change from the fashions of status that existed until the end of the eighteenth century to fashions of attitude during the nineteenth century and the fashion pluralism of postmodernism after the 1960s.

Anthropological clothing theories generally link fashion to the emergence of culture (with its first high points in the Assyrian-Babylonian and Egyptian cultures) and pursue the catalysts of fashion back into the early, mid and late Stone Age.[8]

By contrast, historical costume studies favour the theory that fashion began in the late Middle Ages, when the individual courts of Europe shaped their own styles of fashion, and the urban bourgeois developed an independent style of dressing as well. In the Middle Ages, when clear social distinctions in clothing were clarified—in particular those between courtly and bourgeois clothing and their evident formal differences—not only was etiquette developed, but clothes also began to lay claim to the status of fashion (Norbert Elias[9]). The development of fashion was also connected to the emergence of cities and to the resultant complete distinction between urban, more cosmopolitan and changeable clothing and permanent, rural clothes that were often tied to a region.

In the nineteenth century, the dissolution of dress codes of class during the French Revolution led to an increased 'urbanising, secularising, commercialising and individualising—and was thus viewed as a precondition and accompanying feature of clothes in which continual, rapid changes were no longer oriented on class, but developed into mass fashion'.[10] Juliane Bertschik signals this development as fashion's entry into the modern age and so the beginning of fashion in the contemporary sense of the word. In the nineteenth century, fashion was—by authors at the time like Charles-Pierre Baudelaire and Karl Gutzkow as well—understood as a contemporary expression of growing mass society, which offered the individual the possibilities of both collective conformation and individual dissociation. However, Gutzkow also remarked that by contrast to the fashion of the eighteenth century, the industrially produced ready-to-wear clothes of the nineteenth century characterised the masses rather than individuals.[11] Walter Benjamin evaluated this as a de-individualised, prosaic, mass society.[12] Sociologist Georg Simmel explained the principle of dynamic fashion change on the basis of the reciprocal effects of individualisation and socialisation in 1911.[13] This interprets the reciprocal effects as between individual clothing and social fashion; in other words, dynamic change develops only after a social consensus has been established concerning 'fashion'.

The frequently cited vestimentary diversity on the city streets of the past resulted from a simultaneity of fashion, traditional costume and uniforms up until the First World War; fashion (as added value) and clothes (as a functional, long-term product in the form of traditional costumes and uniforms) existed parallel to each other; that is, during the nineteenth century dress fashion established itself 'as a socially accepted theme among a bourgeois-urban public, mediated via the independent medium of the fashion magazine . . . Here, the change of new fashions is documented, while the providers of ideas are no longer the nobility alone, but also bourgeois eccentrics and representatives of the demimonde, dandies, coquettes, stage stars, professional fashion creators'[14] and, in the course of the twentieth century, youth subcultures.

Radical changes in clothing style, like those during the French Revolution or during the 1920s, are also understood as the thresholds of social and aesthetic modernisation, as well as change in the image of the sexes. In this context, it is noticeable that an entirely new fashion does not necessarily emerge, as in the case of the 1920s; instead, there may be recourse to an historic model, as there was to classical antiquity at the time of the French Revolution. Nonetheless, the *mode à la grecque* of the Directoire displayed a fundamental aesthetic change with respect to the body and clothing—that is, by relation to the previously fashionable Rococo.

While fashion styles followed chronologically before the 1960s, since then they have been presented synchronously. 'The stylistic pluralism of today's clothing

fashion is associated with the principle known as the postmodern, with the masquerade [melting-pot style; author's note], with the short-term staging of individuality as a processual concept of identity based on the oppositional scheme of "in"
and "out" rather than "old" versus "modern"'.[15] This also corresponds to the consciousness of modernity displayed in twentieth-century art (cf. p. 167) and to the
increasing fragmentation and individualisation of social differences. It leads to social differentiation that is more horizontal than vertical, and, inevitably, this also
applies to society's fashionable concepts. In this context, it is certainly possible
for 'in' and 'out' to exist simultaneously. Fashions are no longer a chronological
sequence; they exist alongside one another like styles of fine art. This coexistence
is experienced as succession, leading to an additional, subjective acceleration of
perception in fashion.

Modern, but Not New; New, but Not Modern

New and modern are not fully congruent, any more than are beautiful—in the sense
of liking—and modern. Often something gives pleasure but is not worn because it
is not modern; on the other hand, a person may wear something that he or she does
not like simply because it *is* modern.[16] It is the exceptions that prove the rule here.
Something is modern when it is sanctioned as modern by the expectations of society.
While the concept of innovation (derived from the Latin *novus* for new and *innovatio*)
stands for something newly created, the concept of modernising means renewing
something, in the sense of altering or arranging it according to the latest taste, that
is changing it according to the already communicatively negotiated, predominant
fashion. *New* and *modern* are etymologically different concepts, the Latin *novus* for
new and innovation being one, the Latin *modo*, meaning right now, of today, according to the latest taste, being the other. It is not the fashion that creates taste, therefore;
the development of taste occurs individually according to internal constructions of
reality (cf. p. 9).[17]

In addition to this, products that do not meet with common approval and have
never been modern, like Rei Kawakubo's Quasimodo dresses (cf. pp. 42, 138),
may be anchored in the cultural memory. They owe this to their uniqueness, their
intellectual pretensions, the fascination that they trigger (of whatever kind), and
because of these factors they are photographed, cited in literature and exhibited
in museums.

The definition of *when clothes become fashion originates from the observer.*
Fashion is defined not by the object, clothing, but by observation—that is, by the
signal and the recipient, the observer and the observed. Since fashion is an exclusively communicatively defined social construct, the response 'Then, it is fashion'
interprets not only the question 'When is fashion?', but also the more usual question,
'What is fashion?'.

Communication

Fashion is a social system based on communication. Communication scientist Paul Watzlawick comes to this conclusion: 'It is impossible not to communicate.'[18] This statement applies from human being to human being, from human being to animal and even from human being to product. Sociologist Niklas Luhmann goes one step further with his thesis that society is made up not of human beings but of communications (cf. p. 22). Every communication takes place on several levels. We employ images where language fails and employ language where images fail. Verbal language and writing are created and registered in a serial way, whereas the registering of images is a disperse system, that is it can sample individual points of attention in milliseconds and 'think' them into a whole.

To approach the complex of clothes and fashion as communication, it is necessary to distinguish between social communication and product information. The product clothing—including headwear, shoes and bags—influences visual communication. For their part, abstract processes of communication alter a human being's natural appearance through body painting (earth, blood, make-up), hangings (necklaces of shells, jewellery) or through partial or complete coverings. These processes of communication are activities of man and his environment, of habitat and culture, but they also demonstrate the way in which a human being observes his or her self or that of others.

The fashion designer communicates his creative ideas (cf. p. 33) or established parameters by means of—usually textile—material via the product clothing/accessory. Parameters (design tools) may be laid out in so-called style guides, which are developed by commercially operating trend offices, trend scouts or fashion institutes in order to agree on shared parameters of style, cut, quality, colour and pattern for some time in the future, usually for the season after next. Looking ahead, they provide guidelines in order to avoid lack of orientation and so minimise failed attempts at acceptance and therefore at commercial success. Style guides are distributed across the globe in the shape of books, leaflets and magazines and contribute quite considerably to the standardisation of fashion. This means that designers (especially those who do not belong to the leading group of media shooting stars) will be interested in orienting their work on the style guides to assure economic success. Or—as Peter Sloterdijk puts it—they pursue 'despairingly, in a panic of self-preservation, the same old paths'[19]. The majority of fashion designers, in particular those who work for the industry, remain within a guide (trend)—in other words, within a communicatively negotiated modality of form, cut, processing technique, material, colour and pattern.

After the product clothing has evolved as a communicative process, the next communicative step follows from the model, via presentation and distribution, to its public perception. Via another step, that of socially negotiated acceptance, the product becomes fashion. This means that the interested party approaches the products available to him, that is including the clothes on offer, by means of nonverbal (visual) communication, then valorises, and finally accepts or rejects them. Even when this approach is based on spoken or written language, a communication is existent. In fashion, this is always a sign of the visual, of the image. It is also a visual matter when communication takes place via the Internet, mobile phone or SMS, using verbal and textual descriptions of what a person is wearing, what a person looks like. However, the verbalised media transfer of fashion is increasing, while the direct visual communication (face to face) of fashion is decreasing. In the age of virtual communication, actually produced clothing is decreasing as a means of communication or is reduced to the simple symbolic language of logos. Human activity is configured through objects, but through communication in the postindustrial age. Increased communication between absent parties (mobile telephone, Internet) means that clothes are playing a diminishing role, notwithstanding the millions of photos in various blogs all over the world. (However, in communication between absent parties, their social origins, education and above all appearance play a lesser part than in face-to-face communication.)

The phrase *product language* is a metaphorical expression of the fact that human beings communicate with the product in an unspoken, visual manner that is immediately interpreted verbally in the mind. A product contains—as a statement of difference—purely objective information—'it is a dress' or 'it is a bag'. This may acquire an additional referential aspect via social communication, like 'an erotic dress' or 'a striking bag'. A socially negotiated referential aspect can also make clothes into a symbol, for example of power or a specific political outlook. Watzlawick maintains that *every communication has an aspect of content as well as a referential aspect*. The aspect of content represents the 'what' of a message, the referential aspect the 'how'. The latter says something about how the sender wishes the message to be understood by the recipient. The 'black dress' is factual information, and it is the referential aspect that turns it into either a dress for mourning or the 'little black dress'. As the term referential aspect indicates, it requires a reference. This is created through space, time and activity, like a visit to the opera or the sports field. One characteristic of advertising is the exploding of connotation, in order to draw attention by this very means, such as a bathing costume as an outfit for a visit to the opera or the like.

The referential aspect is not necessarily conveyed automatically, or rather it permits an interpretation by the viewer. By contrast, the factual information is largely unambiguous as a result of fixed, prelearnt termini, and it is restricted to a basic piece of information, like a bag or a (black) dress, precisely because of this. That is, the referential aspect demands a verbal explanation, if it does not become obvious through space, time or activity: 'I am wearing black because black is fashionable, because I am mourning my cat, because I am on my way to the theatre, because I haven't got anything else to wear.' A similar ambiguity emerges in the case of jeans in particular. Perception and communication take place separately. Clearing one's throat can be a noise, or a signal and thus a message. Niklas Luhmann refers to a double contingency. It is the context that lends concrete meaning to objects in a specific situation. As a framework of interpretation, it determines what has which meaning, what is blacked out and what is not. The context shapes perception, identifies the relevant elements and indicates what belongs together and how it should be categorised or labelled. Finally, such frames of interpretation also prestructure our expectancies.

The referential aspect indicates the emotional relation that dominates between partners in communication. Successful communication comes about when partners agree on this aspect. Disruptions emerge in case of disagreement, no matter whether this concerns factual information or referential information. Communication without understanding is always possible, for example in the intercultural sphere; young people swear by a certain type of music, the older generation rejects baggy pants, and specific ethnic groups buy specific things at the supermarket. Unity is not necessarily created even in cultural contact, but the duality becomes more comprehensible.

Fashion is tied to interaction; however, today this functions less from individual to individual but far more from the mass media and their style icons to the individual. Mass media and advertising observe the object and the consumer observes the mass media and advertising (in Luhmann's sense, this is observation of the third order). Accordingly, it is not the object—the clothes—which creates fashion and taste but far more the mass media and advertising. A similar situation occurs in connection with the news in mass media. Correspondents, reporters and journalists observe the actual events for the news, and we observe the news programmes. As a result, it is the news and not the actual events that create information and knowledge. This structure of external reference also exists in fashion information; that is it takes place via reports and photo selections by journalism and the trade. Increasingly, the Internet, where it is possible to find all the photos of a show, and the fashion TV channel, and—even more so—simultaneous videos on iPods are taking over from those sources. Consequently, people who are not trained in the perception of fashion, and that is most people, feel overchallenged and uncertain.

There is a close link between the evolution of the democratic (social) form of fashion and the evolution of the mass media system (whereby each in itself is linked to improved technical possibilities on its way to mass availability). Until the appearance of fashion journals in the second half of the eighteenth century, fashion took place in the narrow sphere of the aristocratic courts (although there was also bourgeois fashion). One needed direct contact with the court in order to know what was being worn at a particular time and what was not, to know what went together and what didn't. The dissemination of such knowledge was very restricted until the end of the eighteenth century, limited to fashion dolls, travel reports and literary works. This does not mean that there was no fashion and knowledge about it in principle, but it was more firmly tied to social circles and dress regulations. It was not until the twentieth century that the distribution of information increased so rapidly. Mass fashion is available to the extent that mass communication is also available to us.

Time

As has been shown in the previous two chapters, the question of when clothes become fashion is explicated by social definitions. Beyond the social definition, a temporal dimension is identified, in the sense of the duration of a fashion. The term *duration* is understood as a period of time. But what is time?

There are infinite scientific treatises on time, ranging from the mathematical to the philosophical. It is valid to assert as a basic insight that 'time is a dimension in itself, which—difficult as it is to "grasp"—is not absorbed in the ordering patterns of history, process, structure and change. We have no sensory organ for time, but we do not conceive it as a merely abstract category like causality, we apprehend it as either something objectively measurable and datable, as something naturally given (day, season, cycles), or as a mode of experience.'[20] Time is not a sensual perception; the perception of time evolves through cognitive processes alone. The experience of time is 'closely and reciprocally related to aesthetic perception.'[21]

For the observation of fashion, it is relevant that time is not a quality of the products (although they can decay) but a definition made by the subject, that is by the human being. In his *Critique of Pure Reason,* Immanuel Kant devoted a separate section to the theme of time. In this, he elucidates the philosophical insight that 'time does not inhere in things as an objective determination', but is 'a subjective condition . . . and the pure form of sensuous intuition'.[22] Accordingly, it is actually impossible to speak of fashion's fast-paced development, as fast pace is a subjective observation—that is it is made by people and therefore another social definition. Fast-paced signifies that the present passes quickly. What is the present, or how do we perceive it? We always become aware of the present only in retrospect—quasi afterwards, for the present is the difference or fluctuation between past and future. As such, the present is fast-moving.

Nonetheless, the question is raised as to why the society perceives fashion, in the habitual sense, as fast-paced (apart from our previous conclusion that it is not fashion but clothes that change quickly; cf. p. 134). From perceptual psychology we know that experience in life leads to perceptual ignorance in face of the supposedly familiar. In other words, sensual monotony explains why the impression arises of time passing faster and faster.[23] From this, it follows that standardised mass fashion in particular conveys the impression of a tremendously fast pace due to seasonal, climatic change, but this is less true of creative fashion and striking designer fashion, which is far more difficult for the layman to date. Uniform mass fashion can be identified easily over a period of years through a comparison of company advertising. The reason for this is that routine activities leave few traces in our memory. Perception is an active activity which—if it is not to become tedious—demands the readiness to exchange a familiar viewpoint for a different perspective now and then. 'Anyone wanting to bring time to a standstill should therefore either experience something fascinating on a daily basis, or simply view the everyday through the "eyes of a child"".[24] To some extent, it is possible to learn a different way of seeing things. On the other hand, among other things it is a natural trait of artists, which is why they often generate the new and unconventional. In addition, an impression of fast pace emerges because there has been an enormous increase in the simultaneity of different fashion styles—known as so-called fashion tribes—and their public visualisation over the last fifty years, while change comes about at different paces within them.

As explained, the factor of time plays an extremely subjective role in our perception of the changes in fashion. In addition, the factor of time plays an essential role in the process of emergence of clothes (not to be confused with the process of emergence of fashion; cf. p. 134), as indeed of every other product. The process of emergence incorporates the purity of the idea—unaltered. In this phase, the product is known as a model or prototype and not fashion, and it exists long before it reaches the public in large numbers, if indeed it ever does. In a manner of speaking, the model knows of no present, as it is the difference or fluctuation between past and present; this is why designers are acknowledged as anticipators. We expect them to anticipate the future. The task of design is to recognise social processes and respond to them creatively (cf. p. 173). This means that the designer imagines his way into the demands and lifestyles of his target group, and he must avoid designing past them for commercial reasons.

The quality of fast pace is prescribed by the seasonal presentation of new collections at fairs and on the catwalk and does not lie—contrary to general assumptions—with the acceptance of fashion, which comes about in a relatively hesitant, step-by-step way (cf. p. 97). The *catwalk presentation* is a combination of design and styling, that is of items of clothing, accessories, jewellery, make-up, and hairstyle (cf. p. 80). The fashion show presents the actual binding and transient fashion, which, however—and this is the paradox—is never worn in this form by the consumer and thus on the streets. Mass fashion also waits until the time is ripe for acceptance before it enters fashion. For this reason, there is always a time gap between avant-garde and mass fashion irrespective of quick response. On the one hand, the transitory aspect of fashion is made visible by the seasonal closing *sales,* which are staged as a ritual of passage from the living to the dead. The goods offered in such sales are ritualised in shops, department stores and display windows by hanging them in rows (procession) and putting them in bargain bins (sacrifice). The formerly elevated, singular presentation of the new is abandoned in the sale of the mass and run-of-the-mill. This seasonal cycle of clothing, the six-monthly fashion shows reported on as generators of the new and the seasonal sale of the new, causes the impression of fashion's fast pace to arise. 'The existence of timeless elements is highly unlikely in a system that only functions as a continual process, driven by the obstinately formulated anxiety that it may arrive at the end (or have already arrived there).'[25] This statement applies to both fashion and art, which makes no more long-term claims today.

Unconsidered with respect to our sense of fashion as fast-paced, the individual mode of experience nonetheless remains decisive. It is defined neither anthropologically nor by the economy, but comes about polyrhythmically. It is oriented on a principle of chance such as a family event, a new partnership, a holiday destination, a sporting activity or an individual desire to attract attention or imitate. In this context, the new follows cultural entropy. In-between times even fashionable clothes are worn for two to three years or longer—usually depending on a person's age, gender and (social) mobility. Only a minority of people indulge in a new outfitting every year. The speed of fashion's renewal is oriented to only a minor extent on market strategies. Short-lived items are usually bought as such in order to supplement the middle-term. So-called classics are subject to their own temporal dynamics (cf. p. 101). However, it is the contradiction and conflict between social pressures, as well as the pressures of the market and one's own real demands and actual well-being, and the instability of body and psyche that cause fashionable stress. It remains a question of the energy required to uphold the system of fashion, as in the case of all other systems (politics, sport, etc.).

From this, we can conclude that neither art and design nor fashion can be explained through the fact of transformation.[26] Above all, in that case it would be unimportant whether change was slow or rapid. Accordingly, fashion also existed in the Middle Ages (cf. pp. 19, 90), when it altered in a way recognisable for us every fifty years. Since the nineteenth century, there has been a change every approximately eight to ten years. In the observation of fashion within a time system (epochs), fashion represents an aesthetic sign system, a style (cf. p. 178). Fashions of attitude or among groups, like that of the rockers or punks, are subject to relatively slight change, and for this reason the term *styles of attitude* is used. By contrast, the desire for change is more pronounced in those communities that see it as promising the most additional benefit (cf. p. 155).

The acceptance of fashion builds on the communicative message, for which a temporal process is required. This already means that fashion will always have a temporal dimension. Not only the fashion cycle of circa eight to ten years has accelerated during the last 200 years, but far more—alongside production—its *mediation,* that is the mediation of realisation from model to fashion and the mediation to a broader class of society. In the USA, legal agreement to make fashion shows simultaneously accessible on the Internet and so possible to download synchronously onto iPods was first reached in 2006: iPod-globalisation versus the clash of cultures? 'The revolutionary moment in America's fashion season occurred one hour after the fashion shows [in New York] . . . had finished. Karl Lagerfeld received an iPod with a video broadcast showing the slim, dark silhouettes of his entire show', Suzy Menkes reported in the *International Herald Tribune* (13 February 2006). 'I love the future—and the idea that this could not have happened only a few months ago', Karl Lagerfeld said in thanks; he had just presented his Lagerfeld collection for Autumn/Winter 2006 in New York. As to his fashion itself, Suzy Menkes regretfully established that it offered nothing new, but 'downloaded' everything that had been viewed as avant-garde fashion over the previous two decades.

As this example illustrates, innovations in the audiovisual and electronic media have altered our experience of time and space, but this acceleration and destruction of space have not yet altered the aesthetics of fashion. This is especially true of commercially exploitable fashion creations, and even in the experimental field, the change in aesthetics as a result of acceleration is still insufficient. Wearable electronics, clothes with alternating colours or colours that change with the onset of night-time, real-time projections on clothing, inflatables or other clothes that change their form are largely still perspectives for the future (cf. pp. 66–77, 122). The question is whether and how rituals and dressing behaviour have altered as a result of the electronic media due to their own temporality, or how much they will alter in the future (cf. p. 140).[27]

Temporal stress culminates in less fashion. Media philosopher Norbert Bolz expresses this clearly: 'The most important distinction in our future culture will be the one between those who have money but little time and those with plenty of time but little money.'[28] 'The pleasure that many women obviously experience when strolling around town is much less pronounced among men . . . Although these women obviously enjoy shopping and also wish sometimes that they had more time available for it . . . in 2004, the majority—no matter whether they had a little or a lot of time—spent a lot less time shopping than they did five years ago . . . our preferences have shifted; as well as saving money, now even those with plenty of time prefer other leisure activities to the shopping trip that demands consumerism and so spend their time e.g. together with friends or in sporting activities.'[29] The present impression is of a casualising and to a great extent a negation of fashionable extravagance (cf. p. 148).

In addition to this, an efficient time factor can be found in countries with seasonal differences. Here, spring is seen as a symbolic new beginning, which also influences the individual's longing to present a new self. (In past centuries, this new beginning was celebrated at length in the form of spring festivals with flower garlands and so forth.) This longing is intensified by the more public presentation of self in the spring/summer as opposed to the private sphere of wintertime. Winter clothing is understood as considerably more functional rather than as a means of attraction.

There remains the temporal relevance of the process of assertion that makes clothes into fashion (cf. p. 95): that of publicity and distribution, and the process of acceptance (cf. p. 97). No change in content in any way comparable to the innovations in the field of electronic media has developed in the print media over the last sixty years. Their online editions also mirror—more or less—the content of the print media, although there has been an obvious increase in information originating from the point of creativity as a consequence of online access to all the model photos or videos of all the collections by the leading designers each season. The fashion magazines themselves continue to appear every month, if not every quarter; fairs and fashion shows take place every six months. In production, 'just in time' and 'made by order' have been a matter of course for about twenty years, even though in mass fashion, so-called vertical providers mean rapid acceleration in both copying and creation, followed by an every-six-weeks rhythm of distribution.

The Temporal Dimension Prompts the Question: When Is Fashion Passé?

The answer to the question of when fashion is passé must be when a society has decided that it is so. Even in its transience, therefore, fashion is explained as an exclusively social perspective. After the end of a fashion that belongs to a form of societal life, fashion continues to exist in its cultural dimension: as an original (artefact) in museums, in photography and advertising, as documentation in fashion magazines and as a personal memory. It is evidence of the zeitgeist, way of life, aesthetics, taste, production and textile technology of an epoch. In this way, fashion continues to exist in different information levels and environments.

Space

Space constitutes a different concept in physics, astronomy, philosophy and the cultural sciences. Different notions of space and differing spatial concepts are also discussed in sociology.[30] In Niklas Luhmann's theory of social systems, the borders of society are not spatially defined and social systems (sport, religion) are not restricted to a territorial space. Luhmann regards forms of spatial differentiation in the modern, functionally differentiated society as 'traditional relics' (his own term). However, Luhmann does point to zones of exclusion in the functionally differentiated society, such as slum districts or favelas.[31]

The relevant aspect for an observation of fashion is that the quality of meaning—the 'how' an item of clothing is experienced—interrelates communicatively with the social environment or the socially defined space. For Georg Simmel, a border was already 'a sociological fact that crystallises in space'.[32] This assumption is also confirmed by the fact that subjectively, the resistance of physical space is decreasing—we are getting from A to B more quickly, and covering longer distances as well—but also because space is becoming irrelevant in the demand for interaction via the electronic media. Those actions that are tied to a physical presence uphold the relevance of a (container) space. Sociologist Markus Schroer points out the continuing importance today of one's own house, community centre, museum, sport stadium and so forth, to which a stabilisation of the system is accredited. This referential aspect is also important for clothes and fashion. Although intimate space is being made public by so-called container TV series, this process actually fulfils the social demand to become famous without previous achievement. The dissolution of delineated space is countered by a strong desire to preserve intimacy and personal space. More than ever, this leads—partially dependent on religion—to increased covering of the body or—partially dependent on society—to an increase in the demarcation of one's body by means of tattooing and piercing, in the sense of the skin as a border that one can design oneself. Additional spaces of one's own—clothing, territory, room—are created around the first space of one's own, the body. Schroer points to the fact that man constructs his environment according to the model or the idea of the physical body.[33] The way that communities decide on space and its immanent vestimentary code is indicated by a study of fashion in public, semipublic and private space (see below).

Fashion and Space

Fashion functions as fashion only in the environment for which it is determined, and this applies globally. This means that a bathing costume at the opera will not be perceived by visitors as fashionable or unfashionable but first and foremost as an incorrect or unsuitable garment. Objects are perceived in context with their surroundings and processed cognitively. Advertising exploits this insight in order to attract more attention, among other things via an unusual locational reference. A bathing costume will not—as long as society has not agreed on this—be accepted as fashion for the opera. Quite apart from the functional and moral components, the bathing costume lacks the added value that refers to the environment of the opera (referential aspect) such as elegance, festive quality or glamour . However, the contemporary, flexible society no longer upholds the vestimentary demands of space that nineteenth-century bourgeois society made, and that continued to have an effect into the 1950s: for example evening wear at the opera.

A further example demonstrates how closely the social expectancy regarding clothes is tied to space and activity, regardless of fashionable status. According to conventions, we expect the banker in the bank to appear in a white or certainly a neat shirt and wear a tie; the banker in the park in casual clothes; the customer in the bank in everyday clothing. As always, the choice of clothing is usually made according to the addressee, which can be a social group, an event (wedding or evening at the opera) or a location, or any combination of these. Space as a location and fashion are bracketed together in varying ways according to the attitudes and lifestyle of social groups (milieus), which are based on complex social, economic, cultural, political and technical factors.

A comparison between situations today and in the 1950s aims to clarify the demands made on fashion in public, semipublic and private space. (This case study relates to Central Europe and lays no claim to be a complex study of milieu.)

The public space of the Sunday walk in 'Sunday clothes', which was still a feature of leisure hours in the 1950s and offered the minor office worker as well as the skilled tradesman and labourer a demonstrative means of social and suggestive (in the sense of self-estimation) improvement, has been superseded by Sunday sport and an increase in types of sport facilitating the display (as well as the suggestion) of a fit body. (Both the fit body and fitness clothing make a social statement.)

Increase in Fashionable Sportswear

In addition, the Sunday walk has been replaced by the Saturday (now day-long) shopping trip. The latest outfit as the demonstration of insider knowledge proves culminating.

Increase in Brand-Name and Avant-Garde Fashion, but also
in Short-Term, Cheap High Fashion

There has been an increase in the urbanisation of young families and urban 'in' districts, a longer time-out from professional life and older mothers of the upper middle classes.

Increase in Brand-Name Fashion, but also in Short-Term,
More Reasonably Priced High Fashion

Everyday shopping; travel to place of work (not white-collar workers)

Increase in Padded Jackets, Anoraks, Comfortable Clothes

The semipublic space of parties and events (awards in all fields and nations, whereby the media celebrate themselves, and after [fashion] show parties) has clearly expanded and become public space, primarily as a result of the desired media presence (photo journalism, TV, Internet pages); fashion—red-carpet-dresses— is made for the sphere of glamour, in which the masses participate and of which they can dream while wearing jeans and T-shirt (comfortable clothes) via Internet or TV. Fashion is shown at parties and events, and since the circle of insiders there tends to remain the same, the fashionable outfit has to change.

Increase in Avant-Garde, Brand-Name Prêt-à-Porter
(Red-Carpet Dresses)

The semipublic space such as at the theatre, the opera and concerts that was once used to present elegant fashion has declined considerably in visitor frequency or for practicality (lack of time or inconvenience to change clothes), but also because of the questioning of culturally pretentious events' 'sacred' character (with the exception of premieres or festivals). It has been absorbed into private space or given a noncommittal character.

Increase in Daytime, All-Round Clothes

By contrast, pop events have increased greatly.

Increase in Jeans, T-Shirts, Comfortable Clothes

A visit to the cinema differs from a visit to the theatre inasmuch as there is no question of being seen during the promenading customary in the theatre interval. While there were breaks at the cinema in the 1950s, even with fashion shows, contemporary cinema has become a black box and thus an anonymous—that is, semiprivate—space. (This transformation is underlined by the interior decor and comfy chairs of modern cinemas.) As a result, comfortable domestic clothes can also be worn at the cinema.

Increase in Jeans, T-Shirts, Comfortable Clothes

By comparison to the 1950s, visits to a restaurant have increased in number, with business clothing defined for semipublic spaces.

Increase in Wearable Daytime, All-Round Clothing

The semipublic space of the workplace has expanded considerably as a result of women's now automatic professional activity. A specific category of women's fashion, so-called business fashion, has been added. Functional, conventional and nonetheless feminine was or is its credo. Meanwhile, men's fashion has experienced this change only as a fashionable variation of the suit with jacket, shirt and tie.

Increase in Daytime, All-Round Clothing

Semipublic space is a sphere of vestimentary uncertainty. There is an increase in its arbitrary or fashionless character, whereby there are no binding agreements (like the space of private parties).

Designer Fashion: 'Too Expensive, Not Necessary'

Private space is obviously increasing as a result of homeworking, home shopping and video on demand, but also due to existing unemployment. Free time and consumerism are going online; most time and attention are devoted to the media, and in younger households above all to the Internet.

*Increase in Jeans, T-Shirts, Comfortable Clothing from
No-Fashion (Clothes) to 'In' Sportswear Brands*

To a minor extent, private-space clothes become public clothes as a result of container-TV, although here 'fucked-up', sloppy clothing is staged as 'naturalness' (even going as far as Rousseau's demand for 'back to nature'—that is, to the 'jungle-container') and thus also as 'natural eroticism'.

Increase in Jeans, T-Shirts, Comfortable Clothing
not Representative

In terms of clothing, private parties (birthday parties) are oriented on social demands and age levels.

Variety of Possibilities: Cocktail Dress, Daytime Clothes
to Casual Clothing

Result:

Increase in jeans, T-shirts, anoraks, comfortable clothes: 5 occasions
Increase in wearable daytime, all-round clothing: 3 occasions
Increase in avant-garde, brand-name prêt-à-porter: 3 occasions
Increase in fashionable sportswear: 2 occasions
Increase in variety of possibilities: 1 occasion

Conclusion: Fashion requires publicity in order to function—that is, before clothes can become fashion. It requires publicity in order to convince others that it functions—as communication. Therefore it becomes possible to check the communicative function as personal experience, for which a suitable environment or a specific social network including blogs is necessary. The relative relaxation of the spatial order as a consequence of flexible life concepts brings flexibility but also unspecific evaluations into fashion. The resulting impression is one of a decrease in fashion as it has been understood previously in favour of functional or comfortable clothing, irrespective of a willingness to experiment among young people (cf. p. 160). At the same time, fashion includes its own mental and imaginative spaces, which are not perceived publicly. The more successful these spaces become, the more they differentiate themselves and create group fashions.

Global Fashion

In general awareness today, space is represented less as a local phenomenon and far more as a global one. Local space has grown in size while global space has shrunk; the 'world has become flat'.[34] Technical and economic developments have impacted on the order, units and delimitations of space; they are changing or dissolving them altogether.

Modern society and its definition of fashion are no longer hierarchically or segmentally differentiated, but functionally, poly-contexturally (a term coined by the German philosopher and logician Gotthard Günther) and heterarchically. The *either/or* has become an *and*. 'Our traditional concept of separate cultures . . . has become untenable. Wishful thinking may still cling to this notion of singular cultures, although they were probably founded on fiction from the start.' As philosopher and art historian Wolfgang Welsch demonstrates, this notion has become obsolete, 'whether due to the inner complexity of cultures or their external network . . . We are cultural hybrids'.[35]

The fact of the simultaneity of the global and the local was clarified for the first time by the *hippies* and their lifestyle and fashion, which had a primarily sociopolitical orientation, still apart from economic interests. A global dissemination of jeans and T-shirts and a resultant increase in vestimentary monotony was first registered in the 1970s. At the same time, however, jeans have been asserted as one of the most democratic items of clothing and almost as a world costume.

In the main, the *uniformity of the product* world is the outcome of economic interdependencies, for everyone wants and above all everyone can have—thanks to digital media and minimum production times—a piece of the big fashion cake. The more coordination there is with the mass trend, the further the market will open, or so the assumption. The fashion industry concentrates its aesthetic influence: the market becomes bigger, the fashion more monotonous. But this sameness must change quickly, a new look must be found; otherwise it becomes tedious. While the tedium was countered in the past by the diversity of clothing types (fashion, costumes, uniforms, servants' clothes), today it is overcome by constant repetition of the supposedly new. As approximately 55 per cent of people in the world today live in cities, clothing and costumes that are local, folk-near and suited to the national environment are gradually petering out, facilitating a global world fashion. By contrast to fashion before the First World War, which existed worldwide only in the upper classes, world fashions today exist in all classes; in the sense of 'one world, one look'—excluding the poorest of the poor, who are regrettably irrelevant as a human address. And so the customer within his or her global, functionally differentiated social group is reassured that he or she is not alone in his or her actions (in particular, this includes the armada of fashion journalists): a reason for the successful global marketing of brand names. While both luxury fashion and mass fashion have arrived in the retail areas of big cities and airport malls, individualised avant-garde fashion—due to its low marketing potentials—continues to exist in a niche. (Some Japanese agencies specialise in selling small European designer brands in Japan, which is why they are often represented more in Japan than in Europe.) And the creative teams in the world's established fashion houses and companies are international. The German sportswear producer Adidas proves that the concept of internationally successful fashion is based on global lifestyles (cf. p. 152) and intercultural design synergies. In addition to a German team, designers working for or in collaboration with Adidas include the British designer Stella McCartney, the US-rapper Missy Elliott and the Japanese designer Yohji Yamamoto.

Apart from this, the content of fashion presents a multicultural world without borders. Here, the Peruvian is combined with the Mongolian, African with Red Indian, or Alpine with Mexican. The foreign overlays or obscures one's own tradition, but it remains at a naive, folklorist level. Ethnic, cultural or social problems are kept at a distance. Ultimately, most creations by Gaultier or Galliano, and especially in mass fashion, are merely concerned with the outward appearance of being culturally different, for no one wants to wear another person's problems on his own body.

The tragedy of fashion is its combination of aesthetics and economic power. As Klaus Staeck (president of the Academy of the Arts in Berlin) wrote, 'Where the economic success criteria of globalised capitalism become a society's prime values, we are threatened with a new kind of totalisation.'[36] Is one of these new totalisations the uniform appearance of people around the globe? Nonetheless, national taste continues to establish differences: the Germans love different colours and patterns than do the Italians, and the English different ones than the French, and so on. Even within designer fashion, the image of fashion displays national characteristics: In Paris people accept glamorous avant-garde, Antwerp is well known for highly intelligent fashion design and London continues to be regarded as a crazy, unconventional fount of ideas.

The Global Lifestyle

One of the most enduring global networks—apart from the economic and the ecological—is on the social level of *sport and pop music*. 'For many people, sport has become a central, if not *the* central source of identification, meaning and satisfaction in their lives.'[37] This statement is so significant because sport spans national and international levels, and social and age groups, as well as the sexes, at least if we consider such different sports as soccer, step aerobics and golf. Beyond all pretension to fitness, this is connected—among other things—to the fact that today's way of life in Western-influenced society is defined less by traditions and more by the demand or wish for each person to constantly define him- or herself on the basis of mobile, multiple, self-reflective, alterable and innovative lifestyle requirements. 'Individualism creates a stimulating psychosocial climate, which simultaneously provokes and annihilates the sovereignty of the individual.'[38]

Logically, the global style of today's clothes is sporting and comfortable rather than elegant, eccentric or hyperfashionable. It consists of anoraks or padded down jackets instead of elegant coats, of jogging shoes instead of high heels, of jeans or camouflage cargo pants instead of narrow skirts or perfectly ironed trousers. These are items of clothing that—and we should take good note of this—became what they are—a global fashion—due to their social usability alone, without the initial influence of design and marketing.

So what is behind this? Cultural philosopher Peter Sloterdijk refers to 'continuing increases in influence and ability' as well as a 'spiralling increase in competence'.[39] Cultural sociologist Richard Sennett talks of the 'flexible person' as a 'culture of the new capitalism' (1998)[40]. The derived *culture of flexibility* leads to either a flexible but unreflected consumption of the new for the sake of the new, or to flexible values like sport (this includes not only active sport, but also sport betting and sport on the Internet) and pop culture. Or the flexible lifestyle leads to people dropping out of any kind of individual, differentiated fashion. Values of the bourgeois middle class, which are traditionally bound to the social and to language, like family occasions, but also educational bourgeois events, like theatre and opera (cf. p. 148), are forced onto the periphery. Religion and faith are being rediscovered as a stabilising value worldwide; however—at least with reference to the Christian church—this may certainly find creative expression as a sporting or pop event.

The valid *conclusion* is this: a priori, the poly-context of flexibility explains the modern and not globalisation, which is no more than 'a sociological fact that crystallises in space'[41].

In the functionally differentiated world society, managers, politicians and the like dress in a similar way. This is equally true of the adherents of subcultures and pop cultures—of hip hoppers, for example. Their appearance is more or less global, because they have created values of their own that are not characterised by traditions and conventions. Accordingly, a distinction must be made between global functional cultures, including subcultures, and local cultures—for example the Bavarians, the Austrians, and so forth, or even the more differentiated Milanese or Düsseldorfers. For the fashionable street image in Düsseldorf certainly differs from that in Milan and that in its turn from the one in London. This means that whatever is functional, subculture or local culture is discerned from the outside as such and terminologically defined so that a specific group can be identified as functional or subcultural and distinguished from the local mainstream. (The pillar of local culture is social consensus, to which political scientist Bassam Tibi gave the dubious term 'leading culture'.)

This explains the simultaneity of the global and the local: an iPod, jeans, padded jacket globalisation versus the clash of cultures and religions, as it were. The modern society and its definition of fashion are globally heterogeneous and locally hierarchic.

However, our traditional understanding of separate ethnic cultures has become untenable in Europe. We are cultural hybrids, which can already be deduced from the fact that the population of the German town Essen (with 583,000 inhabitants), for example, comprises people attributed to 140 different ethnic groups. However, this does not lead—or leads only to a very slight extent—to a truly individual diversity in fashion. On the contrary, it leads to polarisation, that is to international luxury-brand fashion at the high end and international mass fashion at the low end. That is not to say that both do not display variations. While both luxury brand fashion and mass fashion have arrived in the global networks, individualised designer and avant-garde fashion still exists in a niche, which may also be successful as such for some individual designers. The niche existence of this fashion mirrors the crisis of cultural identity among the middle class.

Equally, the global quality of luxury brand fashion and mass fashion corresponds completely with the contradictory demands on life of flexibility and adaptation. On the one hand, luxury brands like Prada, Burberry and Armani are able to do justice to this double demand, and on the other hand, so are brands of mass fashion like Zara and H&M, which can be acquired in big cities all around the globe. Taken together, the two aspects correspond to a definition of fashion; in other words:

Fashion is something about which a community or a group within society has reached agreement. *Fashion is a personal aesthetic perception in the collective.*

Historical Context

Fashion has always been global. It was always restricted less in a national than in a social way. The aristocratic families that dominated Europe politically also led the way in fashion.

Thus the high nobility of Europe dressed according to Spanish fashion in the second half of the sixteenth century and according to French Empire style around 1800 at the time of Napoleon; German Biedermeier fashion took hold of the aspiring European bourgeoisie in the nineteenth century, the French Parisian bustle in the 1880s asserted itself even as far as Japan, and Christian Dior's New Look conquered every world metropolis in the 1950s. Nevertheless, the appearance of the big cities was not monotonous, by any means; on the contrary, it was characterised not only by fashionable clothing but also by a wide range of costumes and colourful uniforms. This spatial expansion is expressed metaphorically as the *world of fashion,* that is, a world that exists *qua exclusio.* This world, like the worlds of art, politics and so on, is a self-referential system like all social systems (cf. p. 21). However, the number of those who can participate in the system of fashion is increasing. The introduction of ready-made fashionable clothes (as a result of improved cutting systems and the sewing machine) in the second half of the nineteenth century meant that more and more people, at least in the big cities, could afford fashion. But as a consequence, the appearance of people in cities began to become more and more similar.

Dressing according to the fashion of the class of society that sets the international tone has always brought social recognition along with it. And in fashion-dominant cultures, in which fashionable clothing variations evolved as social differentiation, the foreign was also a welcome means of distinction: such styles were known as orientalism, chinoiserie, exotism, japonism or Africanism. In addition, there were global materials of the greatest distinction such as silks and satins. Until into the twentieth century, the Western culture represented the leading universal image in the sense of Eurocentrism. The non-Western represented the completely other, which fascinated people from the aspect of tourism at most, but was actually shut out. This is no different today, when designers mix the Peruvian with the Mongolian, Moroccan with Indian, or Alpine with Mexican.

Meaning

Concepts of fashion are oriented primarily not on its utility *value* or value as a commodity, but on emotional and communicative values. The function of protection—whether as protection from heat, cold or nakedness—reduces fashion to clothes (cf. p. 17), which would be adequate in the form of a uniform grey sack with or without a warm fur lining, and could be the same for both sexes. Philosopher Thomas More portrayed this possibility in his work *Utopia* in 1516, and it proves to be a utopia indeed. It is the uniform grey jute sack without jewellery, make-up or hairstyling that is visionary and not the opulent, decorative or unwearable. Even Muslim women wear fashionable clothing and jewellery beneath the chador. Signs on the body give people a visual possibility of understanding. A sign brings about a social act and by this means triggers communication. They constitute a language of signs just like the language of words. Both are based on an intensification of our capacity for abstract thought, which is a precalculating thought of conceivability. But symbolic signs like an amulet or body painting are meaningful only when they are understood by others and are followed by subsequent acts of communication.

Regardless of whether it comprises up-to-date trademarks or prehistoric shell necklaces, the additional utility value of clothing is what a person will judge. People value not the material value of costumes, fashion and accessories but their symbolic function of aesthetics, eroticism, knowledge or power. Lifeless objects are given a symbolic value; in early history, a stick became a staff of office and finally a sceptre, a fur headdress with horns first characterised the priest and later survived as a crown. Attributes were given an emblematic character: various headdresses stood for power and status, gloves became representative of the right hand and thus symbols of honour and jurisdiction; the gauntlet is familiar in this context. But signs are subject to change. Today, a crocodile on a T-shirt provides information about the social value of the garment, and fashionable jeans signal an insider. In this way, people manipulate and communicate their appearance.

Image

Neurophysiologist Wolf Singer explains that man is a communicating and image-creating being: 'just as "he" communicates, "he" also gives himself a portrait, an *imago*'.[42] Clothing and fashion offer an image as a (deceptive) picture, almost as a dimension of mutation. This dimension of mutation can give the villain the appearance of a serious gentleman, just as it may facilitate a street worker's entry into the group that he aims to contact. The image is the external appearance that develops from an individual's abstract calculation, beneath which the wearer's true character may go unrecognised. For clothing is a language of signs like a verbal language. It is possible to use it in order to lie, to pretend something or to express the truth. But what is 'true'? A painting by Malevich can be areas, dots and lines of colour on a surface or an imaginary world of stars, if the viewer chooses to imagine it as such. A fashion can be a collection of textiles, individual parts sewn together or a dress belonging to Marilyn Monroe, if that is what the viewer wishes. Every individual decides alone how much of his or her personality is put into his or her clothes, so expressing his or her innermost being, or whether he or she uses fashion as a mask, as a conventional norm and habituation. Every adaptation to an ideal, including rejuvenation by dyeing one's hair or wearing make-up, is a way of making oneself unrecognisable; it is a matter of image. Every form of clothing can also be a mask; a pair of jeans and a white T-shirt in particular, because they are used to express nothing. They are pure anonymity, as simple as they are meaningless. The self-image of subcultural groups such as mods or punks is also dependent on their complete dress code.

If a well-known person (star, celebrity, sportsman or sportswoman) lends his or her image to a product, whether perfume or underwear, he or she allows it—the product—to become a part of him or her. The result is a transfer of aura from that person to the object. The leading personality becomes a leading product, according to variable bias like the portrait of the designer in the 1970s, the logo as a trademark in the 1980s, the supermodel in the 1990s and superstars since 2001.

The social construct of altering appearance provides an aid to orientation. By designing his body, a person projects or communicates his construct of self to the outside world, or he is observed from the outside in conjunction with this design and—according to the terminology of system theory—he thus becomes a human being, an addressor (cf. p. 156).

The additional function of fashion lies in a creation of *social identity,* which builds upon communication. Being addressed as a social addressee upholds the activity of the consciousness and the organism, for complete isolation leads to hallucinations.[43] Fashions, costumes and uniforms—as socially negotiated forms of clothing—make a person into a social addressor. In order to be addressed as a human being, socially negotiated body styling is necessary. The naked wild man or the witch are not human and are excluded. The naked baby, as it is not yet adult, has a special status; its appearance is usually created by others from the moment of birth so that it is integrated into society. The disabled, however, fluctuate between acceptance and rejection. Individual deviations like tramps, foreign workers and whores are outlawed, ridiculed or granted a special status by society, for example in the case of artists and/or geniuses. A person's picture (imago) must fit into society in order for him to be integrated. This is why a poor farmer in Somalia may paint shoes on his naked feet. Each person experiences his world as culturally preformed. The cultural meaning of clothing lies in other people's social positioning. Clothing is man's closest medium of communication in relation to his surroundings. Each person communicates a self by means of clothes, and others perceive him as an entity together with his clothing. Difference (the individual) is also established comparatively by means of observation or communication. This means that *individuality* must develop qua the inclusion and not qua the exclusion of clothing. Individuals' identities in modern society are defined more by career than by origin, that is more by a present and conceivable future than by the past. Consequently, the self is presented by means of fashion rather than ethnic costume, which is characterised by origins and tradition. Indeed, traditional costumes—in order to remain attractive, meaning up-to-date—are renewed or rather adapt by observing fashion.

The size of the radius of communication explains the mode of clothes' or fashion's social applicableness: limitation or free availability determines their social usability.

Since the 1920s, orientation has been provided by fashion, sport and youth magazines as well as cinema films; since the 1980s, by TV soaps like *Dallas, Denver, Sex and the City* and *Desperate Housewives* to an increasing extent as well, in addition to leading personalities such as Princess Di, Madonna or Shakira in recent years. In a fictive way, the media transform an improbable act of communication—teenagers with Shakira—into a fictively probable act of communication via the media and so call for imitation. A person who lends his or her image to a product is always irreplaceable. And there is no indication that the phenomenon of personality cult will disappear from our culture.

Imitation of such personalities' clothes makes those clothes into fashion. A communicative multiplication effect begins until it has taken hold of the masses, and only combinations and variations lead to an individual image; the pattern is not copied exactly with each imitation (cf. p. 160), but only the idea of the image. A personal creative effort is added; among other things, this also has an impact on the development of taste. People—young people in particular—try out a possible self via the imitation of an ideal, albeit it a temporary one. The result is the problematic, borderline situation between ideal and reality, which is simultaneously a strategy of fashion as the semblance of being. One's own creative styling is reduced to the freedom to combine fashionable items. In the face of today's unmanageable flood of mass-produced garments, the multiplier of combination extends into the infinite and represents the only remaining, inexhaustible means of supposed distinction. In this context, however, the paradox lies in the group-specific similarity of sampling; in other words, the combination is also indicative of gender- and group-specific forms and codes.

The increasing fragmentation of our lifestyle (temporary partners), the contingent nature of where we live and the discontinuity of our professional careers (practical work experience, vocational retraining) are all noticeable today, entirely in the spirit of Richard Sennett's 'flexible man' as a component of the 'culture of the New Capitalism'. Parallel to this, the composition of women's fashion has altered decisively over the last fifty years. Until into the 1960s, this was a *complet* comprising dress and jacket or a suit comprising jacket and skirt made of the same cloth. Since then, the fashion image has disintegrated gradually into individual items: skirt, jeans, blouse, tank top, separate pull-on sleeves, bolero, and blazer. The fragmentation of clothing began with the spread of leisure-time sporting activity around 1900, as a sign of a new body consciousness. Today the do-it-yourself, melting-pot style grants individuality without a person needing to become involved in the process of production or acquiring any knowledge about it. Fashion has become a convention, whereby the huge diversity of styles and garments offered overtaxes the observer. Our body image is continually brought up to date by means of numerous individual items including accessories, so that we remain real in social terms. Reality is actuality—in other words, the human being as an addressor is brought up to date continually, in order to be 'in' (reality)—that is within those fashionable boundaries secured by the majority of consumers. The human being's image or body styling represents the transition from the temporal fact of clothes to the imaginary fact of fashion.

Consciousness—Body

A wide range of philosophical and sociological theories view the human being as ambivalent or as the union of subject and object. The subject is understood as the basic consciousness, as the spirit or the soul, and the object is treated as the body. It is the object on which a subject concentrates his observing, sensually, empirically and practically changing activity. (This pays no regard to standpoints on the question of being, which even go as far as to abolish every ontological concept in Niklas Luhmann's theory of social systems; cf. pp. 21, 175.)

Friedrich Wilhelm Joseph Schelling (1775–1854) believed that the self-consciousness projects both itself and also, via unconscious production, the world of objects.[44] (This corresponds to neuroscientific insight into the brain's self-reference and its construction of reality; cf. p. 8) The *I as a subject* is identical to the *I as an object,* inasmuch as it makes itself into an object in the process of thought. That is, the *subject I* creates the *object I* by means of painting, clothes and the like.

The starting point of Karl Jaspers's (1883–1969) existential philosophy[45] is the ambivalent. He distinguishes between the *self-being* (existence), which constitutes the essential self, and the *being,* which is everything that belongs to a person outwardly; this is interchangeable and dependent on conditions that are not self-defined. These conditions may include the costumes and fashions into which a person is born. Jaspers believes we only become aware of our self-being (existence) in borderline situations like death, struggle, suffering or guilt when the simple being (the externals, author's note) becomes weak. In addition, Jaspers believes that man cannot realise his existence without the conditions of his being. Mere existence does not lead to self-realisation; there is a need for the other and in this context, great significance is attributed to communication.[46] This means that a human being cannot exist without the design of his body. To achieve personal self-realisation, man needs the alteration of his appearance, especially since this develops meaning as communication.

Helmuth Plessner (1892–1985) expanded on the *ambivalence of the subject–object* in his philosophical anthropology: 'Man comprehends himself—due to his reflexive relation to self—as a threefold aspect: as an objective body, as the self (soul) within the body, and as "I". As a consequence of the distance between man and his self, his life becomes an assignment that he is obliged to complete. First, he must make of himself what he is, and that is why he is naturally poled to and dependent on cultivation.'[47]

Georg Herbert Mead (1863–1931) represented the standpoint that spirit and identity develop only from situations of social interaction, via language. In his view, human identity is divided into two part aspects, the *I* and the *me* as its reflection. 'The "me" is the social self, and the "I" is a response to the "me"'.[48] The identity of a person is not directly connected to his actual physiological appearance, but his appearance is decisively important for the formation and development of identity.

Edmund Husserl (1859–1936) perceived *no subject* behind the subject. In his view, there is no pure subject and no pure object; rather, both are always connected by the act of becoming conscious (noesis), by which the object is constituted or rather conceived as meaningful content (noema).[49] The subject is embedded between his brain and society and reacts to conditions of stimulus. Free will expresses itself in a preconstructed social community.

In social philosophy Jürgen Habermas (born 1929) differentiates between *personal identity* as the unit of an unmistakeable life story and *social identity* as an individual's belonging to various reference groups.[50] Fashion gives to a persona the capacity to express precisely this ambivalence. Habermas refers to the ability to mediate between belonging and individual unmistakeability as the I-identity.

According to Niklas Luhmann (1927–1998) and his theory of social systems, the subject (like the world as such) is an illusion and emerges only through communication (cf. p. 22). *Sub-ject* (consciousness) and *ob-ject* (body) are a symbiosis, the unit of which is communication, that is the modus of operation. (This also means that the subject, as the illusion of communication, makes the Internet I, that is the avatar, permissible or conceivable as autarkic.) The body represents the unity of this diversity. The sensory attributes that refer to the body can be organised only in a social way.[51] For this reason, the body is also subject to social impositions and trimmed to acceptance[52], among other things by means of vestimentary overforming or tying up, but also by bodybuilding.

Where the body does not correspond to the ideals of a socially negotiated fashion, it is created artificially. The body subjugates itself to fashions and not the other way around. It is bound by a corset or tight jeans, overformed by a crinoline, or made taller using platform soles. Thus the body quasi lives in a fashion, causing it to bulge, surrendering an individual body odour to it and making fashion individual as a result. Observation of the body in psychology seems to reflect an analogous conclusion when sociologist Peter Fuchs writes: 'The consciousness does not live in the body; it is the body that lives in the consciousness . . . This body is a *socially designated* body and beyond this designation, it is nothing . . . For the body of the human being is an *observed* body.'[53] The observation of the body is dependent on the relevant system. The body is therefore observed differently in medicine or in sport than the way that it is viewed in fashion. Fashion observes the body as a designable, three-dimensional form or as a spatial figure. 'The technical and medical notion of progress is oriented towards freeing man from the bonds of his direct environment as well as liberating him from the inadequacies of his body. In Plato and later in German Idealism one encounters the celebration of the spirit to the cost of the body, the idea of pure, un-adulterated rational understanding which—liberated from the empirical body—can transform itself without effort and move from place to place without restrictions; an idea that is adopted once again in contemporary visions of cyberspace. It is a similar matter with regard to space: it appears exclusively as a dimension that should be overcome . . . In other words, in the modern age, space and body can be found on the list of threatened concepts.'[54] Second Skin, cyborgs, cyberbodies and avatars are suitable examples (cf. pp. 75, 125).

Individuation—Socialisation

Modifications of the body transform a person's natural appearance into a social one. The painted, hair-styled, decorated, clothed body is the social body. As early as 1759, the poet Edward Young noted: 'Born originals, how comes it to pass that we die copies?'[55] Clothes and fashion, just like social rituals and religious rites, make it clear that socialisation is stronger than individuation. Passing on traditions leads to an adaptation or preservation of people's appearance within a community. In this way, it is possible for traditional features to assert themselves despite individual disadvantages: for example when a code of honour demands that a guardsman wear a bearskin cap despite great heat or when social conventions (customary practice) demand the wearing of a tie, which has no practical, functional context whatsoever. This is possible because the society forgets why the man wears a tie.[56] Life praxis and conventions emerge as a result of such forgetfulness. Continuities are asserted via the dimension of stabilisation and/or evolution; that is, there must be sufficient cases in which continuity culminates in an evolutionary advantage. Wearing a tie in the Western world, for instance, probably brings the advantage of generating trust.

   In the phase of *adolescence* in particular, when for example clothes are no longer chosen by one's parents, a young person begins to construct a self-image. Neurosci-entists in the USA have ascertained that the brains of young people between the ages of approximately eleven and twenty-one experience a drastic surge of growth or re-organisation, precisely because a hormonal adjustment is also taking place. Up to the age of twenty-one, the brain—and especially the left-brain hemisphere, as that of the interpreter—is not yet fully developed and is thus more open to experiment without critical analysis, or rather without fixed, preformed opinions. As a consequence, it is more difficult for teenagers to judge situations and establish the correct behaviour than it is for adults or children.[57] While older people instinctively behave in a more rational way, since their brains have already been through this reorganisation and thanks to their experience, youths need to think for a longer time over a decision, or they react emotionally in the heat of the moment, in a way that is often fittingly called 'crackbrained'.[58] Young people consciously seek the presence of friends for their self-portrayal and react more emotionally in the presence of others than they do as individuals. This explains the striking group behaviour and demarcation among youths, which is expressed in a strong vestimentary need to imitate on the one hand and to wear extreme clothes on the other, in particular clothes that adults would be quite unwilling to wear. Wolfgang Welsch talks of 'identity in transition' and the 'social logic of deviation'.[59] In 1955, sociologist René König established that the most mobile of social groups, adolescents, is the group that is also most open to experiment and accessible to short-term and way-out fashions. This fact determined empirically by behavioural scientists and sociologists is confirmed by computer tomography and other technical experimental possibilities in brain research.

Every person is an individual *and* part of the whole—individual being and species. This duality is signalled—more or less, depending on individual need—by means of distinction *and* imitation in the styling of his or her external appearance. After the loss of an unambiguous expression of social roles in the shape of fashion, costume, civil (professional working clothes) and military uniforms as they once existed in the Western world, in some places even up until the First World War, the opportunity for individual self-realisation also followed along with social democratic freedom. (In countries like India, for example, where the social structure is characterised by the caste system, the sari remains widespread as a complexly differentiated national costume.) However, this opportunity—like all opportunities—may also be experienced as pressure to decide.

The individual self-image—individuality—evolves through observation of the self by comparison to others. Sociologist Elena Esposito further specifies this comparative observation of identity: 'The self that observes itself does not discover identity, but the provision, legitimised as such . . . for the fact that everyone differs from others and identifies himself with this difference.'[60] However, Elfriede Jelinek, author and winner of the Nobel Prize for Literature in 2004, sees beyond this observation of being different to the possibility of concealing or preserving her 'true' being. 'I concern myself with my clothes so that I don't have to concern myself with myself.'[61] Jelinek also asks herself whether she is obsessed with clothes that she likes so that no one else can follow her 'track'. 'Otherwise, I could wear what everyone wears, totally normal, then I would also be "invisible" in a certain way, but then there would be a danger that people would look at me . . . I do not dress to make people stare at me because I have acquired something so attractive ['unusual', author's addition] again, I dress in those clothes so that people look at them and not at me.'[62] Jelinek also wants her eccentric hairstyle (a high quiff) to make people take an interest in this hairstyle, but not in the author herself. The hairstyle, as frozen identity, almost turns into a mask. Jelinek wants people to concern themselves with her appearance but not with her true being, and in this way she consciously accepts or even promotes the cliché of the feminine (cf. p. 163) or the eccentric. By allowing the high quiff of hair to become part of her self—entirely in the spirit of Joseph Beuys's statement that 'Beuys is not Beuys without his hat'—Jelinek herself remains elusive, which leads to irritation among some observers.

However, when a person repeatedly alters his or her appearance completely, this irritates the process of observation, since it culminates in the complete failure or extreme difficulty of attributions and categorisation. Since the increasing industrialisation of the bourgeois nineteenth century (with a major revival of the status symbol clothing and accessories in the 1950s), always transforming oneself has become the privilege of women, for whom a frequent change of clothing is available. Irritation became a female matter, while the man radiated visual continuity and thus professional reliability with his unchanging suit. Later, the increase in women's employment led to women also adopting a clear dress image in the form of a skirt or trouser suit, rejecting embellishments and jewellery to a great extent.

Summary

These philosophical and sociological discussions clarify the unit of the referential dimensions *consciousness—body* and *individual—social*. This means that the human being perceives as an individual, even if his or her hairstyle, make-up or clothing follows an ideal type within the community or he or she wears mass fashion. Individuality can also be found in, or may be concealed behind, a uniform or a professional outfit as the expression of a social function. The individual understands himself or herself (or is observed) as a single being within an entirety. In turn, this overall constellation has a defining impact on one's individuality. This corresponds to the definition of fashion as a personal aesthetic perception in the collective.

Gender

In neurophysiology the binary difference between the sexes is confirmed as biological, whereas in gender studies it is questioned and asserted as a sociocultural construct. 'The differences between the sexes are much less cultural than the line taken by a women's movement oriented on androgyny would have us believe. Progress in brain research and biology has destroyed many an illusion.'[63] MIT biologist David Page, whose research focuses on the Y chromosome, notes: 'The genetic differences between men and women overshadow all other differences in the human genome.'[64] The Y chromosome is the key to masculinity: it triggers the production of androgens in the fetus. In the female fetus without the Y chromosome, the androgens are not activated. The environment, Page says, only intensifies or confirms what is already set out. One confirmation of this thesis seems to be the fact that there is not a single community and not a single ethnic group in the entire world whose members do not design their bodies in a sexually differentiated manner.

Gender studies examine the sociocultural intensification of sexual behaviour. The introduction of the (sociological) term *gender* by John Money in 1955 made it quite clear that there is a socially constructed sex. Since the 1990s, however, gender research by theorist Judith Butler[65] has radically questioned the duality of man and woman in terms of biological predisposition—the dual sexual identity—as well. 'Here, not only the socio-cultural, political and economic attributes of gender are regarded as constructs, but also what has been seen to date as a biological substrate, as physical sex.'[66] In her complex, continually expanded theory Judith Butler sees sex as an outcome of denotation (expressed in a simplified form) in the sense of realities that come about as a result of repeated naming. Sociologist Peter Fuchs also writes that it would be incorrect to assume that '[p]eople are born as people, as men or women. These are all actions of denotation with—as we can say today—serious structural consequences . . . The person is not "delineable" . . . nor is he/she the body . . . he/she is a multiple distribution of individually attributed behavioural restrictions, which has an impact in all directions whenever recourse is made to it . . . Here, in all directions signifies that the form "person"—at the moment of its operative use—transforms all persons in operative usage, whether in a confirming, condensing or destructive manner.'[67] This results in a field of reciprocal conditioning effects. Socially constructed gender and its problems can be registered only in context with other aspects like ethnic group, state form, milieu and religion in the past and the present. These are constituted differently in matriarchal and patriarchal societies, because the significance of masculinity and femininity is evaluated differently. To an equal extent, the evaluation and permissibility of the androgynous is dependent on the form of society. The physical attractiveness of the androgynous was first represented in the Western world by the *garçonne* in the 1920s, and in punk and gothic culture or exploitation as self-staging by pop stars since the 1970s. Today, the value perception of the sexes in the sense of a work–life balance model is discussed as politically correct.

Made in 1949, the statement by philosopher and writer Simone de Beauvoir that a woman is not born a woman but made into one presented an essential starting point for the theory of 'doing gender'.[68] This refers to the constant production of gender in (daily) activity and interpretation. Clothes and the complete styling of the body represent a tried and trusted means of 'doing gender', as well as sexually connoted gestures and body presentation. Fashion is the 'material power' that makes the sex publicly visible. Butler refers to the creation of reality through language or rather signs as materialisation. She understands this as the interlocking of forming discourse and matter. Such interlocking can be seen in fashion with the previously reached conclusion that fashion is form and medium (cf. p. 25). Fashion as a medium is imperceptible without communication; it is always constituted at the same time as communication. Now Butler sees power as being contained in the materialising impact of discourse (communication). In this constellation, it is my view that power can be transferred to fashion, which is also firmly established in the media as a body of order and rules together with its normalising effect and creation of conventions. (However, today the aesthetically normative body of rules applies less to gender and far more to the body's constitution—sporty, slim.) Body and gender are defined by fashion and this is defined in turn by communication. The activity lies in the communication, whether it is discursive, verbal or produced by social interaction. Judith Butler defines the constant production of gender as 'performativity', as enduring behaviour in which she includes sex, gender and desire (as the praxis and structure of sexual desire). The medium fashion also communicates desire. An interpretation of Butler's performativity led to links with performance and cross-dressing, drag and transvestism in the 1990s.[69]

The current normative assumption that women are more interested in fashion than men, that they need more clothes, change their clothes more often and enjoy going shopping should be relativised before the pertinent political and social background of man's and woman's social position in the relevant historical context. The following link between neurobiology and an interest in fashion may be regarded as a hypothetical assumption. Brain researchers explain sexually differentiated capabilities: networking between the two brain hemispheres is more pronounced in women; links within each hemisphere are stronger in men. The female brain communicates more quickly and is capable of creating cross-references faster, while men have a greater ability to imagine things in three dimensions. The fashion system has now emerged as an immaterial process of communication triggered by material clothing (cf. p. 133). One might therefore assume that the key to their greater interest in fashion lies in *women's more pronounced communication* by means of body styling.

Historical Context

The history of fashion is characterised by a strong polarisation between men's and women's fashion. In magazines as well, the sexual roles and relations between men and women have been and continue to be understood as a fundamental aspect of social order. The high points of this polarisation were the bourgeois nineteenth century and the 1930s and 1950s when, as Barbara Vinken put it fittingly, 'Her show displays his substance.'[70] Fashion and femininity thus became synonymous. Before the French Revolution, the differentiation *substance—show* took place on the level of social status and not (or less) on the level of sex; the show of the nobility documented the substance of the bourgeoisie. In the twentieth century, the punks and gothics have laid claim to show—largely on the level of the androgynous—and transformed it into the aesthetics of the ugly and dark.

Efforts were made in the various movements for women's emancipation to obliterate the sexual duality manifest in clothing. In the context of fashion history, this meant abandoning the corset as a compulsion to idealise the female body, cutting off women's long hair and adopting short male hairstyles, shortening floor-length hemlines and thus showing the legs, which had been covered because they were associated with the 'sinful womb' for centuries, as well as adopting male leg wear—men's trousers—suits with a jacket, and men's coats including the trench coat, and so forth. In this context, it should be borne in mind that the first pants worn by women—knickerbockers and pantaloons—were originally men's trousers (with the exception of bloomers), as yet with no adjustment to the female figure. All forms of leisure wear and comfortable clothing like jeans, T-shirt, anorak and jogging suit have represented more or less sexually matching clothing since the late 1960s (cf. p. 115).

While the subject of fashion was more than scorned in Germany during the early phase when women's studies became established in the 1970s—as academics wanted to be taken seriously and not reduce women to the topic of fashion yet again—there were fewer such reservations in the USA, or rather the potential of sexual differentiation on the basis of clothing was recognised and integrated into cultural studies. Behavioural science, which also discusses genders and cultures—and was shaped by the cultural sciences until into the 1970s —has been regarded as less opportune in recent years (one might also say: no longer in fashion). Much of what is being investigated, questions for which answers are either being found or not in today's gender studies and sociology, had emerged as the ambivalence between the culture and nature of man in behavioural science.

When Is Fashion Art?

The art is in the viewer.

Jeff Koons

When is Art?

Art defines itself—in a similar way to the question 'When is fashion?'—through the question 'When is art?'. In every epoch, art is defined through its recognition by the ruling secular and ecclesiastical class. The expansion of society's defining classes—politically, intellectually and culturally—means that the concept of art expands as well. This development includes a distinction between high, so-called free art, and low, so-called functional art. Marcel Duchamp, co-founder of conceptual art, offers an explanation of this: '[A] work is made *entirely* by those who look at it or read it and who make it survive by their accolades or even their condemnation.'¹ It is assumed that so-called free art, that is fine art in contrast to applied art, has no purpose whatsoever. Starting out from this assumption, one might come to the—false—conclusion that fashion is art when it has no purpose. However, the current understanding of art implies that any kind of artistic creativity—music, painting, theatre, literature—is bound to a purpose, whether this is to express something or to design it in a creative way, to take enjoyment from it, or to earn a living by it. The freedom of liberal arts, therefore, has become rather dubious, for it also serves a purpose such as representation, decoration or communication. By contrast, the freedom in discussion here lies in the vision and re-alisation of an imagined concept. 'Art is, because it is art, artificial and thus extremely unnatural'², Dariusz Szymanski wrote in his essay 'Why is great art often tedious?'

The fronts between art and design have been laid down firmly since the beginning of the twentieth century. In design, it is a matter of 'socio-politically relevant themes like the use of objects, the organisation of labour-sharing processes, the social and aesthetic consequences of industrialisation, innovative production techniques, the use of new materials, and economic thinking. By contrast, fine art could be viewed as separate from such profane issues . . . Art thus became a reserve for all those things that no longer had any place in the industrialised society; self-determined activity . . . mastery of craftsmanship, mythical ideas, self-reflection and a subjective view of the world.'³

Art always existed, before fashion entered the scene. Art and fashion are concurrent only when fashion approaches applied art and is recruited—like art—from ideas, emotions and experiments, regardless of its wearability or saleability. 'Art is always associated with impertinence . . . By contrast to "trivial" amusing art, "great art" does not appear to concern itself with the viewer.'[4] In the last decade of the twentieth century, elitist designer fashion like that of Viktor & Rolf resulted in an approach towards art, moving away from fashion's pretension to usefulness as a commodity. Even more so, the performative representation of clothing in the fashion show has produced a 'theatrical-artistic-vestimentary synthesis of the arts' like *Voss* by McQueen or the Autumn/Winter 2005/2006 show by John Galliano (cf. pp. 81, 171). Aside from this, however, the majority of models are still produced in the context of wearable design.

Historical Context

At one time, art only reported on and arranged fashion, for it was the task of many painters to portray the rulers of Europe, consolidating their power through a show of fashion, or to document the (vestimentary) characteristics of the common people. Quite frequently, artists like Albrecht Dürer or Lucas Cranach were also fashion advisors who drew fashion, or they designed fantastic costumes for theatrical festivals, as did Leonardo da Vinci. The influence of artist Jacques Louis David on the art, lifestyle and fashion of the Directoire and Empire was exceptional and quite extensive.

The first costume drawings as such concentrated on the representation of regional clothing, being almost the cartography of traditional costumes. First and foremost, they were patterns produced by artists for artists, enabling the reproduction of theatre costumes or authentic (suitable in terms of place, time and action) fashion for painting. It was not until the twentieth century that art became aware of clothing in a different way, and Marcel Duchamp had considerable influence on this development. With conceptualism and his Readymades, Duchamp laid the foundation stone for the use of industrially made products as and in artworks in 1916. Subsequently, other artists such as Giacomo Balla, Vassily Kandinsky, Salvador Dalí, Jean Cocteau, Meret Oppenheim, Joseph Beuys, Andy Warhol and Leigh Bowery took an interest in clothing, although less in its design and far more in the symbolic qualities of clothes as a fetish or a surrogate for, or representative of, the human being. They also made use of clothes and accessories in order to stage their own bodies. Duchamp himself created a clothing artwork for the first time in 1958, at a time when he had already been overtaken by Pop Art. This was a striped men's waistcoat hung on a coat hanger, entitled *Gilet pour Benjamin Péret*. Clothing as a myth—like Nike Air Jordan training shoes—is the theme pursued by Canadian artist Brian Jungen, who transforms the sneakers into Red Indian totems and calls them *Prototypes for New Understanding* (1998–2005).

Context Fashion and Art

It is possible for clothing to become a vestimentary work of art only in *art,* but not in design. Artists like Cindy Sherman, Erwin Wurm and Sigmar Polke adapt the illusory world of fashion in art in order to unmask or ridicule it. Cindy Sherman and Erwin Wurm take dress models by designers, some famous, and place them in different—unusual—contexts. In this way, they undermine in art the criteria that have been created in fashion. Vestimentary works of art like Joseph Beuys's *Felt Suit,* the *Aphrodisiac Smoking Jacket* by Salvador Dalí or the dress sculptures *Dresses* by Wiebke Siem have not been created for the human body. But clothing as applied art is bound to the human body, although it does not necessarily correspond to the notions of clothing as everyday culture. It may also go a step further than this, by means of its concept (Hussein Chalayan's *Afterwords,* 2000/2001; Vivienne Westwood's *Five Centuries Ago*), its overforming or deforming of the body (Rei Kawakubo's *Body Meets Dress*), or its material (Alexander McQueen's *Voss,* Spring/Summer 2001).

Differentiation of the systems of art and fashion is a matter of the context of observation: the designer progresses from the commodity—clothes with their claim to wearability—to art, whereas the fine artist penetrates the world of commodities and transposes the functional object into art (cf. Duchamp). However, one shared aspect of art and fashion is that both create an artificial image of the human being; in addition, clothing represents an extension of the self. In this respect, the new digitalised media (e.g. World Wide Web) differ from the old media such as painting or performance art only inasmuch as their technique is different. Art and clothing alike construct and manipulate the image of the body. This fact is perceived especially when clothing greatly alters the body proportions or deviates considerably from conventions. The image of the body is always the designed body. It displays not nature, but culture. Thus Theodor W. Adorno did not see fashion and art as two irreconcilable rivals but pointed out their close and sometimes beneficial connection.[5]

It was down to art, especially to the body and performance art of the 1960s, that the body was invalidated as a guarantee of authenticity. These trends made clear that the body had always been constructed and manipulated by culture or the media as well. Performances like the *Skinnings* by Victorine Müller, Rebecca Horn's prosthetic extensions of the senses in the shape of flexible shoulder rods, or Vanessa Beecroft's *Displays* of body and skin provide up-to-date examples. Jana Sterbak's *Vanitas, Flesh Dress for an Albino Anorectic* (1987) represents a high point of this art trend to date. She sent a model onto the catwalk wearing a dress made of sixty pounds of hanging raw, bloody and fat-lined beef. This evoked skinned bodies or those anatomical studies from the Renaissance in which one part of the body is intact and dressed, the other half skinned and anatomically dissected. However, Sterbak is not concerned with a perverse aestheticising of anatomy, which permits the texture and pattern of the meat to overturn into a splendid fabric and bold dress pattern at first glance. The attraction of all flesh is the brief formula for vulgar sexual attraction. A woman who is anorectic herself, that is completely without flesh, is literally hung with beef. The colourlessness of the anorectic albino matches the blood-red of the meat with which she is hung.

Additionally, artists and fashion designers attempt to visualise the relation body-space-motion. Both Oskar Schlemmer in his *Triadic Ballet* and Jana Sterbak with her *Remote Control* hoop skirt models (1989) made attempts to do this. In *The Dress . . . I Want You to Feel the Way I Do* (1984/1985), Sterbak presented a dress made of barbed wire and fitted with light filaments in the bodice, which began to glow when the visitor approached. This reaction appears to say 'don't touch me—*noli me tangere*—before you have made an effort to find out how I am feeling'. Here, clothing is shown together with its contradiction between semitransparency and armour, between the (erotic) means of attraction and rejection.

In a similar way, in *Before Minus Now* (2000) Hussein Chalayan portrays the human being as a being defined on the one hand by physical-biological laws and on the other by the mathematical-geometric laws of space. If those laws are obeyed, the aesthetics of the body and the dress thus constructed emerge automatically—in accordance with Albert Einstein's understanding of aesthetics as the necessary result of a correctly solved mathematical problem.

The context crossing of fashion and fine art does not express a desire for fashion to become art; instead, vestimentary design discerns possibilities in art such as freedom, diversity, vision, imagination, pluralism; possibilities that are a matter of course only in the art context. Few other works play more obviously—simultaneously mocking and revealing—with context crossing between art and fashion than *The Immortal Tailor,* a cycle by Alba d'Urbano (cf. p. 53). In addition to this, art in particular is predestined to school our perception.

Fashion as Applied Art

> Fashion is an inspiration, a craft, a technical know-how and not, in our opinion, an art form.
>
> Martin Margiela

A disqualification of applied art on the grounds of its (apparently) immediate usability seems illogical or even absurd. 'Unease over the prejudice often cultivated in the art world that every art that requires a form of reception involving action is discredited as "applied" suggests that it would be a good idea to look more closely at the concept of application . . . For only through application can aesthetic potential . . . be transposed into cultural processes so that its social function and individual value—i.e. significance may be realised.'[6] As already indicated, both fine art and the applied arts have the character of a commodity (cf. p. 167).

Neither haute couture nor prêt-à-porter fashion should be defined a priori as applied art. Haute couture represents the highest form of craftsmanship, in the sense of the artisan, while prêt-à-porter signifies an industrialised version of haute couture, a 'ready-to-wear haute couture' (cf. p. 175). Haute couture is characterised by processing at the highest level of craftsmanship and genuine, tasteful materials. As such, it may be a luxury, but not necessarily art.

Clothing as applied art must become free of the demand for application—that is, from its wearability in a social context. It must expand or even explode the utilitarian language of forms of fashion as a commodity, as is the case with some creations by John Galliano, Alexander McQueen and Viktor & Rolf. That is not to say that its models, no matter how unconventional they are, cannot be worn or that the designer creates them as unwearable from the outset. When no artistic demand is made of fashion, our visual language becomes impoverished to the lowest common denominator—which is the cheapest, most efficient and most functional. The formal language dictated by utility is reduced, but the language of art is opposite to this, because it permits a vocabulary not bound by purpose and consequently permits freedom; it enjoys the free space to invent forms with the potential to stimulate our fantasies and dreams. 'Free design' should represent a challenge, so to speak, to a reality that is oriented on function and purpose. It is an illusion to believe that John Galliano's *Mapping the World* collection (cf. p. 110) or Viktor & Rolf's dresses with their orgies of bows and flounces or bells (cf. pp. 47, 70) ever had any pretension to be worn. The latter display more of a theatrical pretension: they are dresses that pay no account to the demands of everyday life and, apart from their impact as advertising and to attract attention, they lack purpose to the extent that art also claims for itself.

Therefore fashion is applied art when clothes are not designed as a commodity but make an artistic-ideological claim or this claim is incorporated into the object 'clothing' to a dominant degree. As a result, overlaps between the different systems of art and fashion will come about. These crossovers, art crossings (cf. p. 108) or hybrids may be evaluated as applied art and, like designer fashion, as a separate category. Not least, this insight should help to prevent such unsuitable criteria of judgement as 'who is going to wear that', or 'it's all just crazy fantasies', and the like.

When Is Fashion Design?

When Is Design?

An object is not a design object as such; it becomes one as a consequence of the pretension with which the object is used. This pretension is based on a social component. A functional object such as a car tyre may become design when adapted into a table, from which the question emerges: When is design? The car tyre is design when it is recognised and declared as such, and thus becomes socially relevant. With reference to the alienation of objects in design, for example a bucket painted in bright colours becoming a vase for flowers; Uta Brandes and Michael Erlhoff coined the phrase 'non intentional design'. The statement 'When is design?' is then dependent on definition and the surrounding context, in a similar way to Marcel Duchamp's *Urinoir* (cf. p. 11). The statement implicates an aesthetic and semiotic problem. The same artefacts may also exist in different cultures but with different symbolism in each case.

Pretension also determines whether something is a design object—ranging from a unique object to a limited series—or a mass-produced functional object. The design object is not produced contingently, like an artwork for example, but for a specific purpose, that is it is intended to satisfy complex needs and demands. In this way, the design object appears purpose oriented, although the purpose does not necessarily have to be a practical use. A vase can be designed and valued more as a formal aesthetic object than for its function: function and emotion are united. The claim to a relation of form and usage defines design or respectively designer fashion; that is it is defined by means of its own nature. Design must explore the nature—quasi the genetic code—of an anticipated object (e.g. a chair or a dress). Design is created not arbitrarily and not according to a pattern but is constructed with intention. Design must speak for the product and lend it an unmistakable quality. Aristotle invented the concept of *causa finalis*, the planned purpose being the ultimate cause of an action realised. Accordingly, design is essentially dependent on whatever is modified with each new object (chair/dress); each new chair communicates a different way of sitting, each new dress a different corporeal feeling. The quality of design is measured by aesthetic, functional and communicative criteria.

The demands made on a chair to provide a place to sit and on a dress to provide something to wear are timeless, as opposed to those made with respect to their form, material, colour or pattern. While the practical functions refer rather to the physical qualities of functional objects—scissors should cut well—the formal-aesthetic functions refer to purely aesthetic orders. Design is the sum of the functional object and the work of art, of functional aesthetics and artistic expression. We talk of *good* design only when the proportions are right. 'Design is the aspect of art within commerce or industry.'[1] Postmodernism exercises considerable influence on this definition, as the following example shows. One of the best-known design products is the one-piece, rocket-shaped, chrome lemon squeezer *Juicy Salif* (1990) by star designer Philippe Starck, which advanced to become a cult object. Nevertheless, this object is controversial, as its qualities as a lemon squeezer are not entirely satisfactory. The three-legged object topples over easily, the pointed feet can cause holes in a surface and there is no sieve to catch the pips. One can assume that Starck's lemon squeezer is neither a useful object nor an art object but merely an object of prestige (especially as the manufacturer Alessi also offers a version of the lemon squeezer in pure gold). Such design integrates something that lacks attraction into the economy of desire and turns it into luxury; it is a form of advertising for the object and the symbol of a special (emotional) quality.

Every type of design and every kind of acceptance is dependent on subjective viewpoints and interpretations. The basketware of a specific ethnic group belongs in a museum of ethnology as an ethnic symbol; the same basket can also be displayed in a design museum as a functional aesthetic example. Accordingly, 'When is design?' is a social question implicating a social answer.

The designer works with and on the iconic layers of consciousness. He is a creator of the meaning of material and at the same time he bends this material into a form of purpose that exists only as a potential in its nature. His artistic intervention makes the functional article into a design object. The designer experiments, realises the imagined object in drawings or as a prototype and provides technical drawings or instructions for industrial production, but he does not necessarily realise his designs personally up to the point when they are ready for the market; this is in contrast to the craftsman, who hand-produces unique objects himself.

Design is one of several possibilities of form in which something can be created. In design we have also arrived at a pluralism of styles, ranging from neo-objectivism to the biomorphic, to the postmodern, lavish baroque, from hard-edge design to organic design, and to soft design. Design is the '*language of forms as a reflection of the soul of an epoch*'[2]. Form may have a classic component because it is timelessly valid, but it can also mirror a current—modern—aesthetic feeling. The classic design idea permits the form to develop from the sequence of function, to develop its pure, logical form from within the mechanism, like Dieter Rams's designs for Braun. The form may also be autonomous and overform the inner workings of the machine, like the tail-fin bodywork of American cars (road cruisers) in the 1950s. The inventor of tail fins, Harley Earl, oriented his work on the form of an aeroplane and referred to the bodywork as a visible symbol of prestige, a mirror of the soul of that epoch. The social task of design today—that of fashion design as well—consists of making things comprehensible as a reflection of their usage and constructing them according to the standards of ergonomics or pleasure in wearing, so ensuring they are easily available to the user. However, this signals the onset of user aesthetics. Ecological demands and electronic innovations are concealed by nostalgic forms (see car design), prompting the negative conclusion and question 'Is design experiencing a crisis?'. In a similar way, conventional external design conceals the high-tech internal workings of wearables (cf. p. 122).

Today, our notions of design are still shaped largely by the idea that design means luxury and/or intellectual pretensions. (Conversely, design is also misused to justify the unusual or the expensive.) In recent years, this notion has also been put to conscious use by the mass market in order to offer reasonably priced variations based on the formal examples of successful high-priced products. In low design, the primary intention of the formal language of high design brought down to the popular level is fun, which often leads to it being turned into kitsch. By copying the formal repertoire of style-creating high design, design has slipped out of its elitist, pioneering role and is working hard at democratising consumerism from below. The dictate of quality is becoming secondary, as the demands for longevity or timelessness are evaded. To this extent, H&M works with fashion design and is nonetheless concerned with mass products, for the ultimate aim is the ritual of purchase. This ritual of clothing oneself anew, that is of reinvestination (from the Latin *vestire,* to dress), incorporates a cathartic moment of constantly-renewing-oneself and feeling-better, quasi as a therapeutic effect.[3] In addition, a supposedly or actually disadvantaged social milieu in particular will define itself as part of society through the act of being able to purchase—revaluated by milieu-defined brands or design.

Design continues to represent a piece of luxury—but it is becoming available to more and more people. It does not mean an acquisition for life; nowadays it is the expression of a temporary feeling for life. It becomes synonymous with a specific trend while retaining the side effect of being special. Primarily, misused design maintains the current quality of an offer and seeks to arouse desires; its intention is to feed the illusion of permanent freshness and innovation. In our everyday life we are surrounded by things/products/symbols that have a fixed place in the order of normality, that is they have a firmly defined name and a secure function. The standardised, recognisable quality of such things makes them continually reusable; they may also be thrown away after use. They fluctuate continually between a state of usefulness and garbage.

Clothing—From Handicrafts to Design Product

Until into the nineteenth century, clothing was classified as a handicraft product made by tailors, seamstresses, embroiderers, ribbon weavers, trimmers and so forth, quite apart from the weavers, dyers and fabric printers (cf. p. 19). The customer and the tailor shared their ideas about the appearance of clothing—in other words, they inspired each other. The initiation of haute couture by Charles Frederick Worth around 1860 added an entirely new constellation: the couturier as an autonomous provider of ideas and a creative designer, that is the designer of a product who is not necessarily (there are exceptions) capable of tailoring or sewing it. Designers and producers were no longer by any means identical. The handicraft and the purely intellectual or creative work diverged (more or less), although one cannot exist without the other. In haute couture, the place of the exclusive value of handicraft ability was taken by the sometimes much greater appreciation of idea and design. Under the auspices of the—famous—haute couturier, who provided ideas, the best craftsmen/women realise the 'best tailoring art'.[4] The creative, dictatorial or even divine pretension of the fashion creator existed until well into the 1950s, in the case of Christian Dior and Cristóbal Balenciaga, among others.

In the 1960s, there was a second important change or rather extension to the system. Alongside haute couture, the less-exclusive prêt-à-porter was established as 'ready-to-wear haute couture'. In 1965, the first 'Salon du Prêt-à-Porter' was held in Paris, and in 1973 the 'Chambre Syndicale du Prêt-à-porter des Couturiers et Créateurs de Mode' was established, responsible solely for prêt-à-porter fashion. The designer emerged as competition to the haute couturier, who worked more or less autonomously together with a team of craftsmen. The designer entrusts his ideas and designs—under his or her name and sometimes under his or her personal patent of taste—to semi-industrial production and global marketing.

Richard Sennett makes the following comparison in relation to craftsmen and designers: 'Craftsmanship', in other words 'the autonomous activity that derives meaning from within itself can be viewed as counter practice for the fluttered, flexible human being who is caught in incomprehensible, externally-determined references'.[5] Sennett's sociological leitmotif is that today it is no longer a matter of skills learnt, but of a permanent adaptation process. According to Sennett, this is the task of the designer working for industry. Sennett talks of the 'ideology of potency' in today's working world, which requires no content but demands a force radiating outwards. 'Which is why people have lost the ability to become involved in activities—like tailoring and sewing [author's note]—in a truly lasting manner', or so Sennett believes.[6] However, the quality of a design does not lie in its craftsmanship (not given), but far more in its aesthetics, functional and usable value, form, emotion and communication. These (new) emphases of valuation are overtaking haute couture, or rather they are the factors to which it must adapt to today if it wishes to survive. Haute couture can assert itself no longer because it is the highest art of tailoring, but because it is luxury design. Craftsmanship is distancing itself from the product or vice versa, until the marketing of a brand and its efficient and rapid communication become the essentials remaining.

Remember—the designer designs not fashion but clothes, which are credited with the attribute *fashion* or accepted as such as a result of communicative observation.

The definition and answer to the question 'When is fashion?' (as with 'When is art?' and 'When is design?') is given by the viewer. Fashion is an object of the second order—that is it is defined by observation and not through the object itself; it is the clothes that are the object of the first order (cf. p. 27). The generative moment lies in the creative design and the key factor of something new.

Customary since the 1970s, the division into haute couture, prêt-à-porter, custom tailoring, luxury ready-made fashion, ready-made fashion and mass fashion has been retained to the present day, but the structures have become more complex, especially those of prêt-à-porter. Prêt-à-porter has developed into the fashion of the luxury companies, and the chief designers they employ (author design) are more—like Karl Lagerfeld for Chanel—or less—like Christopher Bailey for Burberry—well known and granted more or less creative freedom. So-called designer fashion has been established as a separate category. It is—with exceptions—the fashion in which the name of the label and that of the designer are identical (e.g. in the case of Jean-Paul Gaultier). To a large extent, designer fashion is creative and individual, sometimes even avant-garde. In addition, national style characteristics (influenced by the lifestyle and taste of the local clientele) are certainly evident, as is demonstrated by the fashion shows in New York (wearable), Milan (sexy), Paris (avant-garde) and London (crazy). It is only as a result of so-called breaking down or rather via the introduction of ready-made fashions that the much-cited uniform global look emerges. Companies like Kookai, Zara and Mango as well as Hennes & Mauritz—all based outside the designer strongholds of Paris, London, Milan, Antwerp—have made design into a matter of course for cheap labels (mass goods). In addition, recognised designers have always made collections for department stores and mail-order companies and for mass, ready-made fashion: Heinz Oestergaard for Quelle, Pierre Cardin for Printemps, Yves Saint Laurent for C&A, Karl Lagerfeld for Steilmann and Hennes & Mauritz, Stella McCartney, Viktor & Rolf, Roberto Cavalli and Rei Kawakubo for H&M, among others.

Designer fashion is developing enormous diversity, in terms of style and—increasingly—with respect to age. The styles of the international designers provide classics and opulence, purism and deconstructivism, luxury and provocation, the romantic and the daring, the historical and the futuristic, the strange and the familiar (cf. p. 38). Designer fashion is subject only marginally to the pull of demand on the part of the consumer, but more so to an economy push on the part of company management or to a technology push on the part of innovative textiles, which do not necessarily result in a new aesthetic image, however (cf. p. 122). Due to its extremes, fashion has been ailing since the end of the 20th twentieth century: the near spectacle of designer fashion on the one hand and a culturally impoverished mass fashion on the other. In our time, fashion is disintegrating into an over-individualised haute couture and a partially characterless trademark fashion. John Galliano stands for elite fashion and an artificial, narcissistic fashion language, while companies like Benetton, Nike, Adidas and their consorts set their sights on fashion that is suitable for the everyday and a large middle class. Productive overlaps and penetrations occur only in a minority of cases, for example in the collaboration between Yohji Yamamoto and Adidas.

Pluralism of Styles

Since the 1960s, individual aesthetic concepts have been offered parallel to one another more and more, in both art and design. In fashion, pluralism and sampling have led to the mistaken opinion that anything goes, and also to the false assumption of 'the end of fashion'. Instead, it would be true to say that today's fragmentation of clothing calls for a new communicative definition of fashion (cf. p. 134). The fragmentation of styles and the polemics of theory also led to talk of the 'end of art' in the sense of a new evaluation in art theory. Here, consideration centres on the end of a tradition, in which artists had been involved in a form of artistic production defined by progress and innovation. Art theorist Arthur Danto points to the '[e]nd of an art described as Modernism, which expresses itself now only in cyclic repetitions . . . and the search for its identity'[7]. Parallels can be drawn to fashion with respect to this statement; they show that revivals and retros—sometimes cited as a lack of ideas among the designers—do not apply to fashion alone. They represent a general cultural disposition and furnish retro content and forms as eclecticism and also as abstraction in art and design (e.g. in car design). However, the purely memorial culture is a form of impotence.

The new evaluation of art history demanded by theorists including Hans Belting, Arthur Danto and Heinrich Klotz is equally applicable to fashion history. The twentieth century left behind the notion of a series of epochs, providing basic motifs that cross epochs—for example minimalism and abstraction versus ornamentation and romanticism—and changing, temporary styles subordinate to them. When stylistic terms, attribution and delimitations are undertaken in the following, this therefore serves as an aid to understanding, but makes no claim to exclusive definition. Like the categorisation of artists and designers, the respective definition of styles is never absolutely unambiguous, in either art or fashion.

The styles presented here for discussion in the fashion context have become fixed terms in architecture and interior design primarily: classicism, modernism, postmodernism, constructivism, deconstructivism, purism and minimalism, neo-modernism and post-postmodernism. They refer to artistic tendencies or styles (from the autopoiesis of art) and not trends, which are a symbolically generalised medium of communication. These styles exist alongside rather than after one another, although often the subliminal question arises as to which of these styles is 'more modern'. While the avant-garde tendencies in the first half of the twentieth century followed a primarily linear sequence—futurism, constructivism, surrealism—this has given way to a simultaneity of styles in both art and fashion. However, the traditional retention of stylistic features and categories is seen as partially responsible for the current discussion on the lack of style displayed by fashion, or rather the wearer. This is one reason that, amidst the courting of attention in today's supermarket of (fashion) styles, shock and provocation (cf. p. 38) have a good chance as well as strategic details. The art historian Heinrich Klotz saw (unwanted) stylistic pluralism as a necessary consequence of the new, noncommitted nature of explanatory references; the many -isms (including surrealism) almost as a referential pluralism and a 'collection of labels' of classical modernism.[8]

Modernism

Modernism is contradictory in itself and neither clearly defined nor a self-contained, completed epoch.[9] It can be attributed to the whole of the twentieth century (taking into account certain precursors) and should be defined separately as a political-historical epoch and a style of art. In art, modernism reveals a striving for innovation and progress, a fundamental position critical of consciousness, with contempt for the symbolic and traditional, and an abstracting reduction. As 'classical modernism'[10] or the 'historical avant-garde',[11] it is understood as a heterogeneous style seen as trailblazing at the start of the twentieth century. In contrast to classical modernism, the often so-called second modernism since the end of the twentieth century admits a broader understanding of content.

Modernism sought justification from within and not from the past; in other words, it was equipped with the will to forget or rather to separate itself from the past in order to arrive at the new as a breach with what had gone before. All its efforts were concentrated in a will to innovation quite independent of history. Modernism signified 'conceiving the future by starting out from today . . . Finding orientation in itself alone'.[12] This attitude was also expressed in the fashion of the 1920s and in the lifestyle of that time. The body negation (abstraction) of the sack dress, but also the emphasis on (naked) arms and legs underlined or rather triggered a previously unknown perception of the body, eroticism and movement. The three-part men's suit with a sacklike (because there is no waist seam) jacket (German *Sakko* from the Latin *sacco,* sack) has developed into a gender-crossing, ascetic ideal and a paradigm of modernism.

The Austrian architect and theorist Adolf Loos is considered an important precursor to modernism in architecture and design and its corresponding programme of 'form follows function'. His pronounced rejection of ornament is connected with concentration on an occidental culture and independence. Loos's best-known contribution is the polemic pamphlet *Ornament and Crime* (a lecture given in 1908). In this, he argues that functionality and the absence of ornament represent an economy of human effort in the sense of superfluous baubles, and a sign of more advanced cultural development. He classed the need to decorate walls, the skin and useful objects as the lowest stage of cultural development: permissible for cave dwellers at best. Any ornament that decorates the human body, the body of a building or utility objects, according to Loos, is therefore a reliable indication of criminal energy, childish affectations, sexual licentiousness and excessive hedonism. To Loos's way of thinking, self-control has male connotations; he situates the female on the level of the unconscious, libidinal and erotic. Various discourses on the female and the primitive entered into the interpretation of ornament and the concept of modern art and architecture. In addition, Loos and Hermann Muthesius saw a 'betrayal' of craftsmanship in mechanically produced decor.

However, the assumption that modernism survived without ornament is a myth. The concept 'form follows function' is part of a famous statement by the American architect and prime representative of the Chicago School, Louis Sullivan, one of the first great architects of high-rise buildings, the facades of which—particularly the window fronts—were covered with ornaments. The quotation 'form follows function' from Sullivan's article 'The Tall Office Building Artistically Considered' in *Lippincott's Magazine* from 1896 was taken out of context and therefore misinterpreted. On the contrary, according to Sullivan's logic decor is also a functional element, such as in the case of representative buildings, and thus permissible and possibly even called for. There is a parallel in the Reform Dress, which despite all its apparent functionality certainly permitted decoration with art nouveau ornament. The principle 'form follows function' was realised consistently in the Bauhaus but was supported by geometric patterns. Form ought to be derived from its function, its aim and purpose; afterwards, a function could also be derived, vice versa, from the form. In modernism, not only an aesthetic but also an economic principle entered design.

In painting, the key means of modernism was abstraction,[13] which led to the 'abolition of the work of art'[14] and the pure field of colour.

Fashion and Modernism

At the outset of modernism in fashion, the influential trends were Italian futurism, Russian constructivism and the German Bauhaus (although no clothing was designed there, a well-regarded class of weaving did exist[15]).

Technology and progress, and thus the beauty and noise of the machine, were exalted in the programme of *futurism,* which was founded in Italy. On 20 February 1909, the Italian jurist and poet Filippo Tommaso Marinetti published his first futurist manifesto in the French newspaper *Le Figaro,* so initiating the futurist movement. In relation to clothes, Giacomo Balla summed up the programme in the manifesto *Il vestito antineutrale, Manifesto futurista* (Milan, 11 September 1914). Its focus was on the discussion concerning men's fashion. Artists of Italian futurism such as Giacomo Balla, Tullio Crali, Fortunato Depero and Ernesto Thayaht designed colourfully spectacular men's clothes that caused a considerable sensation. They themselves wore these suits and waistcoats with bold colours and patterns, which were intended to mirror the vibrant diffraction of colours and light, as well as carried accessories with an asymmetric design. An especially provocative impact was made by their 'anti-ties' made of aluminium and their metal shirts.

The ideas of *constructivism* began in Russia, or in parts of today's Ukraine, around 1913 and can be traced until into the 1920s. Their basic demand was for functional clothes that could be produced ready-to-wear. A consistent example of this strict, geometric cut was Alexandr Rodschenko's overall suit (1922) made of woollen cloth with seams, edges and applied pockets trimmed in leather. For use as fabric patterns, the Russian constructivists conceded only the simplest geometric elements of form and clear fields of colour in dramatic contrast to large monochrome areas. Parts of machines, wheels and levers, hammer and sickle were regarded as objective motifs. The painter Alexandra Exter created sportswear and working clothes with strict geometric emphases. Varvara Stepanowa and Ljubov Popova conceived multipurpose geometric designs, while Nadezhda Lamanova lent a feminine touch to them by using folklorist embroidery.

Louis Sullivan's logics of the merging of décor and functionality can be found in the Art Deco evening dresses embroidered with rhinestone ornaments. Futurism and constructivism played equal parts in the development of style for the *fashion of the 1920s.* On the one hand, there was the rectangular form of the sack dress, and on the other the godets inserted into skirts to permit movement, especially in the manically fast legwork of modern dances such as the Charleston. In the 1920s, the woman's torso that had dominated both erotically and fashionably for centuries (with brief exceptions) was completely negated by the new sack form, while arms and legs were liberated for their functional purposes but also became (erotic) eye-catchers. The form of the sack dress was derived from the undershirt form that had been customary for centuries; that is, underwear became outerwear; the informal became formal by means of a qualitative revaluation through material, colour, pattern and embellishment. Recombination and reconnotation generated something new. Gabrielle Chanel realised a type of vestimentary functionalism—equivalent to 'new objectivity' in painting—with her presentation of the little black dress in 1926.[16] In 1954, when she reopened her salon at the age of seventy-one, she consciously created the Chanel suit as functional but still elegant women's clothing and a pendant to the modern men's suit, as well as a conscious contrast to Dior's crinoline-like New Look. She recognised the functional pretension of the traditional rural janker jacket, which—during the time she spent in Switzerland in the war and afterwards—served as her model for the Chanel jacket. In this respect, modernism also took up the past and tradition, but always with an eye on the future.

Neo-Constructivism

Constructivism, with its commitment to modern technology and restriction to geometric forms and patterns, met with renewed favour in the 1960s. Fashion designers like André Courrèges, Lucio Fontana (artist) and Pierre Cardin sought to liberate fashion from the—perhaps already postmodern—artificiality of the 1950s. As neo-constructivism certainly cannot be viewed as a self-contained or completed style either, creations by the Japanese designer Issey Miyake, for example, such as his *Rattan Body* of 1982 and the pleated *Bodyworks* of 1983, may be regarded as a continuation of it, in a comparable way to the architecture of the Centre National d'Art et de Culture Georges Pompidou by Richard Rogers and Renzo Piano in Paris (opened in 1977). These two examples also highlight a transitional phase from constructivism to deconstructivism, while the hippie fashion post-1968 represents a clear pointer to postmodernism.

Postmodernism

Less is a bore—More is more

Robert Venturi, US architect

Postmodernism drew its leading ideas from modernism. Philosophers and key theorists such as Jean-François Lyotard, Jacques Derrida, Michel Foucault and Wolfgang Welsch explained postmodernism using declarations that the artist Jean Dubuffet had already made in his programme in 1951: a move away from anthropocentrism, from the primacy of logic, from the monoculture of meaning and from the prevalence of vision.[17] Art theorist Heinrich Klotz pointed out consequently that the discourse triggering the debate on postmodernism had been one of aesthetics, but that this 'was usurped by philosophy and sociology with considerable disregard for its original reasons' (with reference to Jürgen Habermas and excepting Wolfgang Welsch).[18] One might also attribute postmodernism—according to Klotz—to modernism; as a 'revisionist style' or as a 'crisis of functionalism'.[19] But Lyotard opposed not the rationalism and strength of modernism, but its exclusion of the heterogeneous. In *La condition moderne* in 1979 (not for the first time), Lyotard interpreted the concept of postmodernism as a diversity of intellectual approaches by contrast to the totality of modernism. In Lyotard's work, '[T]he proximity to aesthetic questions was (also) unmistakeable from the very beginning', according to Welsch.[20]

Postmodernism tied in with pop culture and admitted the influences of subcultures and everyday life. Pluralism developed into the heart of postmodernism. It is not seen as self-contained by any means, but after a phase of minimalism and purism in the 1990s it led into so-called post-postmodernism. In postmodernism, strategies of contrast and paradox attained key significance. They do justice to a world that is equally pluralist. The scientific starting points of chaos theory, fractal theory and the concept of dissipative structures explain that the world itself is actually characterised by pluralism and heteronomy, demonstrating that reality is not homogeneous but heterogeneous, not harmonic but multifaceted, and not uniform but diverse.

Charles Alexander Jencks, US architect and theorist, took the concept of postmodernism prevalent in the humanities and literary studies and transposed it to architecture in his book *The Language of Postmodern Architecture,* published in 1977. He pleaded in favour of a double codification—that is for an architecture that addressed both the elite and the man on the street.

The postmodern design also emerged as multifaceted and readily open to dissention between stability and chaos. 'One talks of "Postmodernism" in order to draw attention to the fact that today, those differences still meaningful in "Modernism" are a mere playground for the citation of meanings.'[21] This should 'not lead to the assumption that today everything is "arbitrary" as a result',[22] according to the false attitude of 'anything goes', but postmodernism does liberate the individual. Although postmodernism admits to the validity of history as a court of appeal, its prime aim is not (although it has sometimes been accused of this) to stay the lifeblood of modernism—its reference to the present and the future. Postmodernism expands stylistic language, it resemantises and pluralises, but it does not merely historicise. It is not opposed to modernism, but it rejects the latter's radicalism and has revised its abstraction. The pluralism of postmodernism unites the real and unreal, confronting the rationality of Modernism with various irrational moments such as vision, myth and ecstasy, or adds these aspects to it. The postmodern motto of design is no longer 'form follows function' but 'form produces visions'. Postmodernism is less an epoch than an 'attitude or far more a state of mind', Jean-François Lyotard wrote.[23] 'Today and in the future, we should permit not only those things that can be analysed and mediated. Regardless of its many professional and regular qualities, design must also be bold enough to penetrate into zones of the inconceivable',[24] or, as Theodor W. Adorno put it, 'To do things, of which we are unable to say what they are'[25]. Wolfgang Welsch calls the postmodern artist, architect and designer a 'double agent—equally at home in the world of technology and the realm of marvels'.[26]

In the 1980s, postmodernism aided the aesthetic and conceptual breakthrough of a new, extended concept of design, the creative process of which was firmly rooted in art. The term *artist-designer* was coined. Design galleries were created, the presence of design in the media became enduring and the shelf-object *Carlton* by Ettore Sottsass was the most frequently illustrated artwork of the eighties.

Fashion and Postmodernism

Fashion is more suited to the expression of postmodernism than almost any other medium, because the past in fashion is not something that has been discarded but a wealth of forms that it can employ. In this way, it does not exclude an affirmation of the present and meets the demand—far more than modernism or deconstructivism—for heterogeneity of tastes, expectations and possible combinations of forms. Sociologist Daniel Bell talks of '"cross-cutting" identities', which are satisfied.[27] In postmodernism, it is not only the realisation of the new that represents the focus of creative interest, but also a recombination or a new application of already existing ideas.

The question arises as to whether with his *New Look* of 1947 Christian Dior was aiming for the return of the crinoline and a revival of the notion of elegance or anticipating the fictive aspects of postmodernism. Parallel to Dior's New Look, Arnold J. Toynbee described postmodernism as a late phase of occidental culture in 1947. For Dior, his New Look represented a return to the Belle Epoque and a safe past in which luxury and enjoyment were conceivable without regret. Later, journalist Magde Garland called this 'a "Last Look" at a disappearing world' (as opposed to a New Look).[28] Dior filled the vacuum of meaning during the postwar era and lent an appearance to the need for a new and better reality. His laced waists, huge amount of materials, cartwheel hats and long gloves that a lady never removed in public were all representative of this. However, it was nothing more than a return to bourgeois values and traditional images of the sexes. On the other hand, Dior—entirely in the spirit of postmodernism—had created the fiction of elegance and the illusion of a lady. Although he may have done so unconsciously, Dior was the first designer to introduce to fashion the postmodern credo 'form follows vision' at the cost of the function once demanded by modernism. Insofar as this is true, one may consider it a matter of interpretation whether fashion in advance of art played a visionary, pioneering role. By contrast, modernism was embodied by Gabrielle Chanel, who recreated modernism with her functional suits after 1954 and criticised Dior's heavy, stiff dresses as completely unsuited to the times.

Postmodernism first began in fashion when everyday life and aspects of pop culture were admitted into the *fashion of the 1970s*. Vestimentary rules were pronounced 'the day before yesterday' and fashion shows turned into happenings and actions according to the pattern of art presentations or in collaboration with them. In the hippie life scenario, fashion and life became concurrent and quite separate from consumerism. This led to impulses in fashion design leading in the direction of second-hand fashion and recycling fashion as fresh starting points for individuation and redesigning.

Nevertheless, in the subsequent *1980s fashion* had not—by comparison to postmodern product design, particularly in Italy—abandoned itself entirely to postmodernism, by any means. Fashion was dominated too powerfully by the emancipating character of broad shoulders and oversizing, and by a compulsion to encode via brands and their trademarks. The interplay of 1980s fashion with socio-political movements was greater than its interplay with art and product design. Exceptions were Christian Lacroix, who luxuriated in opulence and the citation of specific ethnic—above all southern France—and historical forms, and Gianni Versace with his neo-baroque designs. This was quite apart from Romeo Gigli, who handled his fashionable silhouettes by adopting the empires of antiquity in a subtle, romantic way, a complete contradiction to the dominant power look of business fashion. But the visionary was to bring an orientation on the future into play as well. Above all, this prompted the use of ecologically defensible materials. Among other things, it was a matter of the renewed consideration of natural fibres (but opposing fur) as an issue that dominated the 1980s. After the plastics and synthetics euphoria of modernism, the oil crises of 1973 and 1979 dampened the mania of producibility.

It was not until in the 1990s that postmodernism's claim to individuality drew general attention to individual designers and the identity of their styles, asserting them alongside well-known brands and luxury fashion: the term *designer fashion* began to replace the term *prêt-à-porter* (cf. p. 176). Fashion by John Galliano, Jean-Paul Gaultier and Vivienne Westwood luxuriated in historical and ethnic vestimentary details, which were perverted, alienated and assembled into a new whole, that is into something that was entirely up to date.

Postmodernism interprets the historical from the standpoint of a changed social situation. In this way, it succeeds in abolishing time and space, as it causes the tradition of history to be assessed as a continuum. Vivienne Westwood pursued precisely this aim in her collection *Five Centuries Ago* from 1997. In this collection she restaged historical paintings such as portraits of Queen Elizabeth I of England using the people of the present day as her actors. In a similar way, John Galliano transposed fin de siècle fashion to the end of the subsequent, twentieth century in 1997. This abolition of time and space symbolises the current age of flexibility, mobility and information, but also the continuity of artistic tradition. It shows how the past continues to live on in the present and how the present revives the past. Of course the old rules of suitability and composition are not neglected, but they are expanded and altered. In postmodernism, the place of the classical ideal of beauty with its symmetry and regularity is taken by a 'dissonant beauty' or 'disharmonic harmony',[29] like that which is manifest in the architecture of the New State Gallery in Stuttgart by James Stirling (1984) or that which had already appeared in the baroque.

Examples of historical eclecticism can be found in many collections by Vivienne Westwood, such as the Watteau outfits in *Les Femmes* (1996) or in her first *Mini Crini* collection from 1984. Nevertheless, it cannot be denied that Vivienne Westwood, for example, demonstrates an occasional tendency to historicism and the traditionalising of styles. As a comparison, the architecture of Frank O. Gehry and Coop Himmelb(l)au is quite liberated from history and arrives at a play of the concave and convex without recourse to baroque forms and ground plans. Sweeping dynamics, ovals and ellipses extend far into space, their statics displaying a fine trust in computer calculation.

The emotional aspect of postmodernism was formulated by Jean-Paul Gaultier with his golden corset top designed for Madonna in 1990 as an expression of sexual emotion. (As someone who repeatedly reinvents herself, Madonna is regarded as the quintessential pop star of postmodernism.) Jean-Paul Gaultier expresses an ethnic mix, as in the collections *Big Journey* (1993/1994) and *Tribal Styles* (1994), and he designed a European national costume mix in 2006 comprising flamenco dress, Romanian blouse and traditional German Bückeburg costume.

John Galliano adopts the ideas and aesthetic concepts of both historical and ethnic clothes and reassembles them—in an apparently playful way—into a new whole. Galliano sees the idea of a seductive woman in the siren of Greek mythology, the courtesan of the Renaissance, the demimondaine of the nineteenth century, the femme fatale at the turn of the century, the vamp of the 1920s, the circus princess and the geisha, and he samples isolated aspects of their fundamental aesthetic concepts in order to create a new image of seductive woman. He regards basic historic and aesthetic concepts as 'functional objects' (in the sense of appropriation art, cf. p. 129) and certainly not as revivals.

These designer collections prompt the question of the reproducibility of artistic-creative models. Many such models, even those that are wearable, have been rejected from the outset as too eccentric for reproduction. The problem with designer fashion and its social acceptance is that clothing as a product has a very direct impact on people—it gets onto their skin, so to speak—and is thus closer to them than any architecture, literature or fine art.

Deconstructivism

Deconstructivism is understood as a philosophical concept, a superdisciplinary scientific theory, and a tendency in art. As a philosophical concept, deconstructivism appeared for the first time around 1972 in connection with the work of the philosopher Jacques Derrida. According to Derrida, the process of deconstruction consists of first tentatively adopting a system of thought or construction in order to subsequently disclose its inconsistencies and failures in implementation. Deconstruction registers what is asserted in order to concentrate immediately on all the things that this assertion fails to state, omits and negates. Accordingly, it directs the focus towards what is not said. Deconstruction must proceed in different ways according to the object of its contemplation—literature, media, architecture or fashion; it cannot always be applied in the same manner. Deconstruction is intended not as a universal method, but as a flexible form of activity adapting to the relevant context.

However, it is possible to discern two fundamental applications: the first comprises reversal, for example of binary distinctions; the second involves a shift in the entire logic of something. If one were to come to a stop after the first motion, a new hierarchy would be reconstructed. For that reason, according to Derrida, the second motion of shift is absolutely necessary. In addition, a deconstruction is never actually completed, for new examples of binary logic will always emerge from it. In this context, those binary opposites may be imagined as something close to a dialectic approach: for example when it is deconstructed, a text that perhaps consists of the customary (binary) thesis and antithesis reveals a large number of further perspectives that are existent concurrently and often conflict with one another. This conflict becomes visible only as a result of the deconstruction. Deconstruction functions by questioning concepts and their history of development as well as conditions and conventions, or when discussions are analysed from a meta-level. The deconstruction always represents a critical analysis of the origins, foundations and limits of our conceptual, theoretical and normative apparatus.

Deconstruction consists in the addition or revealing of an irrational moment and in the visualisation of these processes. Complexity and contradiction, paradox and paralogics correspond to the logic of deconstructivism. The demand for consensus is surpassed by willingness for dissent.

Fashion and Deconstructivism

In design as well as in art and architecture, structures and forms are subject to destruction and renewed construction in the sense of deconstruction, reconstruction and transformation. In clothing, this means that the nonvisible—the construction—is made visible as the interesting and essential aspect. The construction consists of the seams that give clothes their form, the fastenings that enable us to put them on and fix them and the hemlines that establish their delimitations. Deconstructed clothing makes all these things visible. Forms become more important than colours. Deconstructivists understand the creation of clothes as a process of searching for meaning and the continual creation of fresh meaning. Traditional orders and any kind of conventions are exploded; aesthetic habits with respect to body proportions and the criteria of beauty are questioned. In fashion, the Japanese designers Rei Kawakubo (Comme des Garçons) and Yohji Yamamoto paved the way for deconstructivism (cf. p. 104) with their understanding of design at the beginning of the 1980s. In the 1990s, Belgian designers Ann Demeulemeester and Martin Margiela established themselves as the main representatives of deconstructivism.[30]

Belgian Martin Margiela is regarded as a programmatic fashion designer of deconstructivism. Martin Margiela makes the fragmentary aspect of deconstructivism visible by bringing together things that do not belong together, such as a sleeve that is far too wide in an armhole that is far too small. Margiela recycles old fashion; he picks apart, reverses, turns seams and zip fasteners to the outside. In this way, he shows the origin and the artificiality of the tailoring art as well as fashion's soul or lack of it. His recycling (redesigning) is based not on ecological but on aesthetic motivation. In his design, he visualises working processes, the wear and tear of fabrics and traces of use and achieves both new aesthetics and a new authenticity by this means. Quite apart from this, he deconstructs the idea of the logo by always sewing an empty laundry label inside his garments; this is fixed only at the corners so that four white tacking stitches are visible on the outside. However, with this form of logo he also makes use of the logo in principle, as well. Margiela's deconstructed satin dress from circa 1960 that he presented in his Spring/Summer 1996 collection may be regarded as the *pars pro toto* of his deconstruction. He took the original historic dress, photographed the front and back sections, had these photos printed in the original dress size on satin material of the same colour, cut out the front and back, and sewed the pieces together into a new dress.[31] In this way, Margiela succeeded in deconstructing an historical construction and in questioning the story of its development, and also in visualising the process of emergence and creating a new perspective; that is by showing the inside of a dress, which normally remains invisible although it is simultaneously existent. Additionally, with this work he stimulated a fashion of endurance rather than of change, or, in other words, he deconstructed the definition of 'fashion as constant change' and succeeded in constructing a new dress identity while preserving its original identity. As a construction made visible, the once carefully concealed and now turned-out seams and hemlines become the dysfunctional and are so transformed into ornament. The unfinished seams turned to the outside, the crumpled material, and the crooked hemlines result in an aesthetic casualness—which does not meet with overall acceptance in society, however. (It is a different matter when an increase in the casual responds to a demand for comfort, both in wearing and also as ease of social competition in the sense of jeans and T-shirt as 'ugly standard culture of the bourgeois middle class,'[32] as Vivienne Westwood puts it.)

Margiela deconstructs not only the design of clothing, but also its presentations on the catwalk (cf. p. 80). In addition, he has succeeded in the deconstruction or visualisation of time and transience, one of the essential factors of fashion (so questioning this factor as a result). In 1997, Margiela had eighteen of his dresses in an exhibition held in the Museum Boijmans van Beuningen in Rotterdam painted with bacteria, which destroyed them within a very short time. In this way, he investigated the cycle of decay and the consumerism of recurrent purchase and casting off.

John Galliano includes deconstructivism in his postmodern style, almost as a free stylistic citation and demonstration of his creativity. In the haute couture collection *French Revolution* for the House of Dior in 2006, he created a kind of corset belt consisting only of corset laces that he assembled in diagonal lines. It is one of many design quotations that his work offers in this thematic context.

The philosophical and artistic starting points of the stylistic trend are combined in fashion design by Ann Demeulemeester, who is regarded as the main representative of deconstructivism alongside Martin Margiela. In her work, a proximity to Arte Povera also becomes obvious. The broken and run-down is made visible by means of torn-off or pointed hemlines, stockings full of creases, or burst seams and then revaluated into a desirable consumer product. Outlaw and establishment, provocation and pleasure, fear and longing are merged into one. Her creations incorporate a clash of the unfinished and the contingent, the soft and the rigid, the naked and the veiled (irrespective of erogenous zones), which are all subsequently rediscovered in a new harmony. In this way, Demeulemeester creates both anaesthetic and emotional innovation.

Figure 20   John Galliano for Dior, *French Revolution,* haute couture 2006. Photo: Studio Them.
www.them.de.

Hussein Chalayan devoted himself to the deconstruction or the transformation ('morphing') of ethnic and Western-modern clothing in *Ambimorphous,* Autumn/ Winter 2000/2001, whereby he gradually merged traditional Turkish clothing and the little black dress of European fashion tradition. Deconstruction as a change of perspective was realised by the Dutch designer couple Viktor & Rolf in their summer 2006 collection *Upside Down,* which was characterised by the interchange of top and bottom; in other words, a hem decorated with flounces became the décolleté and vice versa (cf. p. 60).

Fashion and Architecture

Deconstructivism also developed as a style in art based on philosophical concept (cf. p. 186). However, Jacques Derrida's philosophical starting point and the architectonic programme are comparable only up to a certain point. Although Derrida and architect Peter Eisenmann worked together on projects and were involved in a dialogue for some years, this eventually culminated in an intellectual separation.[33] The foundation of deconstructivism as a style in architecture was established with the exhibition 'Deconstructivist Architecture' realised by Philip Johnson and Mark Wigley at the Museum of Modern Art in New York (1988). Seven architects participated: Frank O. Gehry, Daniel Libeskind, Rem Koolhaas, Peter Eisenmann, Zaha Hadid, Coop Himmelb(l)au and Bernard Tschumi. Frank O. Gehry's house in Santa Monica and Daniel Libeskind's Jewish Museum in Berlin are regarded as exemplary deconstructivist buildings.

Deconstructivist architecture localises the emotions inherent in buildings, and it breaks down the relation of load-bearing and load as well as traditional statics. It alienates constructive elements by dismantling (deconstructing) functions and forms into their individual components. As a whole, it is an approach almost approximating the shattering of structure. In the sense of conventional visual habits, the collision of different materials, spaces and constructions appears disharmonious, resembling a collage or even a chaotic muddle, as is the case with Frank O. Gehry's house in Santa Monica dating from 1978. It appears dismantled, thrown into confusion and apparently reassembled quite by chance.

The three-dimensionality of clothing suggests a comparison to architecture, which is evident in deconstructivism. Gehry's house may be compared to Martin Margiela's fashion recycling, which is motivated aesthetically rather than ecologically. As in architecture, here the interim space is made visible: Margiela fits a sleeve that is far too wide into an armhole that is far too small (1991/1992), so that the sleeve hangs down below the armpit and a hole remains, or he leaves open the armhole (the correct term ought to be 'sleeve hole') without sewing it up. Margiela undertakes changes to pattern technique, for example by inserting the sleeves into the front rather than the sides, that is in both front and back, as would be customary. In this way, the body is not emphasised as a whole or as something coherent; instead, he underlines the fact that it can be cut up into individual limbs, in a comparable way to the figures Hans Bellmer painted in 1934.

Margiela's obvious armholes—consistently left without sewing up—are intended to reveal the contradiction inherent in the closed cave or walled-up hole. In this way, he visualises the space between the sleeve and the body, just as turning clothes inside out reveals the stiffening and insertions that normally remain concealed between the lining and the upper material. In a comparable way, this happens in the architecture of Bernard Tschumi or in Peter Eisenmann's Wexner Center for the Visual Arts in Columbus, Ohio, USA, when a massive corner pillar rather like a mediaeval tower is slit open vertically to disclose the inner membrane, the actual building.

As direct comparison, fragmentation and a construction completely free of traditions are displayed by both an attic floor built by the architectural office Coop Himmelb(l)au, which falls diagonally over a house front in Vienna, and a blouse with a slipping, asymmetrical top right-hand section created by Ann Demeulemeester in 1997.

Junya Watanabe, co-designer of Comme des Garçons, solves static problems in a different manner when he holds clothes onto the body using an oval metal hoop with fabric stretched over it and jutting at the waist, and thus constructs an asymmetrical hoop skirt. Investigation into the morphological condition of things is a key part of deconstructivism. In a similar way, the rooms are turned to the outside in Gehry's architecture, for example in his *Ginger and Fred* house in Prague or the Vitra Design Museum in Vitra am Rhein. The design principle pursues a disrupted perfection, also

Figure 21a   Ann Demeulemeester, blouse 1997. Ann Demeulemeester, PR.

Figure 21b   Coop Himmelb(l)au, attic Falkestraße, Vienna 1987/1988. © Gerald Zugmann. www.zugmann.com.

understood in the sense of overcoming modernism's perfectionism. This is precisely what Rei Kawakubo is attempting when she tears, rips up and reknots fabric. In the work of Issey Miyake and Yohji Yamamoto, the seams collide and turn outwards, creating spaces that negate the shape of the body.

By contrast, the early happening *Cut Pieces* by Yoko Ono in 1964 (cf. p. 55) was close to the destruction of clothing. Munich artist Ina Ettlinger arrives at the new through a process of destruction; she cuts out and isolates patterns from finished clothing, unravels the woven materials, and so arrives at a new, autonomous form with a fresh connotation between image and sculpture.

The aforementioned programmatic proponent of deconstructivism, architect Peter Eisenmann, gives 'preference to a truly modern aesthetic, in which objects belong at the forefront of the consumer society, replacing humanism'. In this way 'Eisenmann was able to develop a "decentralized" architecture that neglects function and form'.[34] This attitude can be transferred to the collection by Belgian designer Ann Demeulemeester and its catwalk presentation in 1992, when the models shocked the audience by appearing in consciously scruffy, drooping and crumpled nylon stockings of an unattractive brownish-grey colour, even laddered in places. As an element of consumerism that has become matter-of-course, the nylon stockings were deconstructed; at the same time, aesthetics were deconstructed into 'anaesthetics'.[35]

Rei Kawakubo's prime intention is to create forms that no one has seen before and optical stimuli in complete opposition to our customary manner of perception. In 1996 and 1997, she created dresses with an underlay of asymmetric pods that created a fictive body; they were presented as moving dress sculptures under the title *Body Meets Dress* (cf. p. 42). The 'humps' gave the close-fitting dresses and thus the body a new form, in a similar way to the amorphous forms ('nozzles') on the building of Kunsthaus Graz designed by London architects Peter Cook and Colin Fournier (Spacelab) in conjunction with the Graz firm Architektur Consult. In 1998, Kawakubo continued her experiments with a second silhouette of the body and came close to sculptural art. Contemporary world architecture has also developed into sculptures in public space. The Guggenheim Museum in Bilbao, the Jewish Museum in Berlin, the Wexner Art Museum in Columbus, Ohio, and the Art Museum in Denver, Colorado, are as famous as they are not because of their content but due to their architecture as an autarkic object of interest.

Second Modernism

Second modernism emerged as an artistic-aesthetic movement at the beginning of the 1990s from the revision implemented by postmodernism.[36] By comparison to the first, 'classical' modernism, it abandoned the exclusive postulate of progress and incorporated fiction as an increase in aesthetic experience. Modernism granted validity to the creative present as a contrast to tradition. Postmodernism took up tradition—not without the danger of falsification—and transposed it into the present. Second modernism made a demand for authenticity, but of course this represents an exclusively historical value and has never existed in reality.

In fashion, second modernism triggered a commercial departure, based for the most part on the New Economy and its demand for prestige. The minimising of ornament to trademarks and logos and an associated increase in the commercialisation of luxury reduced it to symbols (cf. p. 197).

Purism as the Continuation of Classical Modernism

In the 1990s, abstraction in the sense of a type of purism developed in fashion. This paid homage to bold, nonartificial lines but accepted the validity of asymmetries and overlaps as stylistic means. The Italian fashion designer Giorgio Armani paved the way by adapting the classical aspects of the purist to the zeitgeist. In the 1980s, he had already given a soft, feminine line to the classic tailleur (cf. p. 102) and supplemented the professional woman's wardrobe with the classic trouser-suit. In the 1990s, the understanding of design displayed by Jil Sander and Gabriele Strehle for Strenesse pursued purism as an emancipative symbol. As Alexandra Exter—a representative of Russian constructivism—put it as early as 1923, they attempted 'to free clothes from fashion'.[37] The greatest possible rejection of fashionable embellishment, decoration and similar distraction as their credo can be understood entirely in Loos's sense as a rejection of 'poor' taste and 'childish', that is typically female, behaviour (cf. p. 179). Armani and company echoed the mood between recession and the upsurge of the New Economy with a new simplicity—back to basics—and a consciousness of quality and longevity. Simplicity and understatement were a milieu-specific phenomenon, typical of the Western middle or upper classes. (Even perfume bottles were given the appearance of simple aluminium drinking bottles.) Consumer hedonism, by contrast, developed into a lower-class phenomenon.

However, this extreme reduction of form and simultaneous demand for quality, together with the high intellectual pretensions of nineties design, ultimately led to a dead end. As a consequence, its conceptual clarity and severity was augmented by the added aesthetic value of minimalism. Pure functionalism was thrown into question by such important architects and theorists as Hans Hollein.[38]

Minimalism as an Extension of Purism

Second modernism is also represented in minimalism (not to be confused with minimal art), which is found in a more pronounced form in design—including fashion—than in architecture. Minimalism experiments with materials and geometries, whereby the aim is the aesthetics of the product as such rather than exclusively technology or functionalism. This means that ornamental effects and patterns, that is the fictive, are also permissible in second modernism.

The key representative and creative mind of this trend was Helmut Lang, who made a name for himself in Austria, presented his fashion in Paris, and was particularly admired in the USA. He lent a special something to strict purism through minimal effects: a transparent top was provided with an asymmetrical, coloured bandeau or an arbitrary narrow stripe under it, or the delicate fabric left the seams visible. These were details often not discernible at first glance but which lent the garment an ornamental effect. Helmut Lang's preference for chemical fibres such as nylon and all-poly materials complied with the modernistic demand following the postmodern era of natural materials. He also experimented with materials including rubber. One of his most famous creations was a sack dress (1994) made of rubber with Chantilly lace melted onto the surface—based on the credo 'function plus emotion'. He lent visual forms to ideas by means of asymmetric, apparently arbitrary tapelike gathered materials, and had one arm enveloped in the top or loose pieces of material flutter from it. In addition, he admitted cut-out areas in unexpected places in both women's and men's fashion, with a pretension to eroticism, but also laying claim to nakedness as part of the whole. As well as this, Lang introduced the trimming (with galloon, a satin ribbon) from the outside-leg seams

Figure 22   Helmut Lang, models 2004. Photo: Studio Them. www.them.de.

of dress-suit trousers into men's fashion, as a minimalist ornament on the pants of everyday sportswear.

In a similar way to Helmut Lang, Prada retained the functionality of patterns but impressed the identity of Miuccia Prada onto its models. This consisted of a mixture of fabric patterns from the fifties and polyester jersey, which she had discovered in second-hand shops in New York, as well as pattern styles dating from the 1960s. Personally, Prada called her collection 'bad taste', but young people discovered it as a means of self-portrayal for this precise reason; it was a distinctive feature by comparison to the over-forties generation. Particularly 'ugly' (*Herald Tribune*) were the pea-green 'Formica tile' pattern and the brown to honey-coloured square pattern recalling American motel curtains. International fashion companies like Hennes & Mauritz turned Prada's ideas into mass fashion for contemporary youth. Prada remained on the ball as far as the zeitgeist was concerned; holiday landscapes appeared as prints on pleated skirts, and lavish glass gems as decoration created the illusion of neo-baroque luxury. Miuccia Prada's ideas (and those of her team) have always been the most frequently copied designs.

Hedi Slimane can be cited as the aesthetic successor to Helmut Lang. He revolutionised men's fashion for the House of Dior in 2001–2007 with ideas influenced by his own memories and his personal idols acting as muse. He was a fan of David Bowie by the age of six, and today things have turned full circle; David Bowie wears Hedi Slimane. Designer and muse enter into a synergic effect. Slimane is fascinated by slim, androgynous male bodies which are entirely themselves, nearly consumed by their own imagination and art; men like Karl Lagerfeld, ageing star Mick Jagger, pop star Franz Ferdinand, and rocker Pete Doherty. These men enthusiastically champion the slender silhouette: a tight, crumpled pair of drainpipe jeans in conjunction with heavy rings and biker gloves like those that Karl Lagerfeld wears as a valid cipher of coolness (or possibly as a way of hiding his age). Behind this lie the longings and masculinity of rock 'n' roll, coupled with a neo-dandy's frilly shirts and Bohemian bows, a stylistic hybrid vacillating between second modernism and post-postmodernism. Slimane took snapshots of all manner of things that had impressed him from his sixteenth year onwards. For him, this visual diary represents the manifestations of the moment as well as direct experiences. As he himself puts it, he designs fashion collections almost as an extended form of diary, always chasing after the perfect moment.

Perhaps second modernism would never have been so successful had it not found expression in Yohji Yamamoto's collections for Adidas. Yamamoto made sportswear fit for design and—as a Japanese designer—was thus the first on the European continent to directly adopt the philosophy of American designer Claire McCardell. Prêt-à-porter took to the streets in Yamamoto-Adidas as the sportswear brand Y3, but without losing the intellectual pretension of designer fashion.

Post-postmodernism and Neo-ornamentation

The term post-postmodernism may not sound very elegant, but it is an aid to orientation; like other styles of the twentieth and twenty-first centuries, with respect to time it can be defined only as since the end of the twentieth century.

Among other things, the root of the statement that 'today's art and design is facing a crisis' lies in the return of the ornament. Since Adolf Loos and his treatise on 'Ornament and Crime' (lecture 1908) at the latest, in the Western industrial nations there has been a tendency to equate ornament with poor taste, and it has become anchored as such—as primitive—in cultural memory (cf. p. 179). For decades since the 1920s, according to Pierre Bourdieu, it was possible to signal one's affiliation to the educated upper class by means of an overtly ascetic lifestyle, while a preference for décor became a characteristic of the vulgar[39] or at best of people with close ties to nature, as exemplified by the hippies. The rude words of modernism—appliqué, decoration, ornament and pattern—thought to evidence a lack of design talent in the early and mid twentieth century, have boomed once again since the beginning of the twenty-first. 'Now, even architects Jacques Herzog and Pierre de Meuron, who made their names with severe Calvinist boxes, transform almost every facade . . . into complete ornament.'[40] Ornament and pattern differ inasmuch as ornament is applied to a basic functional form, whereas a pattern is an integral component of the construction materials. Transferred to fashion, the ornament—like styling—is an additive element (applied from the outside) and thus distinguished from the functional model or line and the organic (integral) fabric pattern.

In the 1980s, the brand or logo symbol was used as the smallest conceivable form of ornament, as a statement of prestige. However, luxury brand companies like Louis Vuitton made the singular logo into an all-over pattern and thus into an ornament in the broadest sense towards the end of the 1990s (quite apart from the fact that Louis Vuitton had already introduced the all-over signet comprising the letters LV framed by stylised flowers and stars as a characteristic symbol of its luggage at the end of the nineteenth century.) This return to ornamentation is also connected with the comeback of painting. Artists as lavishly ornamental as Chris Ofili, Takashi Murakami and Olafur Eliasson were exhibited at the Venice Biennial in 2003. The design management at House Louis Vuitton also perceived the new pleasure in patterns at the beginning of the twenty-first century. This is evident in a spirit of emotion and playfulness like that expressed in Pop Art. In 2002, Louis Vuitton produced an edition of luxury bags decorated with fairy-tale characters, and bags with a brightly coloured design by Japanese artist Takashi Murakami appeared in 2003. Murakami refers mainly to Japanese manga comics, removing their motifs from the context and depicting them in isolation or in other contexts (e.g. in repeat patterns). Murakami himself calls his art Superflat.[41] In this way, he refers in only one of various dimensions to the lack of perspective or depth in his pictures, which is typical of Murakami and Japanese painting as a whole.

The rediscovery of ornament and pattern since the 1980s—including the ornamentation of the body by means of tattoos—cannot be interpreted as a short-term trend. Rather, in the age of mass goods, it is ornament that ensures—hypothetical—individualisation.

Models by Prada are covered in special types of ornament: in 2004, these were landscape motifs and sections of romantic village scenes (as a retro to the Bella Italia of the 1950s), which appeared as prints on pleated skirts. In 2005, Prada produced dresses, jackets and T-shirts with big crystals and beaded embroidery, which left a rather restrained impression despite their opulence. Here, it was a matter not of an emotional, but rather of a fictive or elitist use of ornament.

In her Autumn/Winter 2008/2009 Collection, Prada presented dresses and skirts made of lace materials in black or beige. Although these stood for elegance and even created a rather schoolmarmish impression (not least due to the models' hairstyles and make-up), they were suggestive of ornamental wrappings. The sportive, futuristic version was reflected as a contrast in Prada's brand Miu Miu, in dresses made of an XXL lace. These cut-out materials with graphic or floral patterns were worn over tight bodysuits or cycling pants and shirts. Prada thus embraced the neo-ornamentation that had already been evident as facade design in architecture for several years and may be compared with the Institut du Monde Arabe (1981–1987) in Paris from Jean Nouvel or with the National Aquatics Center, called Watercube (2004–2007), in Beijing.

Opulence and superficial luxury entered the mass fashion of the Western world via the detour of the ethno look (in a way similar to that of the hippie era, but with no socio-political background). In 2005/2006, for example, T-shirts ornamented with beads, sequins and gold printing and wide, flounced skirts with a Moroccan-Indian look swamped Europe. Opulent, optionally extendable patterns have developed into a guideline for mass design. Not least, the background to this trend is that people believe short-lived junk goods—usually produced in the Far East—promise more economic benefit than intellectual-minimalist design of first-class quality. 'In accordance with the premise of a consumer society that defines itself not through renunciation but through hedonism, efficiency translated into form has given way to superfluity translated into form.'[42] Since the 1970s, questioning of the value structure of real and false means that the hierarchy of true and false design has entered into the vital distinction between design and styling. More than ever, post-postmodernism backs styling, and this surpasses all ornamentation. Among other things, the provision of accessories for the catwalk is regarded as styling: although suspected of being superfluous trumpery, this offers a powerful optical allure to the dress presentation in a fashion show (cf. pp. 80, 143).

Figure 23   Miuccia Prada for Miu Miu, model 2008/2009. Photo: Studio Them. www.them.de.

Fashion as an Artefact in Exhibitions

In order to communicate fashion as a cultural commodity, an everyday object and also a design product, it is necessary to integrate it as all of these into museums of cultural history as well as design museums. In this way, creative fashion designers are given an opportunity to show their work in a context separate from pure commerce and mass fashion and to present it as predominantly European-oriented design—both aesthetically and conceptually. The fashion designer does not design a priori for museums, of course; the primary aim is for his or her creations to become fashion. But quite apart from this, fashion exhibitions make high standards of art and craftsmanship known to a wider public than elitist fashion shows.

Exhibitions

The genre of art offers designers like Viktor & Rolf or Hussein Chalayan a creative freedom beyond issues of wearability and commercial marketing, and consequently a significant convergence of fashion design and art institutions has taken place since the late 1990s. Museums have shown an increased interest in collecting and/or exhibiting contemporary designer fashion. Examples of such exhibitions include Capucci in the Museum of Art History Vienna, Chanel in the Metropolitan Museum of Art in New York, Armani in the Guggenheim Museum in New York and the New National Gallery in Berlin, Versace in the Metropolitan Museum of Art in New York, Cardin in the Academy of Fine Arts in Vienna, Vivienne Westwood in the Victoria & Albert Museum in London, Hussein Chalayan in the Art Museum in Wolfsburg, Viktor & Rolf in Groningen, Max Mara in Berlin and Gaultier in Paris, Margiela in Antwerp. Museums dedicated to the creative work of a single fashion designer have also been established in recent years, such as the Dior Museum in Granville, the Yves Saint Laurent Museum in Paris, the Zandra Rhodes Museum in London, and the Cristóbal Balenciaga Museum in Guetaria, Spain. In addition, fashion designers may act as guest curators, like Viktor & Rolf for 'Colors' in Kyoto and in Tokyo, or Eva Gronbach for 'in. Femme Fashion' in the Museum of Applied Art, Cologne.

This temporary collaboration between fashion designers and art museums means not that fashion is replacing art, but that it is being viewed increasingly as a cultural commodity—above and beyond mass fashion. Exhibitions—by contrast to fashion shows, shop openings and other media events—provide a democratic setting that concentrates on the object, and they are accessible to everyone. An exhibition offers a neutral communication of designer fashion's aesthetics and concept—in an authentic manner and furnished with narrative qualities.

Exhibitions in particular follow highly innovative approaches with lofty artistic-creative pretensions, although they are equally influenced by a necessity to appeal—for purposes of self-marketing or to win over sponsors, for instance. The fashion biennial 'Looking at Fashion' in Florence (1996) provided an artistic-interpretative exhibition concept as a result of collaboration between representatives of fine and applied art, including clothing. The borderline between clothing and art was highlighted in the exhibition 'untragbar' ('unwearable') in the Museum of Applied Art in Cologne in 2001, which showed sculptural clothing that had become unwearable or, respectively, sculpture that had developed into something wearable.[43] The link between fashion and architecture, which lies in their three-dimensionality, was underlined in the exhibition 'Skin + Bones: Parallel Practices in Fashion and Architecture', shown at the Museum of Contemporary Art, Los Angeles, in 2006/2007.

One pioneering exhibition of recent years focused on the creative works of Yohji Yamamoto and took place in Antwerp. The exhibition triptych 'Rethinking Boundaries' was dedicated to his clothing oeuvre, and three differing concepts were presented in three cities. In 2005, the dresses (Yamamoto himself does not talk of 'fashion') were integrated fully into the historical rooms of the Palazzo Pitti in Florence, radiating peace and an equal value; the fashionable seemed to dissolve into the timeless. Paris followed in the same year. Here, in the Musée de la Mode et du Textile in the Louvre, the focus was on communicating the design process and Yamamoto's design studio. Visitors encountered the most unusual and innovative concept in the Fashion Museum of Antwerp in 2006. Here, it was possible to experience Yamamoto's creations not only visually, but in a tactile and physical way. We are perhaps used to the visual aspect: here are the visitors; there (generally behind glass) are the objects, conforming to the spirit of 'distance creates esteem'. In Antwerp, the lighting took over the function of distancing and so permitted free access to the objects. The bright white light from approximately twenty fluorescent tubes behind each dress or coat made them appear like silhouettes. As fashion exhibitions usually take place in much-dimmed light to protect the fabrics, on this occasion the exhibition scenographer Masao Nihei favoured the concept of glittering light effects. When visitors entered the huge room containing eighty objects thus illuminated, they could imagine themselves in a 'Dream Shop', to quote the title of the exhibition. In addition, this bright light visualised the valence of Yamamoto's favourite colour, black. The objects were distributed in an orderly to haphazard way within the space, and no barriers of any kind prevented the visitors from studying precisely, sketching or simply admiring—from all sides and from top to bottom—every seam, the course of every thread, every hemline, every drape, every fold, every pleat, every pocket, every fastener, every sleeve, and so on. Thus far, however, this would still be a merely visual experience. But unlike the usual exhibition situation, touching and feeling were also allowed: one could stroke the pleat, feel the stiffening inside a voluminous skirt or allow the traditional Japanese techniques like *Yûzen* and *Shibori* to shimmer through one's hands. Visitors were irritated by a tag on the red coat made of crinkled wool from the Autumn/Winter 1995/1996 collection, which is held in shape by a net and quite familiar from a famous photo by David Sims. On this label, written in large letters, one could read the invitation 'TRY ME ON'. Now, the visitor could experience on his or her own body something that only mannequins and one or two favoured customers had been allowed in the past: to feel the warmth and comfort of a Yamamoto coat. Another sixteen models enticed visitors with the same 'TRY ME ON' notice, including a designer evening dress in black silk with asymmetrically draped tubes of fabric from the 2006 collection, and an evening dress with a long train culminating in a large, sequin-embroidered bag with flip fastener, slung over the shoulder and held with long, looping bows. When the wearer walks, this bag sways on her bottom, also leaving an extensive décolleté open at the back. Yohji Yamamoto's credo of 'Rethinking Boundaries' was made quite clear in his creations, which admit no conceivable boundaries, and also in this exhibition concept, which exploded all conventions. But photography was not permitted, meaning that the aura of uniqueness was preserved after all—in the usual way.

However, there is one problem shared by all fashion exhibitions: how can clothes be exhibited in the *absence of the body?* Absence results in a lack of life, for clothes are always a pointer to the body, and to its eroticism in particular (cf. p. 50). The problem is compounded when the explicit aim of models like those by Azzedine Alaïa or John Galliano is an eroticising of the body. The absence of the body and thus of its eroticism leaves behind clothes as an empty casing; our customary perceptual patterns remain unsatisfied. Like a memory, the process of wearing is attached to clothes; to a certain extent, this is the memory of a different form of existence. It can be compensated for only by photography, films and reports to some extent. On the other hand, one is better able to discern the form, construction method and material of originals in exhibitions; here, they can be communicated as applied art. In this context, it is true to say—and this also applies in art—that only originals have an inherent aura, which Walter Benjamin characterised as 'distance, however near it may be'[44]. It was precisely this aura and form of existence that Martin Margiela consciously threw into question when he painted his clothes with bacteria in order to visualise their decay and transience, and thus challenge their aura. This took place in the area around the Museum Boijmans van Beuningen, Rotterdam, in 1997; the presentation was not an installation, but an ex-stallation.

Viktor & Rolf utilised the retrospective exhibition 'The House of Viktor & Rolf'—which took place to mark their fifteenth anniversary as designers in the London Barbican Art Gallery in summer 2008—for a new perception of their creations. Their intention was to avoid the depreciation of déjà vu. Fifty dolls, each sixty centimetres tall, wore Viktor & Rolf creations in authentic miniature form and were displayed in conjunction with the original dresses, an idea that will remind insiders of the *Théâtre de la Mode* in 1945/1946. The difference from the *Théâtre de la Mode,* which had been conceived as a supplement to a real fashion show, was that 'The House of Viktor & Rolf' was to be perceived as a doll's house, or at least the dolls used were porcelain dolls with childish proportions rather than miniature mannequins.

Fashion is documented not only via the clothing object, but also by means of its marketing practices and acceptance. Fashion drawings, fashion photos, fashion journals and advertising are archived in museums and libraries. As the tendency is to attribute the 'status' of a profane commodity to fashion in the cultural scale of values, the memory value of designer models to date has been oriented on whether they influenced fashion, consistently realised the logic of innovation or were successful in an economic sense. As a consequence of the Internet, today the possibility of archivation has increased enormously. Web sites specialising in fashion such as www.firstview.com or www.style.com have presented most models by all the well-known designers since around 1998, and it has been possible to read reports by Suzy Menkes, one of the world's most important fashion journalists and critics, on the Internet page of the *International Herald Tribune* since 1991. This means that one is no longer completely dependent on cultural archives, unless one attaches importance to the original models. Together with digitalised picture archives, to this extent a democratisation of the memory value of clothes and designer fashion has occurred, regardless of their market success.

Epilogue

Fashion is more than the sum of clothing and textiles. It offers insights into society, culture and itself. However, the much-cited proverb 'clothes make the man', the starting point for a novella of the same name written by Gottfried Keller in 1866, does not suffice as an explanation, for it aims only at the semblance of being, reflecting the hope that one is what one wears. It is its semblance that keeps fashion alive: its function as a symbol of eroticism, power, knowledge, aesthetics, pleasure, taste and prestige.

Fashion is defined by the requirement of social validity, which is negotiated in a communicative manner. The unwearable or nonfunctional may also become fashion if a specific community allows it. Fashion provides diversity, including constructs opposing the so-called mainstream. It can be instable or conservative, progressive or reactionary—like the social group that lays claim to it. Fashion is a conglomerate of the current. To be 'in' fashion is equivalent to being 'in' reality; indeed, more than this, it means being real.

Changes in fashion are indicative of changes in society. There is a tendency to label radical changes as the 'end of' a particular era or movement. There is nothing of which the end has not already been prophesied: painting, jazz, skyscrapers, the book, haute couture, and fashion as a whole. However, changes actually signify the beginning of something new. The 'end of' offers inventions the chance to establish themselves as innovation. It is not the pointed logic of exaggeration displayed by even more daring border crossings that fundamentally questions fashion (not clothes), but rather the concentrated power of industry and the public's low aesthetic demands. When too much cultural garbage exists, the standard of the culturally valuable depreciates. New quality characteristics are called for constantly as independent statements of a cultural identity. It is not mass fashion but innovative designer fashion that needs our backing.

No clothing speaks for itself, but only with reference to time, space, the individual or society, and to perceptual patterns permeated by knowledge. In the main, what is offered and worn as 'fashion' is clothing, which is called fashion as a result of commercially strategic definitions and experiences. We have lost the distinction between clothes and fashion, for the banal and comfortable have caught up with it. The short term blocks our view of the essential, which can be defined as those things that will endure in the cultural memory. This is the fashion of the hippies and the hip hoppers, and certainly not empty, insignificant mass fashion. Economic globalisation is one thing, social globalisation is another. The 'one world' character of clothes does not emphasise the discretion of the different but nivellates all the differences. 'The Western' exploits the opportunity to help itself from everywhere, and the original owners of codes and rituals feel prompted to abandon them as a result.

Fashion, with its structure and strategies, is convincingly explained as a social system. It emerges as a self-referential system of operative closure, which develops dynamics in exchange with the environment and varies its state without altering its systemic structures as such. Put in simple terms: fashion remains fashion because the fashion does not remain the fashion. Fashion is neither a phenomenon nor paradoxical, as it is often assumed to be. It is a social construct that is perceived in the form of clothing. It is a personal aesthetic perception in the collective, as the individual becomes meaningful only through the whole.

One noticeable feature of both art and design over the last two hundred years is that manifestos, theories and occasionally ideologies have been the driving forces behind a new system of values. They have provided the criteria permitting the new and enabling us to understand it. Theory promoted acceptance of the abstract, the constructed and deconstructed, the conceptual, the surreal and the fantastic—in which the vestimentary has always participated. Every academic analysis is meaningful only if it refers, like this book, to concrete examples. The impulses of fashion theory are relevant to the practice of fashion design and also to the consumer's understanding of the designers' creations, which always represent the creation of culture and a shaping of the future as well. It may seem that fashion is not countenanced in the present age, but there is certainly a need for it. There is absolutely no doubt as to the relevance of fashion.

Notes

Chapter 1

1. Quoted from Elke Bippus and Frank Hesse's oral presentation 'The Art of Research' at the conference 'Fashion, Body, Cult', Bremen, 5 November 2005.
2. Aristotle, *Metaphysics,* book 1, quoted in Christof Rapp, *Aristoteles zur Einführung* (Hamburg, 2004), p. 170.
3. Quoted in Bernd Stiegler, *Theoriegeschichte der Photographie* (Munich, 2006), p. 76.
4. Charles Sanders Peirce, *Schriften I. Zur Entstehung des Pragmatismus,* edited with an introduction by Karl-Otto Apel (Suhrkamp, 1967), p. 186.
5. Gerhard Roth, 'Das menschliche Gehirn und seine Wirklichkeit', interview with Peter Diehl. http://www.comedweb.de/DE/page.php?pageID=119.
6. Detlef B. Linke, *Kunst und Gehirn. Die Eroberung des Unsichtbaren* (Reinbek, 2001), p. 27.
7. Humberto R. Maturana and Francisco Varela: 'Der Baum der Erkenntnis', in Thomas Kaestle (ed.), *Wann ist die Kunst? Prozess, Moment, Gültigkeit* (Kunstverein Hildesheim, 2005), p. 52.
8. Ibid.
9. Specialist term from the Latin *vestire,* to dress, or *vestis,* clothing.
10. Jan Assmann originally coined the term 'cultural memory' in the context of Egyptology in 1975. The basic thesis is that cultural knowledge is stored for centuries and passed down almost by chance. The future of the cultural memory lies in archives, museums and educational institutions and also on the Internet.
11. Boris Groys, *Über das Neue. Versuch einer Kulturökonomie* (Munich, 1992), p. 70.
12. Jörn Müller, 'Theorie in eigener Sache'. In Kaestle, *Wann ist die Kunst,* p. 39. This opinion is also shared by the media theorist and philosopher Boris Groys. And according to the view of philosopher Arnold Gehlen, art should not deny its fundamental need for explanation but explicitly admit to it: 'Now we plead for a "peinture conceptionelle", which adopts a thesis concerning its existential foundation as the conception of the image and, in connection with such a thesis, gives a conceptual account of itself using the means of depiction and formal principles.' Quoted in Groys, p. 183.
13. http://manifeste.today.net.
14. English translation, *The Fashion System* (Farrar, Straus & Giroux, 1983).

15. Roland Barthes, *Die Sprache der Mode* (Frankfurt/Main, 1985), p. 283.

16. Ibid., p. 10.

17. Gerhard Goebel, 'Notizen zur Semiotik der Mode', in Silvia Bovenschen, ed., *Die Listen der Mode* (Frankfurt/Main, 1986), p. 466. The original version by Gerhard Goebel was titled "Für eine Semiotik der Mode" and appeared in the magazine *Lendemains* (21 February 1981).

18. Goebel, 'Notizen zur Semiotik der Mode', p. 476.

Chapter 2

1. Textiles represent a separate field of research independent of clothing (see www. eurotextile.de). Current states of material are documented and researched, for example at the Research Institute Hohenstein (www.hohenstein.de), and historical textiles at the Abegg Foundation, Riggisberg, Switzerland; here training is also provided in scientific textile conservation and restoration (www.abegg-stiftung.ch).

2. Heide Nixdorff points out that in the so-called male discipline of archaeology, research into textiles is often negated or the textile part of artefacts often cast aside without research. Heide Nixdorff (ed.), *Das textile Medium als Phänomen der Grenze—Begrenzung—Entgrenzung*. Reihe Historische Anthropologie, Vol. 30 (Berlin, 1996), p. 14. In American archaeology, which deviates from the European tradition, the textile belongs to the field of research into "material culture" (by contrast to "social culture") and, as such, is experiencing a current increase in interest, in Europe as well.

Chapter 3

1. A series of exhibitions have been devoted to this subject, including Claudia Pantellini and Peter Stohler, eds, *Body Extensions* (Stuttgart, 2004); Harold Koda, *Extreme Beauty: The Body Transformed,* exhibition book produced by the Metropolitan Museum of Art (2001).

2. 'Clothing' refers to the entirety of clothing with no attribution by gender or specific age; the German *Kleidung* is derived from the Middle High German *kleit,* meaning cloth, and from *klei,* meaning clay-rich earth: Cloth was milled with clay. The word *Kleid* (dress) did not emerge in place of the Old High German *Cotte,* Middle High German *Kotta* and Latin *Tunica* until the twelfth century, just like the term *Kleidung* (clothing) replaced the older *Gewand* from the Old High German *giwant gewendet* (turned) for cloth folded and stored. *Gewand* came from the Middle High German *l_nwāt* for linen cloth.

3. Erving Goffman, *Das Individuum im öffentlichen Austausch. Mikrostudien zur öffentlichen Ordnung* (Frankfurt/Main, 1982), p. 67.

4. On this, see 'Mode und Erotik', in Ingrid Loschek, *Mode—Verführung und Notwendigkeit. Struktur und Strategie der Aussehensveränderung* (Munich, 1991), p. 212ff.

5. On this, see Carsten Niemitz, *Geheimnis des aufrechten Ganges* (Munich, 2004); Niemitz, ed., *Erbe und Umwelt. Zur Natur von Anlage und Selbstbestimmung des Menschen* (Frankfurt, 1989).

6. 'The bosom in full view, at my reckoning three fingers wide. The robe tight round the body. The breasts thrust so high, a candlestick could rest atop.' From the Middle High German poem "Der Kittel", Alsace, mid-fifteenth century.

7. On clothing art and artist's clothing of the nineteenth and twentieth centuries, see Yvonne Schütze, *Kleidung als und im Kunstwerk des 20. Jahrhunderts unter sozialtheoretischer Perspektive* (Berlin, 2001), p. 310ff; and Ingrid Loschek, *Reclams Mode- und Kostümlexikon* (Stuttgart, 2005), p. 344ff.

8. Hippolyte Taine, *Note sur Paris. Vie et opinions de M. Frédéric-Thomas Graindorge* (satirical genre pictures) (Paris, 1867), p. 56.

Chapter 4

1. Here too, it is a matter of vestimentary fashion and the whole of body design, but not of forms that are typical of a specific age, i.e. a general "modern" form e.g. of furniture or cars.

2. Niklas Luhmann, 'Die Gesellschaft der Gesellschaft', in *Die Paradoxie der Identität und ihre Entfaltung durch Unterscheidung*, Chapter 5 (Frankfurt/Main, 1997), p. 1070.

3. Loschek, *Reclams Mode- und Kostümlexikon*, pp. 309–10.

4. Niklas Luhmann, *Die Gesellschaft der Gesellschaft*, unpublished manuscript (1995), p. 462ff. Quoted in Detlef Horster, *Niklas Luhmann, eine Einführung* (Munich, 1997), p. 177.

5. Niklas Luhmann, *Die Kunst der Gesellschaft* (Frankfurt/Main, 1995), p. 218.

6. Niklas Luhmann, *Soziale Systeme. Grundriß einer allgemeinen Theorie* (Frankfurt/Main, 1984), p. 28f.

7. Peter Fuchs, *Der Sinn der Beobachtung. Begriffliche Untersuchungen* (Weilerswist, 2004), p. 129.

8. Dirk Baecker, ed., *Niklas Luhmann. Einführung in die Systemtheorie* (Heidelberg, 2004), pp. 46–7.

9. Based on Fuchs, *Der Sinn der Beobachtung*; Luhmann, *Die Gesellschaft der Gesellschaft*; and Baecker, ed., *Niklas Luhmann. Einführung in die Systemtheorie*.

10. Classics of specialist literature already indicate this, for example Max von Boehn, *Bekleidungskunst und Mode* (Munich, 1918), p. 80 (an analysis of fashion and industrialisation, fashion and the copy that is still valid today); and Norbert

Stern, *Mode und Kultur,* 2 vols (Dresden, 1915) (among other things, emphasis on change within the same).

11. Peter Fuchs, *Ethik Magazin* (February 2001), p. 22ff. See also Niklas Luhmann, *Die Ausdifferenzierung des Kunstsystems* (Bern, 1994), p. 47.
12. See also Karl Rosenkranz, *Ästhetik des Hässlichen* (Leipzig, 1990).
13. Luhmann, *Soziale Systeme,* p. 100.
14. Niklas Luhmann, *Zweckbegriff und Systemrationalität. Über die Funktion von Zwecken in sozialen Systemen* (Tübingen, 1968; Reprint Frankfurt/Main, 1973), p. 20.
15. Yvonne Schütze is of the opinion, mistakenly, that fashion is part of the economy. This is because she exclusively observes clothing in art, but not clothing in fashion. Schütze, *Kleidung,* p. 373ff.
16. Michael Wörz, *Mailing List Systemtheorie* (13 January 2007).
17. Peter Fuchs, 'Zur Beobachtung des Körpers', in *Die Psyche. Studien zur Innenwelt der Außenwelt der Innenwelt* (Weilerswist, 2005), p. 105. On this, see also Schroer, *Räume, Orte, Grenze,* p. 291.
18. Fuchs, *Die Psyche,* p. 117.
19. Niklas Luhmann, Peter Fuchs and Elena Esposito avoid the expression 'third order' as 'inelegant' and refer to observers of the second order here, too.
20. Elena Esposito, *Die Verbindlichkeit des Vorübergehenden. Paradoxien der Mode* (Frankfurt/Main, 2004), p. 10.

Chapter 5

1. Irenäus Eibl-Eibesfeldt, *Die Biologie des menschlichen Verhaltens. Grundriß der Humanethologie* (Munich, 1984), p. 823.

Chapter 6

1. Gerd Binnig, 'Warum ist es einfach, kreativ zu sein?', in Heinrich von Pierer and Bolko von Oetinger, *Wie kommt das Neue in die Welt?* (Hamburg, 1999), p. 303; and Gerd Binnig, *Aus dem Nichts. Über die Kreativität von Natur und Mensch,* 2nd edn (Munich/Zurich,1989).
2. Frank Sulloway, *Born to Rebel: Birth Order, Family Dynamics, and Creative Lives* (Boston, 1996).
3. Tao Ho, 'Das Herz, der Kopf, die Hand: Leidenschaft, Analyse, Produktion'. In Pierer and Oetinger, *Wie kommt das Neue in die Welt?,* p. 246.
4. Ansgar Häfner, 'Kreativität und Wissen', in *Konturen. Zeitschrift der Hochschule Pforzheim* 26 (2006), p. 51.
5. Ibid., p. 49.
6. Groys, *Über das Neue,* pp. 50, 171.

7. Mihályi Csikszentmihályi, *Flow. Das Geheimnis des Glücks* (Stuttgart, 1992).

8. Further along, another girl: rainbow-coloured polyester, polyurethane, and organdy stretch top, a slight opening at the chest, and a right shoulder of Quasimodo-like proportions, a shoulder stuffed with pods. *ArtForum* (December 1996).

9. See Chapter 1, note 10.

10. Immanuel Kant, *Kritik der Urteilskraft* (Berlin 1790), §47, section 1. Kant concerns himself with genius in detail in §46 to §50.

11. Ibid., §46, 3.

12. Semir Zeki, *Inner Vision: An Exploration of Art and the Brain* (Oxford University Press, 1999).

13. Edward de Bono, *The Use of Lateral Thinking,* (Cape, 1968).

14. Bolko von Oetinger, 'Wie kommt das Neue in die Welt?', in Frieder Meyer-Krahmer and Siegfried Lange, eds, *Geisteswissenschaften und Innovationen* (Heidelberg, 1999), p. 73.

15. Erving Goffman, *Frame Analysis: An Essay on the Organization of Experience* (Cambridge, 1974).

16. Mihály Csikszentmihályi, *Flow. Das Geheimnis des Glücks* (Stuttgart, 1992).

17. Roger Willemsen, 'Über das Obszöne', in Barbara Vinken, ed., *Die nackte Wahrheit. Zur Pornographie und zur Rolle des Obszönen in der Gegenwart* (Frankfurt/Main 1997), p. 129.

18. Ibid., p. 129.

19. Ibid., p. 132.

20. Boris Groys in an interview with Sonja Zekri on 'Die RAF-Geschichte wird zum Ready-made', *Süddeutsche Zeitung* (25 July 2003), http://www.perlen taucher.de/feuilletons/2003-07-28.html.

21. Ibid.

22. Ingrid Loschek, *Accessoires. Symbolik und Geschichte* (Munich, 1993), p. 177.

23. Bernard Rudofsky, *The Unfashionable Human Body* (New York 1947), p. 151.

24. Music by Takehisa Kosugi, performed at the Brooklyn Academy of Music, Brooklyn, New York, and at the Paris Opera 1998.

25. Palmers is an Austrian underwear company that is well known in central Europe.

26. Michael Semff and Anthony Spira, eds, *Hans Bellmer* [book for an exhibition in the Staatliche Graphische Sammlung] (Munich, 2006), p. 53.

27. Museum Moderner Kunst Stiftung Ludwig Wien, ed., *Erwin Wurm, the Artist Who Swallowed the World* (Ostfildern, 2006); Sophie Haaser, Museum Moderner Kunst im 20er Haus, ed., *Erwin Wurm* (Vienna, 1994).

28. Nils Binnberg's interpretation that Viktor & Rolf are concerned with the body alone is not tenable, as this is a matter of the difference between clothing and body as a result of textile overforming; see *Mode Depesche,* March 2005.

29. The German sport fashion company Bogner brought an anorak with a down lining onto the market in 1951. It was not until the 1980s that down-padded

coats and anoraks became widely distributed in Europe as a result of the increasing rejection of clothing made from animal fur.

30. Video; see http://husseinchalayan.net/#/videos.2003.2003_s_s_manifest_destiny/. Accessed 18 March 2009.

31. To a certain extent, this is also true of architecture and interior design. 'In a certain sense, Le Corbusier's pilgrimage church at Ronchamp, built in 1955, is the incunabula of biomorphism; Eero Saarinen's TWA Terminal, reminiscent of eagle's wings, in New York and the erotically charged Pop Grottos by the Danish designer Verner Panton or Peter Cook's and Colin Fournier's Kunsthaus in Graz, a blue-shimmering jellyfish from outer space, follow the same track.' In *Die Organische Form* [exhibition catalogue], Wilhelm-Wagenfeld-Stiftung (Bremen, 2003), p. 3.

32. There are peoples who go without clothing, but they do not go undecorated or unpainted. The expression of eroticism and sensuality is dependent on culture, religion and custom. See Loschek, *Mode—Verführung und Notwendigkeit,* p. 78ff.

33. Jane Mulvagh, *Vivienne Westwood. Die Lady ist ein Punk* (Munich, 2001), p. 96.

34. The project *Il sarto immortale* consists of several parts. The first installation, *hautnah,* was in an exhibition by KUNST+PROJEKTE in the Gallery of the City of Sindelfingen in 1995. In *Couture* (1997), two seamstresses in the Kunstverein Wiesbaden made fabrics printed with naked bodies into the items of clothing named here. The title *Il sarto immortale* is based on the fairy tale of the immortal tailor. He creeps into people's bedrooms at night in order to sew and fit a shirt, woven from the threads of their destiny; they are then compelled to wear the shirt and to accept the associated suffering.

35. In the installation *Display,* the project was presented in various exhibitions by means of video, including at Künstlerhaus Bethanien in 2000. At the action *Outside,* posters were displayed on advertising columns and at bus stops showing models wearing parts of the d'Urbano collection, including the name of the artist and the sale price. The posters were comparable to typical advertising posters, like those of H&M, for example. After it had been shown for the first time in public space in the city of Aachen in 1999, the poster action had to be terminated because of a legal complaint; it was realised once again in Berlin, in the course of the exhibition *cross female* in 2000.

36. Through its publication, the individual body is immediately subject to marketing in the fashion industry, via fashion show, display, advertising and so forth. By marketing the artwork via the distribution methods of the fashion industry, d'Urbano ironically questions the meaning and methods of this system. In addition, d'Urbano visualised the discrepancy between the individual, imperfect body and the ideal image of woman conveyed by the media and the staged perfection of the fashion world.

37. There is a comparable conceptual background to the *Torn Dress* that Elsa Schiaparelli produced on the basis of designs by Salvador Dalí in 1937.

38. Ingrid Loschek, *Accessoires. Symbolik und Geschichte* (Munich, 1993), p. 141 f. and 22ff.

39. Ergonomic investigations ascertained that women slip or fall over more often than men, which is connected with the reduced base of high-heeled shoes. Women have to compensate for this uncertainty with conscious physicality, demonstrative balancing and movements that often appear artificial, such as increased hip motion and an exaggeratedly hollow back. This emphasises the breast and bottom, which results not least in an erotic walk and signals helplessness. Barbara Tietze, 'Der Menschliche Gang. Gegenstand ergonomischer Forschung', in *e.g. Schuhe. Vom bloßen Fuß zum Stöckelschuh. Eine Kulturgeschichte der Fußbekleidung,* ed. Michael Andritzky, Günter Kämpf and Vilma Link, Werkbund-Archiv 17 (Gießen, 1987), p. 94ff.

40. Loschek, *Accessoires,* pp. 24–7.

41. Claire Wilcox, ed., *Radical Fashion.* Exhibition book, Victoria and Albert Museum (London, 2001), p. 96.

42. Bradley Quinn, 'Exhibition Review: Radical Fashion? A Critique of the Radical Fashion Exhibition. Victoria and Albert Museum, London'. In *Fashion Theory* 6/4 (2002), p. 443 f.

43. Statement made by Bernhard Willhelm at the conference 'Mode, Körper, Kult', Bremen, 5 November 2005.

44. Ibid.

45. Ibid.

46. Hussein Chalayan, *Exhibition Catalogue* (Groningen/Wolfsburg, 2005), p. 30.

47. Ludwig Wittgenstein, *Tractatus Logico-Philosophicus* (Vienna, 1921), foreword.

48. Bradley Quinn analysed components of Hussein Chalayan's collections in 'A Note: Hussein Chalayan. Fashion and Technology', *Fashion Theory* 6/4 (2002), p. 359.

49. See Courtney Smith and Sean Topham, *Xtreme Fashion* (Munich/London, 2005); Suzanne Lee, *Fashioning the Future: Tomorrow's Wardrobe* (London, 2005); *Mutations/Mode 1960–2000* [book for the exhibition at Musée Galliera] (Paris, 2000).

50. Video; see http://www.husseinchalayan.net/#/videos.2007.2007_s_s_one_hun dred_and_eleven/. Accessed 18 March 2009.

51. Video; see http://www.husseinchalayan.net/#/videos.2007.2007_a_w_ air borne/. Accessed 18 March 2009. In his Autumn/Winter 2007/2008 collection *Airborne,* Hussein Chalayan made his hats and dresses glow by means of integrated LEDs and increased the intensity of light by sewing on Swarovski crystals. The glowing winter hat and the automatically shining party dress radiate an aura of sensuality and emotions.

52. www.lumalive.com.

53. See Sandy Black, ed., *Fashioning Fabrics: Contemporary Textiles in Fashion* (London, 2006).
54. Alexandra Weigand, 'Virtual Aesthetics—Contemplating Images', in Ekkehart Baumgartner, Simona Heuberger, Alexandra Weigand, and Philipp Messner, *Virtual Aesthetics: Considering Perception at the Dawn of the 21st Century* (Innsbruck 2008), p. 38.
55. Ellen Lupton, 'Second Skin. Neues organisches Design', in Gerhard Seltmann and Werner Lippert, eds, *Entry Paradise. Neue Welten des Designs* (Basel, 2006), pp. 122–35.
56. www.core77.com/competition2000/skinthetic/main.html.
57. Peter Sloterdijk, 'Das Zeug zur Macht', in Seltmann and Lippert, *Entry Paradise,* p. 102.
58. Ibid., p. 110.
59. Christoph Keller, 'Wir Cyborgs', in *Body Extensions* [book for the exhibition] (Zurich, 2004), p. 24f. and p. 34.
60. Norbert Bolz, *BANG-design. Design manifest des 21. Jahrhunderts* (Trend Büro, Hamburg, 2006), p. 9. In the United States, use is made of NBIC, an acronym for nano, bio, info and cogno, as a field of research moving into the future.
61. Christiane Luible and Alexander Lindt, 'Extended Body', diploma, University of Applied Sciences, Pforzheim, 1999/2000, p. 4.
62. Taken from an e-mail addressed to the author in September 2005.
63. Caroline Evans, 'Yesterday's Emblems and Tomorrow's Commodities', in *Fashion Cultures: Theories, Explorations and Analysis,* ed. Stella Bruzzi and P. C. Gibson (London, 2000), p. 107.
64. Annika von Taube, 'The Fabric of Life' (interview with Hussein Chalayan), *Sleek* magazine, issue 9 (2005/2006), p. 135. See also http://stylezeitgeist.com/forums/archive/index.php?t-2542.html. Accessed March 2009.

Chapter 7

1. Joseph Alois Schumpeter, *Theorie der wirtschaftlichen Entwicklung* (Berlin, 1911). Quoted from Joseph A. Schumpeter, *Kapitalismus, Sozialismus und Demokratie* (Tübingen, 1997), p. 138.
2. Ibid.
3. Ibid.
4. Hans Robert Jauß, 'Il faut commencer par le commencement!', in *Nachahmung und Illusion.*Poetik und Hermeneutik, vol. 1 (Munich, 1964), p. 563f. On this, cf. also Esposito, *Die Verbindlichkeit des Vorübergehenden,* p. 96ff.
5. Groys, *Über das Neue,* p. 67.
6. Ibid., p. 68.
7. Herbert Anton, 'Modernität als Aporie und Ereignis', in Hans Steffen, ed., *Aspekte der Modernität* (Göttingen, 1965), p. 62.

8. Christoph-Friedrich von Braun, 'Immer Schneller?—Mehr?—Neu?—Besser?', in Pierer and Oetinger, *Wie kommt das Neue in die Welt?*, p. 403.

9. Suzy Menkes, 'High on Haute Couture and Luxe Summit', *International Herald Tribune,* 22 July 1991.

10. St. Augustine, *The Confessiones,* Book 10, 396–8, ca. 400 AD, quoted in Esposito, *Die Verbindlichkeit des Vorübergehenden,* p. 39. Esposito analyses the new in the context of philosophy and literature and draws conclusions for fashion, which are, however, unsuitable and untenable according to evidence from fashion history and fashion theory. See also Esposito, *Die Verbindlichkeit des Vorübergehenden,* p. 112.

11. Eibl-Eibesfeldt, *Biologie des menschlichen Verhaltens,* p. 823.

12. Erving Goffman, *Frame Analysis: An Essay on the Organization of Experience* (Cambridge, 1974), quoted in Franz Liebl, *Der Schock des Neuen. Entstehung und Management von Issues und Trends* (Munich, 2000), p. 72.

13. Gerald Hüther, *Die Macht der inneren Bilder. Wie Visionen das Gehirn, den Menschen und die Welt verändern* (Göttingen ,2004), p. 23.

14. Karl H. Müller, 'Wie Neues Entsteht', *Österreichische Zeitschrift für Geschichtswissenschaften* 11/1 (2000), p. 91.

15. Rudolf Arnheim, *Art and Visual Perception: A Psychology of the Creative Eye* (University of California Press, 1954). German edition: *Anschauliches Denken: zur Einheit von Bild und Begriff* (Cologne, 1972), p. 35.

16. Charles Baudelaire, 'Der Maler des modernen Lebens', in Henry Schumann, ed., *Baudelaire: Der Künstler und das moderne Leben* (Leipzig, 1990), p. 292.

17. Helge Gerndt, *Kulturwissenschaft im Zeitalter der Globalisierung. Volkskundliche Markierungen. Münchner Beiträge zur Volkskunde.* Institute for Ethnology/European Ethnology of the University of Munich, Vol. 31 (Münster, 2002), p. 251.

18. Franz Emanuel Weinert, 'Das Individuum', in Pierer and Oetinger, *Wie kommt das Neue in die Welt?,* p. 275.

19. Egon Friedell, *Kulturgeschichte der Neuzeit. Die Krisis der europäischen Seele von der schwarzen Pest bis zum Weltkrieg,* 3 vols (Munich, 1927–1931), reprint, vol. 1 (Cologne 1997), p. 283.

20. Franz Emanuel Weinert, 'Das Individuum', in Pierer and Oetinger, *Wie kommt das Neue in die Welt?,* p. 269.

21. Karl Popper, *Die offene Gesellschaft und ihre Feinde* (Stuttgart, 1992).

22. Melissa Taylor, 'Cultural Transition: Fashion's Cultural Dialogue between Commerce and Art', in *Fashion Theory* 9/4 (2005), p. 446.

23. Thomas McEvilley, *Art and Otherness: Crisis in Cultural Identity* (New York, 1992), quoted in Michael Haerdter, 'Postmoderne Nomaden', in Kaestle, *Wann ist die Kunst,* p. 95.

24. Groys, *Über das Neue,* p. 91.

25. Ibid., p. 43.

26. Ibid., p. 32.

27. Ibid.
28. Manfred Schmalriede, 'Semiotik und Ästhetik', in 125 Jahre FHG Pforzheim 2002, p. 210.
29. Title of a book by Franz Liebl.
30. Liebl, *Der Schock des Neuen,* p. 97.
31. Michael Wörz, *Mailing Liste Systemtheorie,* 9 February 2006.
32. The origin of the baggy pants style was in black American ghetto areas, where youths deliberately let their trousers slip down in solidarity with prisoners, who are obliged to wear their trousers without a belt. Their music scene consists of gangsta rap and battle rap. In addition, poor children wear clothes that are too big for them so that they can grow into them.
33. Letter from Leopold Mozart dated 22 December 1780 to his son, Wolfgang. Quoted in Wilhelm A. Bauer and Erich Otto, eds, *Wolfgang Amadeus Mozart, Briefe und Aufzeichnungen,* vol. 3 (Kassel, 1971), p. 53.
34. From the work programme of the Vienna Workshops, probably written by Josef Hoffmann in 1905. Quoted in Werner S. Schweiger, *Wiener Werkstätte. Kunst und Handwerk 1903–1932* (Augsburg, 1995), p. 42.
35. http://www.faz.net, accessed 24 April 05.
36. Among others, Karl R. Popper, *The Open Universe: An Argument for Indeterminism* (Totowa, 1982).
37. Groys, *Über das Neue,* p. 68.
38. Quoted in Liebl, *Der Schock des Neuen,* p. 32.
39. This vision of development from the local hiking rucksack into the global backpack was already shared by American writer Jack Kerouac in 1958, when he wrote in his book *Dharma Bums,* 'I have the vision of a great rucksack revolution, thousands or even millions of young Americans who travel with rucksacks.' It took another twenty years or so before this vision became reality.
40. Lecture at the Siemens Foundation, Munich, 23 June 2005.
41. *International Herald Tribune,* 13.02.2006.
42. Esposito, *Die Verbindlichkeit des Vorübergehenden,* p. 112.
43. Peter Bäldle reported on this in the weekend edition 6/7 November 1982 under the heading 'Paris Hauptstadt der Mode'. The only daily fashion newspaper, *Women's Wear Daily,* published a report Christopher Petkanas, 'Comme des Garçons hits Paris', on 17 December 1982.
44. Yuniya Kawamura, *The Japanese Revolution in Paris Fashion* (Oxford, 2004), p. 129.
45. Barbara Vinken, Mode. Spiel mit Grenzen. in, Nixdorff, *Das textile Medium,* p. 109–11.
46. Groys, *Über das Neue,* p. 68.
47. Loschek, *Verführung,* p. 78 ff. and p. 93f.
48. Into the nineteenth century, underpants (slips) for women were regarded as immoral, because they were worn only as erotic underwear (made of cheap

half-silk!) by prostitutes or as a visible covering for the pubic area by artistes and performers (i.e. by a subcultural class). Underpants for men were a much-discussed topic in the medical field until into the nineteenth century, on the one hand with respect to the unhealthy effects of warmth on the testicles (giving an advantage to the loincloth and wrap-around clothes like the kilt and sarong, and also to Arabian loose robes), and on the other hand with respect to preventing masturbation and precocious maturity. At the end of the eighteenth century, Jean Jacques Rousseau—in *Emile,* for example—and Joachim Heinrich Campe concerned themselves with this topic in the context of an excurse on education and schooling. In addition, the doctor Bernhard Christoph Faust made a statement on the subject in *Wie der Geschlechtstrieb der Menschen in Ordnung zu bringen und wie die Menschen besser und glücklicher zu machen* (Braunschweig, 1791), quoted in *Zeitschrift für Sexualmedizin,* July 1981. See also Wolfgang Brückner, 'Zu Thesen über die Männerunterhosen im 19. Jahrhundert', in *Anzeiger des Germanischen Nationalmuseums,* 1998, pp. 225–8. See also Leo Schidrowitz, *Sittengeschichte des Intimen* (Vienna/Leipzig, 1926).

49. See Ingrid Loschek, 'The United Look of Fashion', in *Die Welt als Laufsteg. Zeitschrift des instituts für Auslandsbeziehungen,* no. 52 (April 2002), pp. 36–8.
50. Black, *Fashioning Fabrics,* pp. 31, 35.
51. Personal conversation with Bernhard Willhelm at the conference 'Mode, Körper, Kult', Bremen, 5 November 2005.
52. Max von Boehn, *Bekleidungskunst und Mode* (Munich, 1918), p. 84.
53. Müller, *Wie Neues Entsteht,* p. 100.
54. http://www.indexmagazin.com/interviews/miguel_adrover.html. Accessed February 2007.
55. http://www.designerhistory.com/historyoffashion/chaneltwo.html. Accessed March 2007.
56. See Rudolf Dekker and Lotte van de Pol, *Frauen in Männerkleidern. Weibliche Transvestiten und ihre Geschichte* (Berlin, 1990); Andrea Stoll and Verena Wodtke-Werner, eds, *Sakkorausch und Rollentausch. Männliche Leitbilder als Freiheitsentwürfe von Frauen* (Dortmund, 1996); Susanne Benedek and Adolphe Binder, *Von tanzenden Kleidern und sprechenden Leibern. Crossdressing als Auflösung der Geschlechterpolarität?* (Dortmund, 1997); J. J. Allen, *The Man in the Red Velvet Dress: Inside the World of Cross-Dressing* (New York, 1996).
57. The brothers Daniel and Markus Freitag in Zurich first made a courier bag by sewing together old truck tarpaulins, car belts and bicycle inner tubes in 1993 (recycling). The functional Freitag bag became a cult object and is sold and distributed in various versions all over Europe. See http://www.freitag.ch.
58. See http://www.wearable-technologies.de.
59. A network research project of ITV Denkendorf, BPI Hohenstein and IPE University Stuttgart.

60. See http://www.core77.com/competition2000/sustain/main.html. Accessed March 2007.

61. See, http://www.cutecircuit.com. Accessed March 2009.

62. Bruce Grenville, ed., *The Uncanny, Experiments in Cyborg Culture,* exhibition book, Vancouver Art Gallery (Vancouver, 1999), p. 44.

63. Donna Haraway, 'A Cyborg Manifesto, Science, Technology, and Socialist-Feminism in the Late Twentieth Century', in *Simians, Cyborgs and Women, The Reinvention of Nature* (New York, 1991), pp. 149–81; http://www.stanford.edu/dept/HPS/Haraway/CyborgManifesto.html. Accessed March 2009.

64. See http://www.secondlife.com. Accessed March 2009.

65. Birgit Richard, *Sheroes. Genderspiel im virtuellen Raum* (Bielefeld, 2004).

66. Christiane Funken, 'Körpertext und Textkörper. Zur vermeintlichen Neutralisierung geschlechtlicher Körperinszenierungen im elektronischen Netz', in Barbara Becker/Irmela Schneider, eds, *Was von Körper übrig bleibt* (Frankfurt/Main, 2000). The power of the belt is expressed in its symbolism, cf. Loschek, *Accessoires,* pp. 54–9.

67. Julia Bertschik, *Mode und Moderne. Kleidung als Spiegel des Zeitgeistes in der deutschsprachigen Literatur (1770–1945)* (Cologne, 2005), p. 11.

68. Georg Simmel, 'Die Mode', in *Philosophische Kultur. Gesammelte Essais* (Leipzig, 1911), p. 31.

69. Bertschik, *Mode und Moderne,* p. 16.

Chapter 8

1. Esposito, *Die Verbindlichkeit des Vorübergehenden.*

2. Thomas Schnierer examines the rules of these dynamics in Schnierer, *Modewandel und Gesellschaft. Die Dynamik von 'in' und 'out'.* PhD dissertation, Ludwig-Maximilian-Universität, Munich (1995).

3. Arthur Schopenhauer, *Parerga und Paralipomens* (Leipzig, 1851), p. 394, quoted in Bertschik, *Mode und Moderne,* p. 12.

4. *Journal des Luxus und der Moden,* special paperback edition of the old historic magazine, selected and commentated by Christina Kröll (Dortmund, 1979), p. 166.

5. Louise Godard de Donville, *Signification de la mode sous Louis XIII* (Aix-en-Provence, 1978), p. 30.

6. Richard Dawkins, *The Selfish Gene* (Oxford, 1976).

7. Bertschik, *Mode und Moderne,* p. 3. However, both Bertschik and Elena Esposito mention some 'phenomena still open' in fashion, which are explained from the standpoints of behavioural science and neuroscience in my opinion; see also Loschek, *Verführung.*

8. Loschek, *Verführung,* pp. 11–34; Loschek, *Reclams Mode- und Kostümlexikon,* p. 9.

9. Ralf Baumgart, Volker Eichener, *Norbert Elias. Zur Einführung* (Hamburg, 1991), pp. 58, 127.

10. Bertschik, *Mode und Moderne,* p. 8.

11. Karl Gutzkow, *Der Mensch des neunzehnten Jahrhunderts,* 1837, quoted in Bertschik, *Mode und Moderne,* p. 12. Gutzkow was always interested in clothes as a contemporary political symbol.

12. Walter Benjamin, Gesammelte Schriften, vols 1 and 2 (Frankfurt/Main, 1980), p. 580f. Quoted in Bertschik, *Mode und Moderne,* p. 13.

13. Simmel quoted in Bovenschen, *Die Listen der Mode,* p. 180.

14. Bertschik, *Mode und Moderne,* p. 8.

15. Ibid., p. 16.

16. Esposito succumbs to the false assumption that we always find whatever is in fashion beautiful. Esposito, *Die Verbindlichkeit des Vorübergehenden,* p. 166.

17. Esposito also falls prey to the idea that '[i]t is fashion that creates taste and not the other way around'. Ibid., p. 167.

18. Paul Watzlawick, Janet H. Beavin and Don D. Jackson, *Menschliche Kommunikation. Formen, Störungen, Paradoxien* (Bern, 1969), p. 53.

19. Peter Sloterdijk, *Das Zeug zur Macht,* p. 111.

20. Boris Groys, *Zeiterfahrung und ästhetische Wahrnehmung. Information text on a post-graduate course* (University of Frankfurt, 2004), p. 2.

21. Ibid.

22. Immanuel Kant, *Critique of Pure Reason: Transcendental Aesthetics,* section 2, 'Of Time', § 6.

23. Many experiences leave us with the feeling that we have had a long holiday, while a monotonous stay on the beach appears brief when we look back.

24. Hassan Al-Hakim, 'Wie lange dauert die Gegenwart', in Kaestle, *Wann ist die Kunst,* p. 91.

25. Kaestle, *Wann ist die Kunst,* p. 16.

26. The arguments of both Silvia Bovenschen ('Fashion refers to the permanence of change', p. 13), and of Elena Esposito ('in which continual change becomes the only constant', p. 16) are grossly inadequate in this respect.

27. A graduate course at the University of Frankfurt directed by Boris Groys has been investigating this set of themes under the heading 'Experience of Time and Aesthetic Perception' since 2004. See Chapter 8, note 20.

28. Quoted in Christa Wehner, 'Die Zeitsparer, Eine Zielgruppe wird besichtigt', in *Der Verbraucher im Zeitstress, Motor oder Bremse des Konsums,* conference bulletin ed. Gesellschaft für Konsum- Markt- und Absatzforschung (Nuremberg, 2004), http://gfk-verein.de.

29. Ibid. In April 2004, a GfK questionnaire in Germany on time and consumption indicated that all pleasure-oriented dimensions—pleasure in shopping, lifestyle, fashion consciousness, hedonism—had lost their importance, some considerably, since 2001.

30. Schroer, *Räume, Orte, Grenze.*

31. Niklas Luhmann, 'Inklusion und Exklusion', in Luhmann, *Soziologische Aufklärung* (Opladen, 1995), p. 260. Quoted in Schroer, *Räume, Orte, Grenze,* p. 152.

32. Quoted in Schroer, Räume, Orte, Grenze, p. 134.

33. Ibid., pp. 278–83.

34. Thomas L. Friedman, *The World is Flat* (London, 2006).

35. Wolfgang Welsch, 'Transkulturalität. Zur veränderten Verfasstheit heutiger Kulturen', in *Zeitschrift für Kulturaustausch* 45/1 (1995), pp. 39–44. This concurs with Boris Groys's view that 'the future belongs to tautology', in Kaestle, *Wann ist die Kunst,* p. 28.

36. Klaus Staeck, *Die Zeit ist reif! Aktion für mehr Demokratie,* http://www.sozi okultur.de/_seiten/1006006495.htm.

37. Norbert Elias and Eric Dunning, *Gesammelte Schriften 07. Sport und Spannung im Prozeß der Zivilisation* (Frankfurt/Main, 2003), p. 6.

38. Sloterdijk, *Das Zeug zur Macht,* p. 102.

39. Ibid., p. 98.

40. Richard Sennett, *Der flexible Mensch. Die Kultur des neuen Kapitalismus* (Gutenberg, 1996).

41. Simmel, quoted in Schroer, *Räume, Orte, Grenze,* p. 134.

42. Statement by Wolf Singer at the congress 'Kulturzone 06', 13 July 2006, Frankfurt/Main.

43. Peter Fuchs and Andreas Göbel, eds, *Der Mensch—das Medium der Gesellschaft?* (Frankfurt/Main, 1994), pp. 239–63; Loschek, *Verführung,* pp. 23f., 42.

44. Friedrich Wilhelm Joseph Schelling, *System des transzendentalen Idealismus* (Tübingen, 1800), pp. 10, 14. See http://www.scribd.com/doc/47769/Schelling-Friedrich-Wilhelm-Joseph-System-des-transzendenten-Idealismus.

45. Karl Jaspers, *Philosophie,* 3 vols (Berlin, 1932). Quoted in Jürgen Grzesik, ed., *Texte der Existenzphilosophie* (Munich, 1968), pp. 81–5.

46. Ibid.

47. Helmuth Plessner, *Die Stufen des Organischen und der Mensch* (Berlin, 1965). Quoted in Josef Rauscher, 'Philosophische Anthropologie', lecture 1998/1999, p. 7. http://www.vaticarsten.de/theologie/theologiedokumente/philosophie/ rauscher_anthropologie.pdf. Accessed March 2009.

48. Georg Herbert Mead, *Mind, Self and Society* (Chicago, 1934), p. 178.

49. Edmund Husserl, *Ideen zu einer reinen Phänomenologie und phänomenologischen Philosophie I,* 1913. Quoted in Anton Hügli and Paul Lübcke, eds, *Philosophielexikon. Personen und Begriffe der abendländischen Philosophie von der Antike bis zur Gegenwart* (Reinbek, 1991), p. 419.

50. Jürgen Habermas, *Stichworte zu einer Theorie der Sozialisation.* Frankfurt/ Main 1968/1973, p. 131.

51. Fuchs, *Psyche,* pp. 116–7.

52. Ibid., p. 99.
53. Ibid., p. 100–1.
54. Schroer, *Räume, Orte, Grenze,* p. 276.
55. Quoted in Esposito, *Die Verbindlichkeit des Vorübergehenden,* p. 76.
56. Loschek, *Accessoires,* p. 141f.
57. Jay Giedd, 'Neurologie', *Bild der Wissenschaft* (February 2006), p. 30f. loc. cit.
58. Ibid., p. 31.
59. Wolfgang Welsch, *Ästhetisches Denken* (Stuttgart, 1993), p. 168.
60. Esposito, *Die Verbindlichkeit des Vorübergehenden,* p. 79. See also Luhmann, *Die Kunst der Gesellschaft,* p. 153.
61. Elfriede Jelinek, 'Die Mode—keine Spur!', in Ingeborg Harms, ed., *Figurationen. Gender, Literatur, Kultur,* vol. 2 (Cologne, 2000), p. 77.
62. Ibid., p. 78.
63. Christine Brinck, 'Was ist weiblich? Anders von Anfang an', *Die Zeit* (3 March 2005), no. 10, http://www.zeit.de/2005/10/Erziehung_1. Accessed March 2009.
64. Ibid.
65. Judith Butler, *Gender Trouble* (London, 1990).
66. Therese Frey Steffen, *Gender* (Leipzig, 2006), p. 2.
67. Fuchs, *Der Sinn der Beobachtung,* pp. 133–4.
68. Simone de Beauvoir, *Le deuxieme sexe* [The Second Sex], vol. 2 (Paris, 1949), p. 206; see also Candace West and Don H. Zimmerman, "Doing Gender", *Gender and Society,* 1/2 (1987), pp. 125–51.
69. Judith Butler takes up these themes in *Undoing Gender* (Routledge, 2004). On this, see also Gertrud Lehnert, *Wenn Frauen Männerkleider tragen. Geschlecht und Maskerade in Literatur und Geschichte* (Munich, 1997).
70. Barbara Vinken, 'Mode. Spiel mit Grenzen', in Nixdorff, p. 101; Vinken, *Mode nach der Mode* (Frankfurt/Main, 1993), p. 19; see also Barbara Vinken, *Fashion Zeitgeist: Trends and Cycles in the Fashion System* (Oxford, 2005), p. 13.

Chapter 9

1. Dieter Daniels, *Duchamp und die anderen. Der Modellfall einer künstlerischen Wirkungsgeschichte in der Moderne* (Cologne, 1992), p. 205.
2. *Festspielhaus Baden-Baden* (February 2006), p. 35.
3. Annette Tietenberg: 'Das Muster, das verbindet', in *Patterns. Muster in Design, Kunst und Architektur* (Basel, 2005), p. 9.
4. Dariusz Szymanski, *Festspielhaus Baden-Baden* (February 2006), p. 70.
5. Theodor W. Adorno, *Ästhetische Theorie* (Frankfurt, 1970), p. 265.
6. Michael Lingner, 'Dann ist Kunst. Konditionen der Kunstkonkretion', in Kaestle, *Wann ist die Kunst,* p. 57f.

Chapter 10

1. Welsch, *Ästhetisches Denken,* p. 201.
2. Claude Lichtenstein, in *Sportdesign—zwischen Style und Engineering,* exhibition book (Museum of Design Zurich, 2004), p. 85.
3. Roman Meinhold, *Der Mode-Mythos: Lifestyle als Lebenskunst* (Würzburg, 2005), p. 100. Meinhold also draws attention to self-renewal by means of confession in the Christian faith, p. 61f.
4. Even at the beginning of the twentieth century, a school of tailoring was known as a college of tailoring art, and a well-known book on tailoring brought out by Butterick Publishing Company in London was called *The Art of Dress Making* (1927).
5. Alex Rühle, 'Radikaler Höhlenbewohner. "Schreiben ist qualvoll": Ein Besuch be idem amerikanischen Soziologen Richard Sennet', *Süddeutsche Zeitung* (28 February 2006), p. 13.
6. Ibid.
7. In face of the discussions regarding appropriation art (cf. p. 129), Arthur C. Danto sees this as a philosophical question of art and non-art. Arthur C. Danto, 'Geschichten vom Ende der Kunst', in Danto, *Reiz und Reflexion* (Munich, 1994), pp. 384, 389. See also Hans Belting, *Das Ende der Kunstgeschichte* (Munich, 1995), p. 22.
8. Heinrich Klotz, *Kunst im 20. Jahrhundert. Moderne—Postmoderne—Zweite Moderne* (Munich, 1994), p. 22.
9. Welsch writes of 'apparent clarities' in which 'neither the concept of Modernism nor that of Postmodernism is less problematic'. Welsch, *Ästhetisches Denken,* p. 79.
10. Klotz, *Kunst im 20. Jahrhundert,* p. 53.
11. Ibid.
12. Ibid., p. 22.
13. Wassily Kandinsky's *First Abstract Painting,* 1910/1911, as well as Kasimir Malevich's *Black Circle* from around 1923, demonstrate a composition, in contrast to Ad Reinhardt's *Black Painting* from 1960–1966 or the drippings produced by Jackson Pollock after 1946.
14. Klotz, *Kunst im 20. Jahrhundert,* p. 31.
15. Among others, see Schütze, *Kleidung,* pp. 56–8.
16. Ingrid Loschek, *Reclams Mode- und Kostümlexikon,* p. 310; and Loschek, *Modedesigner. Ein Lexikon von Armani bis Yamamoto* (Munich, 2007), p. 48.
17. Welsch, *Ästhetisches Denken,* p. 82.
18. Klotz, *Kunst im 20. Jahrhundert,* p. 8.
19. Ibid. By contrast, Bernhard E. Bürdek believes that Klotz attaches this opinion too firmly to the forms of objects. Bernhard E. Bürdek, 'Vom Mythos des Funktionalismus', in Bürdek, Reinhard Kehl, Florian P. Fischer, and Jürgen

W. Braun, *Vom Mythos des Funktionalismus,* ed. by Franz Schneider Brakel (Brakel-Köln, 1997), p. 13.

20. Welsch, *Ästhetisches Denken,* p. 84.
21. Dirk Baecker, *Wozu Kultur* (Berlin, 2003), p. 23.
22. Ibid.
23. Jean-François Lyotard, *Philosophie und Malerei im Zeitalter ihres Experimentierens* (Berlin, 1986), p. 97.
24. Welsch, *Ästhetisches Denken,* p. 217.
25. Theodor W. Adorno, *Ästhetische Theorie* (Frankfurt, 1970), p. 264.
26. Welsch, *Ästhetisches Denken,* p. 217.
27. Daniel Bell, *The Winding Passage: Essays and Sociological Journeys 1960 to 1980* (Cambridge, 1980) p. 243.
28. Marietta Riederer, *Wie Mode Mode Wird'* (Munich, 1962), p. 61.
29. Welsch, *Ästhetisches Denken,* p. 9ff.
30. Although the Belgian 'Groupe des Six' made a name for themselves in the 1980s, their work was not based on a unified stylistic tendency. Thus, fashion by Dries Van Noten and Dirk Bikkembergs cannot be attributed to deconstructivism.
31. Loschek, *Modedesigner,* p. 135.
32. Quoted from Martina Glomb, lecture at the University of Applied Sciences, Pforzheim, 15 May 2007.
33. This debate is documented in the exchange of letters between Derrida and Eisenman; see Peter Eisenman, *Aura und Exzeß. Zur Überwindung der Metaphysik der Architektur* (Vienna, 1995). Apart from the same name and a superficial similarity of practice, there is no explicit connection between deconstruction in philosophy and philology and deconstructivism in architecture. See Mark Wigley, *Architektur und Dekonstruktion. Derridas Phantom* (Basel, 1994).
34. Andreas Papadakis and James Steele, *Architektur der Gegenwart* (Paris, 1991), p. 169.
35. Welsch, *Ästhetisches Denken,* p. 9.
36. The term *second modernism* was already used to refer to the art of the 1950s, but Heinrich Klotz among others saw that art—with respect to both its spiritual and aesthetic claims—as a continuation of the modernism prior to the Second World War, since modernism had not been interrupted in all countries, the exceptions being the USA, Scandinavia and Brazil. It was not until postmodernism cut in that a new aesthetic discourse of modernism was triggered; Klotz, *Kunst im 20. Jahrhundert,* p. 195. In contrast, designer Otl Aicher refers to industrial mass production as a whole as second modernism, while he speaks of third modernism as the period after the Second World War, employing the example of the house by Charles and Ray Eames; Bürdek, *Vom Mythos des Funktionalismus,* pp. 13–14. We have yet to see a complete, definitive definition of second modernism. Characteristic of sociology are terms like 'new incomprehensibility'

(Jürgen Habermas), 'risk society' (Ulrich Beck) and 'the flexible human being' (Richard Sennett).

37. Quoted in Schütze, *Kleidung,* p. 52.

38. Jürgen W. Braun, 'MAN transFORMS. Ein Ausstellungsprojekt von Hans Hollein', in Bürdek, *Vom Mythos des Funktionalismus,* p. 79.

39. Pierre Bourdieu, *Die feinen Unterschiede. Kritik der gesellschaftlichen Urteilskraft* (Frankfurt/Main, 1982).

40. The perforated copper shutters of the Fünf Höfe facade facing onto Theatinerstraße in Munich are exemplary of this; Alexander Hosch, *Süddeutsche Zeitung* (7 August 2006).

41. Takashi Murakami, Superflat (Tokyo, 2000).

42. Tietenberg, *Muster,* p. 9.

43. Other exhibitions examining the overlapping of art and fashion include 'Künstler ziehen an', Dortmund, 1998; 'Addressing the Century: 100 Years of Art & Fashion', Kunstmuseum Wolfsburg, 1999; 'untragbar. Mode als Skulptur', Museum für Angewandte Kunst, Cologne, 2001.

44. Walter Benjamin, 'Das Kunstwerk im Zeitalter seiner technischen Reproduzierbarkeit', in *Zeitschrift für Sozialforschung,* 1936, quoted in Benjamin, *Gesammelte Schriften I,* 2nd edn, ed. by Rolf Tiedemann and Hermann Schweppenhäuser (Frankfurt/Main, 1980), p. 473.

Bibliography

Addressing the Century: 100 Years of Art & Fashion, Kunstmuseum Wolfsburg, 1999.

Allen, J. J., *The Man in the Red Velvet Dress: Inside the World of Cross-Dressing,* 1996.

Anna, Susanne, and Heinzelmann, Markus, eds, *untragbar. Mode als Skulptur.* Ausst.-Kat. des Museums für angewandte Kunst Köln, Ostfildern-Ruit, 2001.

Arnold, Rebecca, *Fashion, Desire and Anxiety,* New Brunswick, 2001.

Bachmann, Cordula, *Kleidung und Geschlecht. Ethnographische Erkundungen einer Alltagspraxis,* Bielefeld, 2008.

Baecker, Dirk, ed., *Niklas Luhmann. Einführung in die Systemtheorie,* Heidelberg, 2004.

Baecker, Dirk, *Wozu Kultur,* Berlin, 2003.

Barnes, Ruth, and Eicher, Joanne B., *Dress and Gender: Making and Meaning in Cultural Contexts,* Providence/Oxford, 1993.

Barthes, Roland, *Die Sprache der Mode,* Frankfurt/Main, 1985.

Bartlett, Djurdja, 'Let Them Wear Beige: The Petit-Bourgeois World of Official Socialist Dress', *Fashion Theory* 8/2 (2004), pp. 127–64.

Baumgart, Ralf, and Eichener, Volker, *Norbert Elias. Zur Einführung,* Hamburg, 1991.

Baumgartner, Ekkehart, Heuberger, Simona, Weigand, Alexandra, and Messner, Philipp, *Virtuelle Ästhetik. Betrachtungen zur Wahrnehmung am Beginn des 21. Jahrhunderts,* Innsbruck, 2008.

Baudrillard, Jean, *Der symbolische Tausch und der Tod,* Munich, 1982.

Baudrillard, Jean, *Das System der Dinge: Über unser Verhältnis zu den alltäglichen Gegenständen,* Frankfurt/Main, 1991.

Becker, Barbara, and Schneider, Irmela, ed., *Was von Körper übrig bleibt,* Frankfurt/Main, 2000.

Belting, Hans, and Schulze, Ulrich, *Beiträge zu Kunst und Medientheorie: Projekte und Forschungen an der Hochschule für Gestaltung Karlsruhe,* Ostfildern, 2000.

Benedek, Susanne, and Binder, Adolphe, *Von tanzenden Kleidern und sprechenden Leibern. Crossdressing als Auflösung der Geschlechterpolarität?,* Dortmund, 1996.

Benjamin, Walter, *Gesammelte Schriften,* vols 1 and 2, ed. Rolf Tiedemann and Hermann Schweppenhäuser, Frankfurt/Main, 1980.

Bertschik, Julia, *Mode und Moderne. Kleidung als Spiegel des Zeitgeistes in der deutschsprachigen Literatur (1770–1945),* Cologne-Weimar-Vienna, 2005.

Beylerian, George M., Dent, Andrew, and Quinn Bradley, eds, *Ultra Materials. Innovative Materialien verändern die Welt,* Munich, 2007.

Binnig, Gerd, *Aus dem Nichts. Über die Kreativität von Natur und Mensch,* Munich, 1989.

Bippus, Elke, and Mink, Dorothea, *Fashion Body Cult/Mode Körper Kult,* Stuttgart, 2007.

Black, Sandy, ed., *Fashioning Fabrics: Contemporary Textiles in Fashion,* London, 2006.

Body Extensions, exhibition companion book, Zürich, 2004.

Bolton, Andrew, *Wild: Fashion Untamed,* New York, 2004.

Bolton, Andrew, *The Supermodern Wardrobe,* London, 2002.

Bolz, Norbert, *Bang design. Design-manifest des 21. Jahrhunderts,* Trend Büro Hamburg, 2006.

Bolz, Norbert, 'Mode oder Trend? Ein Unterschied, der einen Unterschied macht', *Kunstforum International,* no. 141 (1998), pp. 196–201.

Bono, Edward de, *The Use of Lateral Thinking,* Cape, 1968.

Bourdieu, Pierre, *Die feinen Unterschiede. Kritik der gesellschaftlichen Urteilskraft,* Frankfurt/Main, 1982.

Bourdieu, Pierre, *Soziologische Fragen,* Frankfurt/Main, 1993.

Bovenschen, Silvia, ed., *Die Listen der Mode,* Frankfurt/Main, 1986.

Christina von Braun and Inge Stephan, eds, *Gender & Wissen. Ein Handbuch der Gender-Theorien,* Cologne, 2005.

Braddock, Sarah E., and O'Mahony, Marie: *Techno Textiles. Revolutionary Fabrics for Fashion and Design,* vol. 1, London, 1998; vol. 2, London, 2005.

Brand, Jan, and Teunissen, José, eds, *Global Fashion, Local Tradition: On the Globalisation of Fashion,* Ausst.-Begleitbuch Centraal Museum, Utrecht, 2005.

Brandstetter, Gabriele, Völckers, Hortensia, and Mau, Bruce, *ReMembering the Body,* London, 2000.

Breward, Christopher, *Fashion,* Oxford, 2003.

Breward, Christopher, and Evans, Caroline, eds, *Fashion and Modernity,* Oxford, 2005.

Breward, Christopher, and Gilbert, David, *Fashion's World Cities,* Oxford, 2006.

Bruzzi, Stella, and Gibson, P. C., eds, *Fashion Cultures: Theories, Explorations and Analysis,* London, 2000.

Brydon, Anne, and Niessen, Sandra, *Consuming Fashion: Adorning the Transnational Body,* Oxford, 1998.

Buckley, Cheryl, and Fawcett, Hilary, *Fashioning the Feminine: Representation and Women's Fashion from the Fin de Siècle to the Present,* New York, 2002.

Butler, Judith, *Gender Trouble* (1990) [Das Unbehagen der Geschlechter], Frankfurt/Main, 1991.

Buxbaum, Gerda, ed., *Fashion in Context,* Vienna, 2009.

Calefato, Patrizia, 'Fashion and Worldliness: Language and Imagery of the clothed Body', in *Fashion Theory,* 1/1 (1997), pp. 69–90.

Calefato, Patrizia, *The Clothed Body,* Oxford, 2004.

Chi, Immanuel, 'Eingetragen—Abgetragen. Zur Phänomenologie der Gebrauchsspur in der Mode', *Kunstforum International,* no. 141 (1998), pp. 154–61.

Clark, Judith, *Spectres: When Fashion Turns Back,* exhibition companion book, Victoria and Albert Museum, London, 2004.

Cordwell, Justine M., and Schwarz, Ronald A., *Fabrics of Culture: The Anthropology of Clothing and Adornment,* New York, 1979.

Craig, Jennifer, *The Face of Fashion: Cultural Studies in Fashion,* London, 1994.

Csikszentmihályi, Mihályi, *Flow. Das Geheimnis des Glücks,* Stuttgart, 1992.

Davies, Hywel, *Modern Menswear,* London, 2009.

Davis, Fred, *Fashion, Culture, and Identity,* Chicago, 1992.

Dekker, Rudolf, and Lotte van de Pol, *Frauen in Männerkleidern. Weibliche Transvestiten und ihre Geschichte,* Berlin, 1990.

Design and the Elastic Mind, Museum of Modern Art, New York, 2008.

Dettmar, Ute, and Küpper, Thomas, *Kitsch. Texte und Theorien,* Stuttgart, 2007.

Doswald, Christoph, ed., *Double-Face: The Story about Fashion and Art from Mohammed to Warhol,* St. Gallen, 2006.

Eibl-Eibesfeldt, Irenäus, *Die Biologie des menschlichen Verhaltens. Grundriß der Humanethologie,* Munich, 1984.

Elias, Norbert, *Die Gesellschaft der Individuen,* Frankfurt/Main, 1991.

English, Bonnie, *A Cultural History of Fashion in the Twentieth Century: From the Catwalk to the Sidewalk,* Oxford, 2007.

Esposito, Elena, *Die Verbindlichkeit des Vorübergehenden. Paradoxien der Mode,* Frankfurt/Main, 2004.

Evans, Caroline, *Fashion at the Edge: Spectacle, Modernity and Deathlessness,* New Haven, 2003.

Evans, Caroline, 'Yesterday's Emblems and Tomorrow's Commodities', in *Fashion Cultures: Theories, Explorations and Analysis,* ed. Stella Bruzzi and P. C. Gibson, London, 2000.

Evans, Caroline, and Frankel, Susannah, *The House of Viktor & Rolf,* London, 2008.

Fabo, Sabine, 'Ephemeriden—Mode, Kunst, Medien. Strategien des Flüchtigen', *Kunstforum International,* no. 141 (1998), pp. 162–71.

Fausch, Deborah, Singley, Paulette, El-Khoury, Rodolphe, and Efrat, Zvi, *Architecture in Fashion,* New York, 1994.

Fischer-Lichte, Erika, *Ästhetik des Performativen,* Frankfurt/Main, 2004.

Frey Steffen, Therese, *Gender,* Leipzig, 2006.

Fuchs, Peter, *Die Psyche. Studien zur Innenwelt der Außenwelt der Innenwelt,* Weilerswist, 2005.

Fuchs, Peter, *Der Sinn der Beobachtung. Begriffliche Untersuchungen,* Weilerswist, 2004.

Fuchs, Peter, and Göbel, Andreas, eds, *Der Mensch—das Medium der Gesellschaft?,* Frankfurt/Main, 1994.

Garber, Marjorie, *Vested Interests: Cross-Dressing and Cultural Anxiety,* New York, 1992.

Gaugele, Elke, *Schurz und Schürze. Kleidung als Medium der Geschlechterkonstruktion,* Cologne/Vienna, 2002.

Geiger, Annette, Hennecke, Stefanie, and Kempf, Christin, eds, *Spielarten des Organischen in Architektur, Design und Kunst,* Berlin, 2005.

Glynn, Prudence, *Skin to Skin: Eroticism in Dress,* New York, 1982.

Goffman, Erving, *Frame Analysis: An Essay on the Organization of Experience,* Cambridge, 1974.

Goffman, Erving, *Das Individuum im öffentlichen Austausch. Mikrostudien zur öffentlichen Ordnung,* Frankfurt/Main, 1982.

Goffman, Erving, *The Presentation of Self in Everyday Life,* New York, 1959.

Grenville, Bruce, ed., *The Uncanny: Experiments in Cyborg Culture,* exhibition companion book, Vancouver Art Gallery, Vancouver, 1999.

Griggs, Claudine, *S/he: Changing Sex and Changing Clothes,* Oxford, 2003.

Groys, Boris, *Über das Neue. Versuch einer Kulturökonomie,* Munich, 1992.

Gründl, Harald, and EOOS Designs, *The Death of Fashion: The Passage Rite of Fashion in the Show Window,* Vienna, 2007.

Hartung, Elisabeth, *Zweite Haut—Kunst und Kleidung. Seconda pelle—Arte e Abito,* exhibition book, Women's Museum Evelyn Ortner, Meran, 2001.

Horster, Detlef, *Niklas Luhmann, eine Einführung,* Munich, 1997.

Hussein Chalayan, exhibition catalog, Groningen/Wolfsburg, 2005.

Hüther, Gerald, *Die Macht der inneren Bilder. Wie Visionen das Gehirn, den Menschen und die Welt verändern,* Göttingen, 2004.

In_Rete, 2006 miniaturtextilcomo. XVI Mostra Internazionale d'Arte Contemporanea, exhibition book, Museo di Palazzo Mocenigo, Venice, 2007.

Janalik, Heinz, and Schmidt, Doris, *Kleidung, Körper, Körperlichkeit. Textil—Körper—Mode,* part 2, Baltmannsweiler, 1997–1998.

Kaestle, Thomas, ed., *Wann ist die Kunst? Prozess, Moment, Gültigkeit,* Kunstverein Hildesheim, 2005.

Kawamura, Yuniya, *Fashion-ology: An Introduction to Fashion Studies,* Oxford, 2004.

Kawamura, Yuniya, *The Japanese Revolution in Paris Fashion,* Oxford, 2004.

Keupp, Heiner, Ahbe, Thomas, et al., *Identitätskonstruktionen. Das Patchwork der Identitäten in der Spätmoderne,* Reinbek, 2006.

Klotz, Heinrich, *Modern-Postmodern-Zweite Moderne,* Munich, 1994.

Koda, Harold, *Extreme Beauty: The Body Transformed,* exhibition companion book, Metropolitan Museum of Art, New York, 2001.

Koren, Leonard, *New Fashion Japan,* Tokyo, 1984.

Lange, Barbara, *Visualisierte Körperkonzepte. Strategien in der Kunst der Moderne,* Berlin, 2006.

Leach, Neil, *Camouflage,* Cambridge, Mass., 2006.

Lee, Suzanne, *Fashioning the Future: Tomorrow's Wardrobe,* London, 2005.

Lehnert, Gertrud, 'Die Angst, gewöhnlich zu sein. Über die Performativität von Mode und das Spiel mit 'Geschlecht', in Gerhard Johann Lischka, ed., *Mode-Kult,* Cologne, 2002.

Lehnert, Gertrud, *Wenn Frauen Männerkleider tragen. Geschlecht und Maskerade in Literatur und Geschichte,* Munich, 1997.

Lehnert, Gertrud, ed., *Die Kunst der Mode,* Oldenburg, 2006.

Lehnert, Gertrud, *Mode, Weiblichkeit und Modernität,* Dortmund, 1998.

Lerche-Renn, Heidi, ed., *Kleid und Menschenbild,* Cologne, 1992.

Liebl, Franz, *Der Schock des Neuen. Entstehung und Management von Issues und Trends,* Munich, 2000.

Liessmann, Konrad Paul, *Zukunft kommt! Vom Unglück des Hoffens auf die Zukunft,* Vienna, 2007.

Linke, Detlef B., *Kunst und Gehirn. Die Eroberung des Unsichtbaren,* Reinbek, 2001.

Loschek, Ingrid, *Accessoires. Symbolik und Geschichte,* Munich, 1993.

Loschek, Ingrid, 'Authentisch kopiert', *Zeitschrift der Gesellschaft für Historische Waffen- und Kostümkunde,* 45/1 (2003), pp. 67–76.

Loschek, Ingrid, 'Blendwerk—Vom Natürlichen zum Künstlichen', in Vitus Weh, ed., *Glanz und Verderben. Die unheimliche Konjunktur des Kristallinen.* Bozen-Wien, 2009.

Loschek, Ingrid, *Fashion of the Century. Chronik der Mode von 1900 bis heute,* Munich, 2001.

Loschek, Ingrid, 'Kostümkunde. Gestern—Heute—Morgen', *Zeitschrift der Gesellschaft für Historische Waffen- und Kostümkunde* 39/1–2 (1997), pp. 4–9.

Loschek, Ingrid, *Modedesigner. Ein Lexikon von Armani bis Yamamoto,* Munich, 2007.

Loschek, Ingrid, 'Mode—Gestalten—Inszenieren-Interpretieren', in Neue Kleider, ed., *Museum August Kestner und Fachhochschule Hannover,* Hannover, 2008.

Loschek, Ingrid, *Mode im 20. Jahrhundert. Eine Kulturgeschichte unserer Zeit,* Munich, 1995.

Loschek, Ingrid, 'Mode- und Architektur in der zweiten Hälfte des 20. Jahrhunderts—ein stilistischer Vergleich', *Zeitschrift der Gesellschaft für Historische Waffen- und Kostümkunde,* 40/1–2 (1998), pp. 17–32.

Loschek, Ingrid, *Mode—Verführung und Notwendigkeit. Struktur und Strategie der Aussehensveränderungen,* Munich, 1991.

Loschek, Ingrid, 'Mode zwischen Identifikation und Identität', *Zeitschrift für Balkanologie* 31/2 (1995), pp. 156–63.

Loschek, Ingrid, *Reclams Mode- und Kostümlexikon* (Weiterführende Literatur), Stuttgart, 2005.

Loschek, Ingrid, 'Schuhikonen. Von High Heels zu Birkenstocks', in *Schuhtick. Von kalten Füßen und heißen Sohlen*, Mainz, 2008.

Loschek, Ingrid, 'The United Look of Fashion', *Die Welt als Laufsteg. Zeitschrift für Kulturaustausch des Instituts für Balkanologie*, 52/4 (2002), pp. 36–38.

Loschek, Ingrid, 'Von Avantgarde bis Klassik. Was die Entwürfe von Newcomern und Global Playern so anziehend macht', *Deutschland. Forum für Politik, Kultur, Wirtschaft und Wissenschaft*, 1 (2004).

Loschek, Ingrid, 'Von der Geste zum Ritual in der Mode', in Alba d'Urbano and Tina Bara, eds, *Eine Frage nach der Geste*, Salzburg, 2008.

Loschek, Ingrid, 'Mode. Gestalten—Inszenieren—Interpretieren', in *Neue Kleider?!*, Hannover, 2008.

Luhmann, Niklas, *Die Ausdifferenzierung des Kunstsystems*, Bern, 1994.

Luhmann, Niklas, *Die Gesellschaft der Gesellschaft*, Frankfurt/Main, 1997.

Luhmann, Niklas, *Die Kunst der Gesellschaft*, Frankfurt/Main, 1995.

Luhmann, Niklas, *Soziale Systeme. Grundriß einer allgemeinen Theorie*, Frankfurt/Main, 1984.

Luhmann, Niklas, *Zweckbegriff und Systemrationalität. Über die Funktion von Zwecken in sozialen Systemen*, Tübingen, 1968; Neudruck Frankfurt/Main, 1973.

Lyotard, Jean-François, *Philosophie und Malerei im Zeitalter ihres Experimentierens*, Berlin, 1986.

Maar, Christa, and Burda, Hubert, eds, *Iconic Turn. Die neue Macht der Bilder*, Cologne, 2005.

Magnago Lampugnani, Vittorio, et al., ed., *Architekturtheorie 20. Jahrhundert. Positionen, Programme, Manifeste*, Ostfildern-Ruit, 2004.

Martin, Richard, 'A Charismatic Art: The Balance of Ingratiation and Outrage in Contemporary Fashion', *Fashion Theory* 1/1 (1997), pp. 91–104.

Mauch, Daniela, *Zur Ausdifferenzierung der Sportmode. Eine systemtheoretische Untersuchung*, Reihe Mode- und Textilwissenschaft vol. 3, Baltmannsweiler, 2005.

Maynard, Margaret, *Dress and Globalisation*, Manchester, 2004.

McEvilley, Thomas, *Art and Otherness: Crisis in Cultural Identity*, New York, 1992.

McQuaid, Matilda, *Extreme Textiles*, exhibition companion book, Cooper-Hewitt National Design Museum, New York, 2005.

Mead, Georg Herbert, *Mind, Self and Society*, Chicago, 1934.

Meinhold, Roman, *Der Mode-Mythos. Lifestyle als Lebenskunst*, Würzburg, 2005.

Mentges, Gabriele, and Nixdorff, Heide, eds, *Zeit.schnitte. Textil—Körper—Mode*, Dortmunder Reihe zu kulturanthropologischen Studien des Textilen, Dortmund, 2001.

Mentges, Gabriele, and Richard, Birgit, eds, *Schönheit der Uniformität*, Frankfurt, 2005.

Meyer-Krahmer, Frieder, and Lange, Siegfried, eds, *Geisteswissenschaften und Innovationen,* Heidelberg, 1999.

Mulvagh, Jane, *Vivienne Westwood. Die Lady ist ein Punk,* Munich, 2001.

Mutations//Mode 1960–2000, exhibition companion book, Musée Galliera, Paris, 2000.

Newark, Tim, *Camouflage,* exhibition companion book, Imperial War Museum, London, 2007.

Neuburger, Susanne, Buxbaum, Gerda, and Pamminger, Walter, *Das doppelte Kleid. Zu Mode und Kunst,* Galerie Schloss Ottenstein, Vienna, 1996.

Niemitz, Carsten, *Geheimnis des aufrechten Ganges,* Munich, 2004.

Niemitz, Carsten, *Erbe und Umwelt. Zur Natur und Anlage der Selbstbestimmung des Menschen,* Frankfurt, 1989.

Nixdorff, Heide, 'Bekleidung als Ausdruck der leiblich-seelischen Entwicklung des Menschen', *Mensch und Kleidung,* 17/18 (1983), pp. 15–22.

Nixdorff, Heide, ed., *Das textile Medium als Phänomen der Grenze—Begrenzung—Entgrenzung,* Reihe Historische Anthropologie, vol. 30, Berlin, 1996.

Nixdorff, Heide, 'Das Tier im Outfit des Menschen. Faunistische Elemente der Kleidung und ihre sozialanthropologischen und historischen Bezüge', in Jutta Beder, ed., *Vortragsreihe zur 600-Jahr-Feier der Kölner Universität,* Textilkunst und Kleidung. Kulturhistorische Beiträge, vol. 1, Cologne, 1990.

O'Mahony, Marie, C*cyborg: The Man-Machine,* London, 2002.

Die Organische Form, exhibition catalog, Wilhelm-Wagenfeld-Stiftung, Bremen, 2003.

Pape, Cora von, *Kunstkleider. Die Präsenz des Körpers in textilen Kunst-Objekten des 20. Jahrhunderts,* Bielefeld, 2008.

Pantellini, Claudia, and Stohler, Peter, eds, *Body Extensions,* Stuttgart, 2004.

Papadakis, Andreas, and Steele, James, *Architektur der Gegenwart,* Paris, 1991.

Parkins, Wendy, *Fashioning the Body Politic: Dress, Gender, Citizenship,* Oxford, 2002.

Pierer, Heinrich von, and Oetinger, Bolko von, *Wie kommt das Neue in die Welt,* Hamburg, 1999.

Poschardt, Ulf, *Anpassen,* Hamburg, 1998.

Poschardt, Ulf, 'Mode und Militär', *Kunstforum International,* no. 141 (1998), pp. 138–43.

Quinn, Bradley, *The Fashion of Architecture,* London, 2004.

Quinn, Bradley, *Techno Fashion,* Oxford, 2002.

Rath, Jan, *Unravelling the Rag Trade: Immigrant Entrepreneurship in Seven World Cities,* Oxford, 2002.

Richard, Birgit, 'Die oberflächlichen Hüllen des Selbst. Mode als ästhetisch-medialer Komplex', *Kunstforum International,* no, 141 (1998), pp. 48–95.

Richard, Birgit, *Sheroes. Genderspiel im virtuellen Raum,* Bielefeld, 2004.

Richard, Birgit, 'Smarte Mode und intelligente Textilien', in Gerhard Johann Lischka, ed., *Mode-Kult,* Cologne, 2002.

Richards, Ann, 'Form als Formation in Natur und Design—"Ein Kräftediagramm"', *Textilforum,* January 2003.

Roach-Higgins, Mary Ellen, and Eicher, Joanne B., eds, *Dress and Identity,* New York, 1995.

Rosenkranz, Karl, *Ästhetik des Hässlichen,* Leipzig, 1990.

Roth, Gerhard, *Das Gehirn und seine Wirklichkeit,* Frankfurt/Main, 2000.

Rudofsky, Bernard, *The Unfashionable Human Body,* New York, 1947.

Schaschl-Cooper, Sabine, et al., ed., *Cooling Out: On the Paradox of Feminism,* exhibition book, Kunsthaus Baselland, Zürich, 2008.

Schnierer, Thomas, 'Modewandel und Gesellschaft. Die Dynamik von "in" und "out"', PhD dissertation, Ludwig-Maximilian-Universität, Munich, Opladen, 1995.

Schroer, Markus, *Räume, Orte, Grenze. Auf dem Weg zu einer Soziologie des Raums,* Frankfurt/Main, 2006.

Schütze, Yvonne, *Kleidung als und im Kunstwerk des 20. Jahrhunderts unter sozialtheoretischer Perspektive,* PhD dissertation, University Wuppertal, Berlin, 2001.

Seltmann, Gerhard and Lippert, Werner, eds, *Entry Paradise. Neue Welten des Designs,* Basel, 2006.

Sennett, Richard, *Der flexible Mensch. Die Kultur des neuen Kapitalismus,* Frankfurt/Main, 1996.

Simmel, Georg, 'Die Mode', in *Philosophische Kultur. Gesammelte Essays,* Leipzig, 1911.

Slimane, Hedi, u.a., *Rock Diary,* Zürich, 2008.

Smith, Courtney, and Topham, Sean, *Xtreme fashion,* Munich, 2005.

Smith, Courtney, and Topham, Sean, *Xtreme Houses,* Munich, 2002.

Sommer, Carlo Michael, *Soziopsychologie der Kleidermode,* Regensburg, 1989.

Sommer, Carlo Michael, and Wind, Thomas, *Mode. Die Hüllen des Ich. Psychologie heute,* Weinheim, 1988.

Sportdesign—zwischen Style und Engineering, exhibition companion book, Museum für Gestaltung, Zürich, 2004.

Stankowski, Anton, and Duschek, Karl, eds, *Visuelle Kommunikation. Ein Design-Handbuch,* mit einem Vorwort von Otl Aicher, Berlin, 1993.

Steele, Valerie, 'Fashion', in *Glamour: Fashion + Industrial Design + Architecture,* exhibition companion book, San Francisco Museum of Modern Art, San Francisco, 2004.

Steele, Valerie, ed., *Fashion Theory: The Journal of Dress, Body and Culture,* New York, 1997.

Steele, Valerie, *Fetish, Fashion, Sex and Power,* New York, 1996.

Steffen, Hans, ed., *Aspekte der Modernität,* Göttingen, 1965.

Stern, Norbert, *Mode und Kultur,* 2 vols, Dresden, 1915.

Stoll, Andrea and Wodtke-Werner, Verena, eds, *Sakkorausch und Rollentausch. Männliche Leitbilder als Freiheitsentwürfe von Frauen*, Dortmund, 1996.

Sulloway, Frank, *Born to Rebel: Birth Order, Family Dynamics, and Creative Lives*, Boston, 1996.

Tietenberg, Annette, 'Das Muster, das verbindet', in *Patterns. Muster in Design, Kunst und Architektur*, Basel, 2005.

Troy, Nancy, *Couture Culture: A Study in Modern Art and Fashion*, Cambridge, Mass., 2003.

Veblen, Thorstein, *Theorie der feinen Leute*, New York, 1899.

Verhelst, Bob, and Debo, Kaat, *Maison Martin Margiela*, Antwerp, 2008.

Vinken, Barbara, *Fashion Zeitgeist: Trends and Cycles in the Fashion System*, Oxford, 2005.

Vinken, Barbara, 'Mannekin, Statue, Fetisch', *Kunstforum International*, no. 141 (1998), pp. 144–53.

Vinken, Barbara, *Mode nach der Mode. Kleid und Geist am Ende des 20. Jahrhunderts*, Frankfurt, 1993.

Vinken, Barbara, 'Kultkörper, verworfen und heilig: Marie-Antoinette', in Gerhard Johann Lischka, ed., *Mode-Kult*, Cologne, 2002.

Vinken, Barbara, ed., *Die nackte Wahrheit. Zur Pornographie und zur Rolle des Obszönen in der Gegenwart*, Frankfurt/Main, 1997.

Welsch, Wolfgang, *Ästhetisches Denken*, Stuttgart, 1993.

Wilcox, Claire, ed., *Radical Fashion*, exhibition companion book, Victoria and Albert Museum, London, 2001.

Wilson, Elizabeth, *Body Dressing*, Oxford, 2001.

Wilson, Elizabeth, *Bohemians: The Glamorous Outcasts*, London, 2000.

Wilson, Elizabeth, *In Träume gehüllt. Mode und Modernität*, Hamburg, 1989.

White, Nicol, and Griffiths, Ian, *The Fashion Business: Theory, Practice, Image*, Oxford, 2000.

Willingmann, Heike, 'Kleid auf Zeit. Über den Umgang mit der Vergänglichkeit von Bekleidung', in Gabriele Mentges and Heide Nixdorff, eds, *Zeit.schnitte. Textil—Körper—Mode*, Dortmunder Reihe zu kulturanthropologischen Studien des Textilen, vol. 1, Dortmund, 2001.

Woodward, Sophie, *Why Women Wear What They Wear*, Oxford, 2007.

Zeki, Semir, *Inner Vision: An Exploration of Art and the Brain*, Oxford, 1999.

Index